MESSAGE OF THE FATHERS OF THE CHURCH

General Editor: Thomas Halton

Volume 21

MESSAGE OF THE FATHERS OF THE CHURCH

LITURGICAL PRACTICE IN THE FATHERS

by

Thomas K. Carroll and *Thomas Halton*

Michael Glazier
Wilmington, Delaware

About the Authors

THOMAS K. CARROLL holds doctorates in theology and liturgy, was a peritus at Vatican II, and has written and lectured widely on patristic topics. He is presently on the faculty of the University of Dallas.

THOMAS HALTON holds M.A. and Ph.D degrees in Ancient Classics from University College, Dublin and the Catholic University of America, where he is now Professor of Greek and Latin. He is a past President of the North American Patristic Society and has lectured and written widely on patristic subjects in Europe and North America. He is Editorial Director of the *Message of the Fathers of the Church* and *Studies in Christian Antiquity*. Recently, he co-authored (with Robert D. Sider), "*A Decade of Patristic Scholarship 1970-1979.*"

First published in 1988 by Michael Glazier, Inc., 1935 West Fourth Street, Wilmington, Delaware 19805.

Library of Congress Catalog Card Number: 88-81138
International Standard Book Number:
  Message of the Fathers of the Church series:
    (0-89453-312-6, Paper; 0-89453-340-1, Cloth)
  LITURGICAL PRACTICE IN THE FATHERS
    (0-89453-324-X, Paper; 0-89453-361-4, Cloth)

Typography by Angela Meades.

Printed in the United States of America by Edwards Brothers, Ann Arbor.

Contents

Abbreviations

ACW   Ancient Christian Writers
ANF   Ante-Nicene Fathers
CCL   Corpus Christianorum, Series Latina
CSEL Corpus Scriptorum Ecclesiasticorum Latinorum
FOTC Fathers of the Church
GCS   Die griechischen christlichen Scriftsteller der ersten
      drei Jalrhunderte
LNPF A Select Library of Nicene and Post-Nicene Fathers
      of the Christian Church
OECT Oxford Early Christian Texts
PG   Patrologia Graeca
PL   Patrologia Latina
PLS   Patrologia Latina, Supplementum
SC   Sources Chrétiennes

EDITOR'S INTRODUCTION

The *Message of the Fathers of the Church* is a companion series to The *Old Testament Message* and The *New Testament Message*. It was conceived and planned in the belief that Scripture and Tradition worked hand in hand in the formation of the thought, life and worship of the primitive Church. Such a series, it was felt, would be a most effective way of opening up what has become virtually a closed book to present-day readers, and might serve to stimulate a revival in interest in Patristic studies in step with the recent, gratifying resurgence in Scriptural studies.

The term "Fathers" is usually reserved for Christian writers marked by orthodoxy of doctrine, holiness of life, ecclesiastical approval and antiquity. 'Antiquity' is generally understood to include writers down to Gregory the Great (+604) or Isidore of Seville (+636) in the West, and John Damascene (+749) in the East. In the present series, however, greater elasticity has been encouraged, and quotations from writers not noted for orthodoxy will sometimes be included in order to illustrate the evolution of the Message on particular doctrinal matters. Likewise, writers later than the mid-eighth century will sometimes be used to illustrate the continuity of tradition on matters like sacramental theology or liturgical practice.

An earnest attempt was made to select collaborators on a broad inter-disciplinary and inter-confessional basis, the chief consideration being to match scholars who could handle the Fathers in their original languages with subjects in which they had already demonstrated a special interest and competence.

About the only editorial directive given to the selected contributors was that the Fathers, for the most part, should be allowed to speak for themselves and that they should speak in readable, reliable modern English. Volumes on individual themes were considered more suitable than volumes devoted to individual Fathers; each theme, hopefully, contributing an important segment to the total mosaic of the Early Church, one, holy, catholic and apostolic. Each volume has an introductory essay outlining the historical and theological development of the theme, with the body of the work mainly occupied with liberal citations from the Fathers in modern English translation and a minimum of linking commentary. Short lists of Suggested Further Readings are included; but dense, scholarly footnotes were actively discouraged on the pragmatic grounds that such scholarly shorthand has other outlets and tends to lose all but the most relentlessly esoteric reader in a semi-popular series.

At the outset of his *Against Heresies* Irenaeus of Lyons warns his readers 'not to expect from me any display of rhetoric, which I have never learned, or any excellence of composition, which I have never practised, or any beauty or persuasiveness of style, to which I make no pretensions.' Similarly, modest disclaimers can be found in many of the Greek and Latin Fathers and all too often, unfortunately, they have been taken at their word by an uninterested world. In fact, however, they were often highly educated products of the best rhetorical schools of their day in the Roman Empire, and what they have to say is often as much a lesson in literary and cultural, as well as in spiritual, edification.

St. Augustine, in *The City of God* (19.7), has interesting reflections on the need for a common language in an expanding world community; without a common language a man is more at home with his dog than with a foreigner as far as intercommunication goes, even in the Roman Empire, which imposes on the nations it conquers the yoke of both law and language with a resultant abundance of interpreters. It is hoped that in the present world of continuing language barriers the contributors to this series will prove opportune interpreters of the perennial Christian message.

Thomas Halton

INTRODUCTION

In the mythical age, or age of the gods, space and time were the symbols of the sacred and the eternal. In Israel, they were institutionalized, and one became the Temple, and the other the Sabbath. But in Christ each *became flesh and made His dwelling among us* (Jn. 1:14): *destroy this temple, was Jesus' answer, and in three days I will raise it up ... Actually He was talking about the temple of His body* (Jn. 2:19-21); elsewhere He said to them: *the sabbath was made for man, not man for the sabbath. That is why the Son of Man is Lord even of the sabbath* (Mk. 2:27-28). Thus, there is the new space, or Temple, that is the Church, one, holy, catholic and apostolic, and the new time, or Sabbath, that is *Anno Domini*, the Year of the Lord, with its division of days and nights, weeks and seasons, to reveal God's grace in time—the beginning in space of eternal glory.

The New Testament with its emphasis on the *Hour of Jesus* bears witness to this divine invasion of space and time. When asked for a messianic sign at Cana, Jesus replied: *My hour has not yet come* (Jn. 2:4), but at the Last Supper He said: *Father, the hour has come! Give glory to your Son that your Son may give glory to you* (Jn. 17:1). Again, He slipped through the hostile crowd on one occasion, *because His hour had not yet come* (Jn. 7:30), whereas, in Gethsemani, He said: *this is your hour—the triumph of darkness* (Lk. 22:53).

This *hour of Jesus*, or time of darkness and light, of sin and glory, began when *evening came* (Gen. 1:5), *and darkness came over the whole land* (Lk. 23:44), and *morning followed* (Gen. 1:5), *as the first day of the week was dawning* (Mt. 28:1) . . . the eighth day! This New Testament day is the octave, so to speak, of the Old Testament first day, the day of separating light from darkness (cf. Gen. 1:5), but its origin is to be found solely in the fact of the resurrection of Christ on the day after the Sabbath. Unlike the Jewish Sabbath, or seventh-day *rest of God*, at the end of creation, this is the first day of the new creation, and there will be no other day to follow—no more weeks, nor seasons, nor years. Now *the first streaks of dawn* have appeared, and the *morning star will rise in our hearts* (2 Peter 1:19), until we are *blameless on the day of Our Lord Jesus Christ* (1 Cor. 1:8). This day and its dawn is Christ, God's grace in time, and glory in eternity. A fully developed theology of this day, as the primary symbol of God's grace in time, can be seen in Cyprian's (d. 258) *Commentary on the Lord's Prayer*:

[1]For since Christ is the true Sun and the true Day, as the sun and the day of the world recede, when we pray and petition that the light come upon us again, we pray for the coming of Christ to provide us with the grace of eternal light. Moreover, the Holy Spirit in the psalms declares that Christ is called the Day. He says: *The stone which the builders rejected has become the cornerstone. This is the Lord's doing; it is wonderful in our eyes. This is the day which the Lord has made; let us exult and rejoice therein* (Ps. 118:22-24). Likewise Malachias the prophet testifies that He is called the Sun when He says: *But unto you that fear my name, the Sun of justice shall arise, and healing is in His wings* (Mal. 3:20). But if in holy Scripture Christ is the true Sun and the true Day, no hour is excepted for Christians, in which God should be adored frequently and always, so that we who are in Christ, that is, in the true Sun and in the true Day, should be insistent throughout the whole day in our petitions and should pray; and when, by the law of the world, the revolving night,

[1]Text: CSEL 3,1.292=FOTC 36.158

recurring in its alternate changes, succeeds, there can be no harm from the nocturnal shades for those who pray, because to the sons of light even in the night there is day. For when is he without light who has light in his heart? Or when does he not have sun and day, to whom Christ is Sun and Day?

At *about the sixth hour* (Lk. 23:44) of *Preparation day* (Jn. 19:31), the sixth day of Genesis, when *God created man in His image* (Gen. 1:27), *a darkness came over the whole land* (Lk. 23:44): so *evening came* (Gen. 1:5) before the Sabbath, and after a long night, forty hours of darkness and silence, *morning followed* (Gen. 1:5), after the Sabbath, in keeping with what Moses, according to Basil the Great[2] (d. 379), called *mia hemera* or one day, rather than *first day* (Gen. 1:5). Of this night Scripture says: *the night will be as clear as day, it will become my light, my joy* (Ps. 139:12).

Certainly, by the middle of the second century, if indeed, not much earlier, the resurrection of Christ had shed its light on the Paschal night of Israel, and biblical event and cosmic experience combined to enrich the Lord's Day with the Word of Scripture and the fragrance of spring. Thus was born the Paschal night of the Church, as a vigil and fast in expectation of the day and the feast. Night and day made the symbol of redemption complete, and again by the time of Cyprian (d. 258) every night was computed as the day:

[3]Moreover, let us who are always in Christ, that is, in the light, not cease praying even in the night. Let us, most beloved brethren, who are always in the light of the Lord, who remember and retain what we have begun to be after receiving grace compute the night as day. Let us believe that we walk always in the light (cf. 1 Jn. 1:7); let us not be hindered by the darkness which we have escaped; let there be no loss of prayers in the hours of the night, no slothful or neglectful waste of

[2]Cf. PG 29.59
[3]Text: CSEL 3,1.294=FOTC 36.159

opportunities for prayer. Let us who by the indulgence of God have been recreated spiritually and reborn imitate what we are destined to be; let us who in the kingdom will have day alone without the intervention of night be just as alert at night as in the day; let us who are destined to pray always and to give thanks to God, not cease here also to pray and to give thanks.

In the first and second centuries day and night constituted the primary symbol of biblical time: *for the darkness itself is not dark, and night shines as the day. Darkness and light are the same* (Ps. 139:12). But the Sabbath debates of the third century brought to the fore the planet week which emphasized the Lord's Day as the *arche* or principle of the week.

A treatise entitled *On Sabbath and Circumcision*, attributed to Athanasius (295-373) proposed a theology of the week, which was more fully developed by Basil (d. 379) in his *Third Homily on the Hexaemeron*. Here Basil explains why Moses used the word *one* rather than the word *first* to show how the week, by returning on itself, forms a unity:

[4]God, who created time, gave it the periods of the days as measures and signs, and, measuring it by the week, He established that the week, returning always upon itself (*anakuklousthai*) should mark the measure of time. And the week itself constitutes one single day, returning seven times on itself. Here is the form of the cycle, which has its beginning and end in itself. Now the property of the aeon is to return on itself and never to end. This is why the principle of time is called not the first day, but one day, so as to indicate, by its name, its relationship with the aeon. Having the characteristics of oneness and of incommunicability, it is properly and fittingly called one.

Here two ideas are encountered. There is first of all the Pythagorean notion of time being ruled by the seven day period: "the first day, according to the Pythagoreans, ought

[4]Text: PG 29.59

to be called the *one* (mia) of the monad, and not the *first* (prote) of the hebdomad, because it is unique and cannot be communicated to the others".[5] Secondly, there is the Hellenistic idea of time, in which the week represents a closed cycle returning perpetually on itself, having therefore neither beginning nor end, and thus representing eternity. The connection between the monad of Greek thought and the biblical *mia* was uniquely Basil's: he is no less clear on the cosmic week which is the figure of the future age, *the eighth day*, or the *day of the Lord*:

[6]The Day of the Lord (*hemera Kyriou*) is great and celebrated (cf. Joel 2:1). Scripture knows this day without evening, without succession, without end; the Psalmist calls it also the *eighth day* because it is outside of this time of seven days. Whether you call it day or age, the sense is the same. If this state is called day, it is one (*mia*) and not multiple; if it is called aeon, it is alone (*monakos*) and not part of a whole (*pollostos*). To raise our spirit toward the future life. (Moses) called *one* the image of the aeon, the first-fruits of days, the contemporary of the light, the holy Lord's Day (*kyriake*) honored by the resurrection of the Lord (*kyrios*).

The scriptural and doctrinal development of the mystery of Christ by the preaching of the Greek and Latin Fathers and by the councils of the fourth and fifth centuries enabled the biblical event to enlighten cosmic experience, and to make the heavens, so to speak, *declare the glory of God* (Ps. 19:1). This is the age of Basil in the Greek East, and Ambrose in the Latin West, when revelation and nature were at one, and the sun and moon were made by God to *serve as signs, and for the fixing of seasons, days and years* (Gen. 1:14):

---

[5]Jean Daniélou, *The Bible and The Liturgy*, University of Notre Dame Press 1956, pg. 265.

[6]Text: PG 29.52

[7]We think that *season* means the changes of the periods of time—winter, spring, summer, and autumn—which, due to the regularity of the movement of the luminaries, are made to pass by us periodically. It is winter when the sun tarries in the southern parts and produces much night shadow in the region about us, so that the air above the earth is chilled and all the damp exhalations, gathering around us, provide a source for rains and frosts and indescribably great snows. Afterwards, returning again from the southern regions, it arrives in the center, so that it divides the time equally between night and day, and the longer it tarries in the places above the earth, much milder a climate does it bring back in turn. Then comes spring, which causes all plants to bud, brings returning life to most trees, and preserves the species for all land and water animals by a series of births. And now, the sun, moving thence toward the summer solstice in a northerly direction, offers us the longest days. And, because it travels through the air a very great distance, it parches the very air above our heads and dries up all the land, aiding in this way the seeds to mature and hurrying the fruits of the trees to ripeness. When the sun is most fiery hot, it causes very short shadows at midday because it shines upon our region directly from above. Those days are longest in which the shadows are shortest, and again, the shortest days are those which have the longest shadows. This is so for us who are called Heteroscians (Shadowed-on-one-side), who inhabit the northern part of the earth. Yet, there are some who for two days of every year are entirely shadowless at midday, upon whom the sun, shining from the zenith, pours equal light from all sides, so that it even lights up the water in the depth of the wells through narrow apertures. Consequently, some call them Ascians (Shadowless). But, those beyond the spice-bearing land have shadows that change from one side to the other. They are the only inhabitants in this world who cast shadows to the south at midday; whence some call them Amphiscians (Shadowed-on-both-sides). All these phenomena happen when the sun has already passed across to the northern

[7]Text: PG 29.117-148 = FOTC 46.95-103

regions. From them it is possible to conjecture the intensity of the burning heat which exists in the air from the solar beam, and what effects it produces. The season of autumn, welcoming us in turn from summer, breaks the excessive stifling heat and, gradually lessening it, by its moderate temperature leads us unharmed out of itself into winter, that is to say, while the sun again turns back from the northerly regions to the southern. These changes of the seasons, which follow the movements of the sun, govern our lives.

Let them serve, He says, *for the fixing of days* (Gen. 1:14), not for making days, but for ruling the days. For, day and night are earlier than the generation of the luminaries. This the psalm declares to us when it says: *He placed the sun to rule the day, the moon and stars to rule the night* (Ps. 136:8). How does the sun rule the day? Because, whenever the sun, carrying the light around with it, rises above our horizon, it puts an end to the darkness and brings us the day. Therefore, one would not err if he would define the day as air, lighted by the sun, or as the measure of time in which the sun tarries in the hemisphere above the earth. But, the sun and the moon were appointed to be for the years. The moon, when it has completed its course twelve times, measures a year, except that it frequently needs an intercalary month for the accurate determination of the seasons, as the Hebrews and the most ancient of the Greeks formerly measured the year. The solar year is the return of the sun from a certain sign to that same sign in its regular revolutions. . . .

May He who has granted us intelligence to learn of the great wisdom of the Creator from the most trivial objects of creation permit us to receive loftier concepts of the Creator from the mightly objects of creation. And yet in comparison with the Creator, the sun and moon possess the reason of an ant or gnat. Truly it is not possible to attain a worthy view of the God of the universe from these things; we can only be led on by them, as also by each of the tiniest of plants or animals to some vague and faint impression of Him.

When the Fathers spoke about the year of the Church, as the ancients did about the *anni circulus*, or yearly cycle, they did so in the same symbolic way. For both the circle was the opposite of all development, and as something completely round it was the symbol of God's eternity. In it there is neither before nor after, greater nor less, and it contains the highest degree of oneness and likeness. It has neither beginning nor end, and it returns upon itself and stretches out in all directions: it is at the same time the deepest rest and the highest exercise of power. Thus the circle is an image of life without development or growth; eternal life, or pleroma, where Christ and His Church stand in the realm of Abiding Spirit.

The mystical Christ, gloriously risen and reigning with His bride, the Church, who in her inmost being is already with Him in heaven (cf. Tertullian, *On Baptism*, 15: *una ecclesia in caelis*) is the real presence of this cosmic symbol, that is, the yearly cycle. In the eternity of His Father in heaven, Christ is the everlasting day: *that city needs neither sun nor moon, because the glory of the Lord shines upon it and the Lamb is its brilliant light* (Rev. 21:23). In the year of His Church on earth He is *the true day which shines on day, the true sun which sheds everlasting light* (Ambrose), as the Roman Liturgy sings in her *Lauds*: He is also *the day which is splendid with the light that knows no evening (phos anesperon)*, as the Greek Liturgy sings in her *vespers*. But in addition Christ is especially the true year without winter, or darkness or death whilst the world's day is simply the *aeon*, or age that is passing: indeed, *Christ is the Lord of all the ages* (cf. 1 Tim. 1:17). Thus the mystery of Christ was woven through days, weeks and seasons into the cosmic cycle of the year, and the cosmic cycle became, as it were, a first prefiguring of the mystery and gave to every hour of time a new unity and significance.

[8]Every day is the Lord's Day ... therefore Christians eat the flesh of the Lamb daily: they consume each day the flesh of the Word, for *Christ our passover has been sacrificed* (1 Cor. 5:7). He was sacrificed on the evening of the Day of Preparation, in

[8]Text: SC 7 bis. 264

keeping with the law of the Pasch, which was eaten in the evening,—in the evening of the world that you might nourish yourselves on the flesh of His Word, you who are always evening until the morning comes ... *In the evening weeping shall have place and in the morning gladness* (Ps. 30:6): so, too, you shall rejoice and be glad in the morning, that is in the world to come (Origen, *On Genesis*, Hom. X).

This volume, entitled *Liturgical Practices in the Fathers,* is another book on the liturgical year. Recently, Thomas Talley wrote historically on *The Origins of the Liturgical Year:* previously, Nocent had written spiritually and pastorally on the same topic, which Karl Adam had earlier considered theologically. The furrow has been well ploughed: yet this book is different. In allowing the Fathers to speak for themselves they become the text and are no longer the footnotes. Nevertheless, there is much common ground, acknowledged when necessary, and avoided where possible.

Ultimately every book on the liturgical year considers the symbolism of time revealing God's grace at work in our space now. In the Old Testament, *God called the light "day", and the darkness He called "night"* (Gen. 1:5): thus day became the starting point of biblical time and night the counterpoint as *day pours out the Word to day, and night to night imparts knowledge* (Ps. 19:3). By the rotation of weeks, seasons, and years this *one*, or *first day* of the Old Testament Creation became the New Testament's *one day of* the resurrection, on the *first day* of the week. This day which *the Lord has made* (Ps. 118:24), continues in the time of the Church through the presence of divine grace in our space; and by the same rotation of weeks, seasons and years this day is daily becoming the new and eternal day of the new and glorious space, that is *God's dwelling among men* (Rev. 21:3).

[9]The Lord came in the evening of the declining world and near the end of its appointed course, but at His coming, since

[9]Text: SC 16.180=FOTC 71.312

He Himself is *the Sun of Righteousness* (Mal. 4:2), He restored a new day for those who believe. Because, therefore, a new light of knowledge arose in the world, in a certain manner, He made His own day in the morning, and, as it were, the *Sun of Righteousness* brought forth its own morning, and in this morning those who receive His precepts are filled with bread (Origen, *On Exodus*, Hom. VII).

The sequence of biblical time is more logical than historical, and can be seen in the structure of this book: nevertheless there is also visible in the arrangement of the material a certain historical sequence, which illustrates the progress of God's grace through the march of time that is history. Hence the division of the material into the following chapters: 1) *The Lord's Day and Week*, which begins in the first century; 2) *The Lord's Night and Season*, which begins in the second century; 4) *New Weeks of the Lord*, which begins in the third century, and 5) *New Seasons of the Lord*, which begins in the fourth century. The third chapter on *New Days of the Lord* follows the logical sequence, but historically belongs for the most part to the fourth and fifth centuries; indeed each chapter outgrows its period of origin, and moves chronologically from the earliest of the Greek Fathers to the Latin Fathers of the sixth century.

Hence by way of Epilogue Isidore of Seville (d. 636) is included to provide a complete picture of what the liturgical year had in his age become, as the mystery of Christ, clarified by patristic teaching, gave to time its full significance.

The patristic texts used throughout are for the most part the translations of my collaborator, editor and friend, Thomas P. Halton. Many of these texts, like that of the Epilogue, are appearing in English for the first time. He and I, together, are pleased to present this volume as a tribute to the priests and people of Mullahorn, Co. Cavan, the parish in Ireland whence we sprang *ex eodem stirpe. O tempora! O mores!*

Thomas K. Carroll

Chapter One

THE LORD'S DAY AND WEEK

The influence and interplay of sun and moon on the Jewish division and computation of time into seven days of one week can indeed be seen in Genesis' first story of creation: but this biblical account with its emphasis on six days of divine work and a seventh day of divine rest differs from every mere solar or lunar calculation, and is the source, however distant, of our Christian understanding of the day and the week.

God and not man is the subject of the Genesis story and God's repose or rest in all that He has made is its message. Consequently in the blessing and hallowing of the seventh day, which unlike the other six has neither morning nor evening, eternity becomes the goal of time, rest of activity, and God of creation. Thus in this creation text there is no mention of the Sabbath of Israel, nor indeed is there any command to our first parents to cease from work on the seventh or Sabbath day. Such notions are man's eventual response to the unfolding of the divine plan in the saving events of history, as days and weeks, seasons and years proclaim the wonder of God from the call of Abram to the hour of Christ, an hour which ended the "time" of Israel, and began the "time" of the Church. Hence the consideration in this chapter of The Lord's Day and Week under the following headings: 1. New Names for the New Day; 2. A Pagan Name for the New Day; 3. A Jewish Name for the New Day.

1. New Names for the New Day

Among all primitive peoples the lunar cycle of time with its emphasis on weeks and months (as we shall see in a later section of this chapter), had a sacred character; but the Genesis story of creation belongs more to the developed civilizations of solar time, which worshipped the sun as Buddha's "universal sovereign," and Plato's "image of the good." Nevertheless, something of the sacred quality of lunar time remained in the blessing of the seventh day, and in the later development of the decalogue Sabbath: *Remember to keep holy the Sabbath day. Six days you may labor and do all your work, but the seventh day is the Sabbath of the Lord, your God. No work may be done then either by you, or your son or daughter, or your male or female slave, or your beast, or by the alien who lives with you. In six days the Lord made the heavens and the earth, the sea and all that is in them; but on the seventh day He rested. That is why the Lord has blessed the Sabbath day and made it holy* (Ex. 20:8-11).

The terms "seven" and "Sabbath," their origin and meaning continue to engage biblical scholars: however, the observance of the seventh day as a day of rest and worship in the Old Testament is beyond dispute, but in the New Testament, and in the patristic age that follows, the continuance and influence of the Sabbath day becomes our problem. According to some the Sabbath in the Old Testament began as a day of rest and became a day of rest and worship, whereas the Sunday of the New Testament began as a day of worship and, in the history of the Church, became a day of worship and rest to parallel the Old Testament Sabbath.[1] Others, representing a more fundamentalist view see one day in seven for rest and worship established at creation, incorporated into the mosaic code and formally presented as moral law: thus the Lord's resurrection on the first day of the week effected a

[1]Rordorf, W. *Sunday*: The History of the Day of Rest and Worship in the earliest centuries of the Christian Church. London, SCM.1968

legitimate, if not immediate, shift from Jewish Sabbath to Christian Sunday.[2] More radically it has been recently argued that Sunday observance did not begin in the Jerusalem Church, which continued Sabbath observance until the second destruction of the city in 135 A.D., but in the Roman Church in the time of Hadrian (117 A.D.-135 A.D.), when Roman repression of the Jews prompted the Church to adopt the symbolism of the powerful pagan cults rather than the practices of Jewish piety.[3] On this question of Lord's Day as Christian Sabbath the message of the Fathers is of particular importance. In their use of new names for a day that had been traditionally numbered can be seen their developing understanding of this day as a) the first day of the week; b) the Lord's Day; c) the eighth Day.

THE FIRST DAY OF THE WEEK

In the New Testament the first day of the Jewish week is proclaimed as an entirely new day from which will arise gradually a new Sabbath, a new week, a new season, and ultimately a new year. Apart from the old Sabbath this first day of the week is the only day to receive explicit attention in the New Testament: according to all the evangelists (cf. Mt. 28:1ff.; cf. Mk. 16:1ff.; cf. Lk. 24:1ff.; cf. Jn. 20:1ff.), who never indicate the day on which an event took place, this was the day of the Lord's resurrection. It was also the day of His apparition to His disciples (cf. Mt. 28:9ff.; cf. Lk. 24:13ff.; cf. Jn. 20:19ff.), and the day He bestowed on them the gift of the Spirit (cf. Acts 2:1ff.; cf. Jn. 20:19-22): similarly it was the day on which He sent them forth, enlivened by His Spirit, as ministers of salvation (cf. Jn. 20:21-23; cf. Acts 1:8). Above all by the time of Paul, and as far away as Troas, this day already associated with numerous episodes in the Christian event, had become the

[2]Berkwith, R.J. & Stott, W. *This is the Day*: the Biblical Doctrine of the Christian Sunday in its Jewish & Early Christian Setting, London. 1978

[3]Bacchiocchi, S. *From Sabbath to Sunday*: A Historical Investigation of the rise of Sunday observance in early Christianity, Rome. 1977

day, or rather, the evening of His supper: *On the first day of the week when we gathered for the breaking of bread, Paul preached to them. Because he intended to leave the next day, he kept on speaking until midnight. As it happened there were many lamps in the upstairs room where we were assembled. Paul talked on and on, and a certain young lad named Eutychus who was sitting on the window-sill became drowsier and drowsier. He finally went sound asleep and fell from the third story to the ground. When they picked him up he was dead. Paul hurried down immediately and threw himself on him, clutching the boy to himself. 'Don't be alarmed,' he said to them. 'There is life in him.' Afterwards Paul went upstairs again, broke bread and ate. Then he talked for a long while-until his departure at dawn* (Acts 20:7ff.).

The Pauline emphasis on the Lord's Supper as an act of worship (cf. 1 Cor. 11:17-34), and on its established time, *the first day of each week* (1 Cor. 16:2), indicates a new day of worship for Christians, which Pliny, the governor of Bithynia (c. 112), describes in his letter to the Emperor Trajan:

[4]Others, whose names were given to me by an informer, admitted the charge of being Christian at first, but later on denied it, saying that they had ceased to be Christian two or more years previously, and some as long as twenty years before. To your statue, and to the images of the gods in the same way, they all did reverence, and they all reviled the name of Christ. They also confessed the sum total of their guilt in this way: on a fixed day, before dawn, they met regularly to chant verses alternately among themselves in honor of Christ, as if He were a God; and also to bind themselves by oath, not for any criminal purpose, but rather to abstain from robbery, theft and adultery, from violating any breach of trust, especially a deposit when called upon to restore it. After this ceremony they usually dispersed but reassembled later to take food of an

[4]E.H. Warmington, ed. *Pliny*, Loeb Classical Library, V.59.289

ordinary harmless kind. This practice, in fact, they had given up after my edict (issued on your instructions), which banned all political assemblies. This decision made me all the more extract by torture from two serving women, whom they call deaconesses, a confession I found nothing but a degenerate sort of a cult carried out to extravagant lengths. (BK.X. ep.XCVI.5-8)

> Thus, "the first day of each week" in Paul, and "the fixed day" of Pliny, indicates for Christians a new day of worship, which brought into question, in the new world of the Church, the decalogue Sabbath of Israel. Some early writers, like Ignatius of Antioch (c. 107), anticipate the dominant trend of second-century Christianity toward a forthright rejection of Sabbath observance along with Jewish practices in general. In his *Epistle to the Magnesians*, Ignatius writes:

[5]Do not be led astray by wrong views or by outmoded fables that count for nothing. For if we go on observing Jewish rites we admit we never received grace. The divine prophets themselves lived Christ Jesus' way. That is why they were persecuted, for they were inspired by His grace to convince unbelievers that God is one, and that He has revealed Himself in His Son Jesus Christ, who is His Word proceeding from silence and who was pleasing in all things to Him who sent Him.

Those, then, who lived by ancient practices arrived at a new hope. They ceased to keep the Sabbath but lived by the Lord's Day, on which our life as well as theirs shone forth, thanks to Him and His death, though some deny this. Through this mystery we got our faith, and because of it we stand our ground so as to become disciples of Jesus Christ, our sole teacher. How, then, can we live without Him when even the prophets, who were His disciples by the Spirit, awaited Him as their teacher? He, then, whom they were expecting, raised them from the dead, when He came.

[5]Text: SC 10.87

We must not, then, be impervious to His kindness. Indeed, were He to act as we do, we should at once be done for. Hence, now we are His disciples, we must learn to live like Christians—to be sure—whoever bears any other name does not belong to God. Get rid, then, of the bad leaven—it has grown stale and sour—and be changed into new leaven, that is, into Jesus Christ. Be salted in Him, so that none of you go bad, for your smell will give you away. It is out of place to talk Jesus Christ and to practice Judaism. For Christianity did not believe in Judaism, but Judaism in Christianity. People of every tongue have come to believe in it, and so been united together in God.

> Again the *Letter to Diognetus*, although it may not be as early as the second century, says:

[6]As for Jewish scruples with respect to food, along with their superstition about the Sabbath, their bragging about circumcision and their hypocrisy about fast days and feasts of new moons I hardly think that you need to be told by me that all these things are ridiculous, and not worth arguing about. How can it be anything but godlessness that makes me accept some of the things made by God for man's use as created good and reject other things as useless and superfluous? And is it not impious to pretend that God forbids a good deed on the Sabbath day? And are they not asking for ridicule when they boast of the mutilation of the flesh as a sign of their being chosen by God, as if for this reason they were especially beloved by him? Again when they constantly gaze at the stars and watch the moon, in order to observe months and days with scrupulous care and to distinguish the changes of the seasons which God has ordained, in order to cater to their own whims, making some into festivals, and others into times of fasting, who could call this evidence of religion rather than of folly? All this being so, I think that you have learned enough to see that Christians are right in holding themselves aloof from the

[6]Text: SC 33.60

silliness and trickery of Greeks and Jews alike, and from the officiousness and noisy conceit of the Jews. But as far as the mystery of the Christians' own religion is concerned, you cannot expect to learn that fully from man.

Other writers of the second century like Justin (c. 150), under the influence of Stoic natural law theory, rejected the details of Sabbath ceremonial (see *Dialog with Trypho*, 12), but preserved those elements of Mosaic law that were expressions of eternal moral law.

Barnabas (c. 130), probably an Alexandrian Jewish Christian, is the only writer of this century to treat the Sabbath commandment explicitly as part of the decalogue: his metaphorical interpretation of this commandment became popular in the latter half of the second century, partly in the context of controversy with Judaism, from which the Church was increasingly concerned to differentiate itself, and partly in the context of controversy with Marcion, who repudiated the Old Testament entirely:

[7]Furthermore, it is also written concerning the Sabbath in the decalogue ... *sanctify also the Sabbath of the Lord with pure hands and a pure heart* (Exod. 20:8) ... and ... *if my sons keep the Sabbath, I will have mercy upon them* (Jer. 17:24). Now concerning this Sabbath He speaks at the beginning of creation ... *and He rested on the seventh day* (Gen.2:2). This means that when this Son will come and destroy the time of the lawless one and judge the godless, and change the sun and the moon and the stars, then He shall indeed rest on the seventh day. Furthermore He says: *thou shalt keep it holy with pure hands and a pure heart* (Exod. 20:8). If, then, anyone is able in the here and now to hallow the day which God sanctified, by being pure in heart, we are completely deceived: know that we cannot sanctify it until that time when we shall enjoy true repose; when we shall be able to do so simply because we have been made just ourselves and

[7]Text: SC 172.182

shall have received the promise, when there is no more sin, but all things have been made new by the Lord; then we shall be able to sanctify it, having been made holy ourselves. Furthermore, He says to them: *I will not abide your new moons and your Sabbaths* (Isa. 1:13). You see what He means: the present Sabbaths are not acceptable to me, but that Sabbath which I have made, in which, after giving rest to all things, I will make the beginning of another world. Therefore, we also celebrate with joy the eighth day on which Jesus also arose from the dead, was made manifest, and ascended into heaven.

> The attempt to steer a course between Judaism and Marcionism forced Christian writers such as Irenaeus and Tertullian to clarify elements of continuity and discontinuity between the religion of the Old and New Testaments. In the case of the Sabbath the metaphorical interpretation of Scripture enabled them to explain how the commandment could be both God-given and valuable, and yet not binding on Christians in its literal sense.
>
> "The first day of the week" could easily become for Jewish Christians a new temporary Sabbath in anticipation of the eternal Sabbath. For Tertullian the detailed Mosaic legislation was secondary to the fundamental morality of the decalogue, which was the basis of Abraham's faith and righteousness. (cf. Tertullian, *Adversus Judaeos*)

[8]It follows accordingly, that, in so far as the abolition of carnal circumcision and of the old law is demonstrated as having been consummated at its specific times, so also the observance of the Sabbath is demonstrated to have been temporary.

For the Jews say, that from the beginning God sanctified the seventh day, by resting on it from all His works which He made; and that thence it was, likewise, that Moses said to the People: *Remember the day of the Sabbath, to sanctify it* (Ex. 20:8): *every servile work ye shall not do therein, except what pertaineth unto life* (Ex. 12:16). Whence we (Christians)

[8]Text PL 2.605 ANF 3.155

understand that *we* still more ought to observe a Sabbath from all "servile work" always, and not only every seventh day, but through all time. And through it arises the question for us, *what* Sabbath God willed us to keep? For the Scripture points to a Sabbath eternal and a Sabbath temporal. For Isaiah the prophet says, *Your Sabbaths my son hateth* (Isa. 1:13), and in another place is said *My Sabbaths ye have profaned* (Ez. 22:8). Whence we discern that the temporal Sabbath is human, and the eternal Sabbath is accounted divine; concerning which He predicts through Isaiah: *And there shall be.* He says, *month after month, and day after day, and Sabbath after Sabbath; and all flesh shall come to adore in Jerusalem, saith the Lord*, which we understand to have been fulfilled in the times of Christ, when 'all flesh'—that is, every nation—'came to adore in Jerusalem' God the Father, through Jesus Christ His Son, as was predicted through the prophet: *Behold your God, cities of Judah* (Isa. 40:9). Thus, therefore, before this temporal Sabbath, there was withal an eternal Sabbath foreshown and foretold; just as before the carnal circumcision there was withal a spiritual circumcision foreshown. In short, let them teach us, as we have already premised, that Adam observed the Sabbath; or that Abel, when offering to God a Holy victim, pleased Him by a religious reverence for the Sabbath; or that Enoch, when translated had been a keeper of the Sabbath; or that Noah the ark-builder observed on account of the deluge an immense Sabbath; or that Abraham in observance of the Sabbath, offered Isaac his son: or that Melchizedek in his priesthood received the law of the Sabbath.

But the Jews are sure to say that, ever since this precept was given through Moses, the observance has been binding. Manifest accordingly it is, that the precept was not eternal nor spiritual, but temporary, which would one day cease. In short, so true is it that it is not in the exemption from work of the Sabbath—that is, of the seventh day—that the celebration of this solemnity is to consist, that Joshua the son of Nun, at the time that he was reducing the city Jericho by war stated that he had received from God seven days, making the circuit of the city; and thus, when the seventh day's circuit had been performed, the walls of the city would spontaneously fall (cf.

Josh. 6:1-20). Which was so done; and when the space of the seventh day was finished, just as was predicted, down fell the walls of the city. Whence it is manifestly shown, that in the number of the seven days there intervened a Sabbath day. Whencesoever they may have commenced, must necessarily include within them a sabbath-day; on which day not only must the priests have worked but the city must have been made a prey by the edge of the sword by all the people of Israel. Nor is it doubtful that they *wrought servile work* (Ex. 12:16). When, in obedience to God's precept, they drove the preys of war. For in the times of the Maccabees, too, they did bravely in fighting on the Sabbaths, and routed their foreign foes, and recalled the law of the fathers to the primitive style of life by fighting on the Sabbaths. Nor should I think it was any other law which they thus vindicated than the one in which they remembered the existence of the prescript touching *the day of the Sabbath* (Ex. 20:8; Deut. 5:12-15).

Whence it is manifest that the force of such precepts was temporary, and respected the necessity of present circumstances; and that it was not with a view to its observance in perpetuity that God formerly gave them such a law.

> The same spiritual approach to the Decalogue was further developed in opposition to Marcion who separated the Law from the Gospel. Again Tertullian, for whom the ceremonial aspect of the Law was diminished while its moral aspect was increased, is our witness in his writings against Marcion:

[9]Concerning the Sabbath I have this to say: the question could not have arisen if Christ had not publicly declared Himself to be Lord of the Sabbath.... Thus men wondered ... was it proper for Christ to proclaim the Creator to be God, and at the same time to impugn His Sabbath?... But let me say this: If Christ interfered with the Sabbath He simply acted after the Creator's example in as much as in the siege of Jericho the carrying of the Ark of the Covenant round the walls for

[9]Text: PL 2.383 = ANF 3.155

eight days, including the Sabbath by the Creator's express command (cf. Josh. 6:14-15), broke the Sabbath by working— or so those people think who have the same opinion also of Christ, being unaware that neither did Christ break the Sabbath nor did the Creator as I shall shortly show. Even so, the Sabbath was on that occasion broken by Joshua so that this too might be taken as referring to Christ. Even if it was through hatred that He made an attack on the Jews' most solemn day because (as Marcion alleges) He was not the Jews' Christ, even by this hatred of the Sabbath He, the Creator's Christ, acknowledged that Creator, following up His cry made by the mouth of Isaiah: *Your new moons and Sabbaths my soul hateth* (Isa. 1:13). Now in whatever sense this was spoken we know that in circumstances of this kind a sharp reproof has to be put in action against a sharp provocation. Next I shall argue the case in reference to the actual subject in which Christ's rule of conduct has been thought to destroy the Sabbath. The disciples had been hungry; on that very day they had plucked the ears of corn and rubbed them in their hands: by preparing food they had made a breach in the holy day. Christ holds them guiltless and so becomes guilty of infringing the Sabbath: the Pharisees are His accusers. Marcion takes exception to the heads of the controversy—if I may play about a bit with the truth of my Lord—written document and intention. A plausible answer is based upon the Creator's written document and on Christ's intention, as by the precedent of David who on the Sabbath day entered into the temple and prepared food by boldly breaking up the loaves of the shewbread. For he, too, remembered that even from the beginning since the Sabbath day was first instituted, this privilege was granted to it. I make exception from fasting. For when the Creator forbade the gathering of two days' supply of manna, He allowed it only on the day before the Sabbath, so that by having food prepared the day before He might make immune from fasting the holy day of the Sabbath that followed. Well it is then that our Lord allowed the same purpose in breaking down the Sabbath—if that is what they want it called: well it is also that He gave effect to the Creator's intention by the privilege of not fasting on the Sabbath. In fact

He would have once and for all broken the Sabbath, and the Creator besides, if He had enjoined His disciples to fast on the Sabbath, in opposition to the fact of Scripture and of the Creator's intention. So then, as He did not keep His disciples in close constraint, but now finds excuse for them; as He puts in answer human necessity as begging for considerate treatment: as He conserves the higher privilege of the Sabbath, of freedom from sorrow rather than abstention from work: as He associates David and his followers with His own disciples in fault and in permission: as He is in agreement with the relaxation the Creator has given: as after the Creator's example He Himself is equally kind: is He on that account an alien from the Creator? After that the Pharisees watch if He will heal a man on the Sabbath, that they might accuse Him— evidently (accuse him) as a breaker of the Sabbath, not as the setter forth of a strange god: for perhaps I shall everywhere insist on this point alone, that nowhere was there any prophecy of a different Christ. But the Pharisees were utterly in error about the law of the Sabbath, having failed to notice that it is under certain conditions that it enjoins abstention from works, under a specific aspect of them. For when it says of the Sabbath day, *No work of thine shalt thou do in it* (Ex. 20:10), by saying *thine* it has made a ruling concerning that human work which any man perform by his craft or business, and not about divine work. But the work of healing or of rescue is not properly man's work but God's. So again in the law it says, *In it thou shalt do no manner of work, save that which is to be done for every soul* (Ex. 12:16), that is, with the purpose of setting a soul free for the work of God can be done even by the agency of a man, for the saving of a soul, yet God is the doer of it: and this as man Christ also was going to do, because He is also God. Because of His desire to lead them towards this understanding of the law by the restoration of the withered hand, He asks them, *Is it lawful to do good on the Sabbath, or not? to set a soul free, or to destroy it?* (Lk. 6:9): so that by giving approval to that sort of work which He purposed to do for the soul, He might give them warning of what works the law of the Sabbath forbade, human works, and what works it enjoined, divine works, which were to be done for every soul.

He called himself Lord of the Sabbath because He was protecting the Sabbath as belonging to Himself. Though even if He had broken it He would have had the right to do so as being its Lord, and even more so as He who instituted it. But He did not utterly destroy it in order that henceforth it might be clear that the Sabbath was not broken either by the Creator, even at a time when the Ark was carried around the walls of Jericho ... and although He has shown a certain distaste for Sabbaths in calling them your Sabbaths, elsewhere ... He has put His own Sabbath in a different light, ... declaring them to be 'true, and delightful and inviolable.'

This metaphorical approach to the Sabbath of Israel, common among Christian writers of the late second and early third centuries, led later writers to see the first day of the old Jewish week as the beginning in time of the eschatological Sabbath of Genesis, a new day of creation, which had in fact begun with the resurrection of Christ on the first day of the Jewish week, and was already being called by Christians in the second century, the Lord's Day.

THE LORD'S DAY

In the New Testament, as we have already seen, the resurrection of Christ, and all subsequent expressions of this event, such as certain of the apparitions, took place on the first day of the week. To this day, then, as to the first day of Genesis, when God separated light from darkness, the Christ event gave a new meaning, which the early Christians soon expressed in a new name—the Lord's Day.

The very term is fraught with meaning: used by the emperors from the time of Nero to express their divinity, it was also used in Acts, together with the word Messiah or Christ, to proclaim the gospel of the first Pentecost: *therefore let the whole house of Israel know beyond doubt that God has made both Lord (Kurion) and Messiah this Jesus whom you crucified* (Acts 2:36). Thus, through His resurrection the Christ of Jewish expectation became in the

Word's fullest sense the Lord of the universe, and the first day of the Jewish week of numbers, on which He rose from the dead, was named the Lord's Day, just as the seventh day of the same numerical week was special and named accordingly the Sabbath.

The Lord's Day, *kyriakē hēmera*, differs somewhat from the Old Testament's "Day of the Lord," *Hēmera tou kyriou*, which refers to the day on which God will come in judgment: thus, if the early Christians wished to avoid this confusion and ambiguity, and at the same time wanted to name the first day of the week after their Lord or *Kyrios* they would have to use the adjective form of *Kyriake* or Lord's Day: "On the Lord's Day I was caught up in ecstasy, and I heard behind me a piercing voice like the sound of a trumpet": Scholars offer four possible interpretations of "Lord's Day" in this text: (a) the eschatological day of the Lord; (b) the Saturday Sabbath; (c) Easter Day; (d) the first day of the week of the resurrection. But since this adjectival form is also found in Paul in reference to the Lord's Supper, the possible interconnection of the act of worship and the day of worship cannot be ignored. Certainly at the dawn of the second century the Lord's Day meant the day of His resurrection and triumph, the first day of the week, when Christians assembled to celebrate the Eucharist, and the Revelation text must be read in this context. The *Didache* (c. 100) is our earliest witness:

[10]On every Lord's Day—His special day—come together and break bread and give thanks, first confessing your sins so that your sacrifice may be pure. Anyone at variance with his neighbor must not join you, until they are reconciled, lest your sacrifice be defiled. For it was of this sacrifice that the Lord said, *Always and everywhere offer me a pure sacrifice; for I am a great King, says the Lord, and my name is marveled at by the nations* (Mal. 1:11).

[10]Text: SC 248.192

Ignatius of Antioch (c. 107) is equally clear in his *Letter to the Magnesians:*

[11]Those, then, who lived by ancient practices arrived at a new hope. They ceased to keep the Sabbath and lived by the Lord's Day, on which our life as well as theirs shone forth, thanks to Him and His death, though some deny this. Through this mystery we got our faith, and because of it we stand our ground so as to become disciples of Jesus Christ, our sole teacher. How, then, can we live without Him when even the prophets, who were His disciples by the Spirit, awaited Him as their teacher? He, then, whom they were rightly expecting, raised them from the dead, when He came.

The *Gospel of Peter* 35 and 50 (c.150) gives further evidence of the "Lord's Day" being the accepted technical term for the first day of the week, and by the second half of the second century the references become more numerous and less ambiguous: "a reference to weekly Sunday worship seems very probable but not certain in the letter of Bishop Dionysius of Corinth to Bishop Soter of Rome (c.170): 'today we have kept the Lord's holy day, on which we have read your letter!

At about the same time, however, a passage in the Acts of Peter (Act. Verc. 29) clearly identifies *dies dominica* (the Lord's Day) with the next day after the Sabbath, and the Acts of Paul represents the Apostle as praying on the Sabbath as the Lord's Day drew near.'"[12]

It is also possible to detect, a century before the law of Constantine, a desire for rest on the Lord's Day on purely pragmatic grounds. It cannot have been easy for many Christians to find adequate time for worship on a day which was for pagan and Jew an ordinary workday. Hence Tertullian speaks of "deferring (on the Lord's Day), even

[11]Text: SC 10.88
[12]Carson, *op. cit.* 299

our business affairs, lest we give place to the devil."[13]
Likewise, the Syriac *Didascalia* (c.250):

[14]Now then, whenever you teach, command and warn the people to be constant in coming to church ... lest any one diminish the Church by not assembling and cause the body of Christ to be short of a member. Let no one take thought of others only, but of himself as well, listening to that which our Lord said: *Every one that gathereth not with me, scattereth* (Mt. 12:30). Since therefore you are the members of Christ, do not scatter yourselves from the Church by not assembling. Seeing that you have Christ for your head, as He promised— for you are partakers with us—be not then neglectful of yourselves and do not then deprive our Savior of His members: do not rend and scatter His body by making your worldly affairs of more account than the word of God; but on the Lord's Day leave everything and run eagerly to your Church for she is your glory. Otherwise, how can you stand before God who do not assemble on the Lord's Day to hear the word of life and be nourished with the divine food which lasts forever?

This need for rest on the Lord's Day is more fully expressed much later by Martin of Braga, in the post-Constantinian Church:

[15]Go often to church and to the holy places and pray to God: do not neglect the Lord's Day, but hold it in reverence, because on it the Son of God, our Lord Jesus Christ, arose from the dead. Do not perform servile work on the Lord's Day in field or meadow or vineyard: ... cook only what is necessary to nourish the body ... do not journey on the Lord's Day ... except for a good purpose, such as walking to holy places, visiting a brother or a friend, consoling the sick, or carrying counsel or aid for a good cause to one in trouble. In this way

[13]Text: PL 1.1191
[14]Text: R.H. Connolly, ed., 124
[15]Text: PL 72.18 = FOTC 62.84

the Christian should honor the Lord's Day. It is quite disgraceful that the pagans who do not know the faith of Christ, but worship idols and demons, should honor the day of Jupiter or any other demon and abstain from work, when demons certainly never created and do not have any day. Yet we, who worship the true God and believe that the Son of God rose from the dead, do not honor the day of the resurrection, the Lord's Day. Do not do wrong to the resurrection of the Lord, but honor it and hold it in reverence for the sake of the hope which we have in it. For just as He, our Lord Jesus Christ, the Son of God, who is our Head, rose from the dead on the third day, so, too, do we hope that we who are His members shall rise in our flesh at the end of the world.

> As we have already seen, the basic idea behind the term Lord's Day from the beginning has been the resurrection. According to Justin (c.150) Christians gather on this day, "since it is the first day, on which God, transforming darkness and matter, made the universe, and Jesus Christ, our Savior rose from the dead on the same day."[16] Likewise, for Tertullian it is "the day which commemorates the Lord's resurrection."[17] This early emphasis on the resurrection prevailed and by the fourth century, especially among the Greeks, it became customary to refer to the Lord's Day as the day of the resurrection as in the *Apostolic Constitutions* (c.360):

[18]On the day of the resurrection of the Lord, which we call the Lord's Day, you must always come together to give thanks to God, and to bless Him for all the benefits which He has bestowed upon us through Christ by rescuing us from the bonds of ignorance and error: thus let your sacrifice be spotless and pleasing to God who to His universal Church said: *In every place I am offered incense and a pure offering; for I am indeed a great King says the Lord God Almighty, and my*

[16]Text: PG 6.430
[17]Text: PL 1.1191
[18]Text: cf. ANF 7.470

name is wonderful among the nations (Mal. 1:11).

> The *Apostolic Constitutions* (c.360) also presents the Sabbath as a memorial of the first creation, and the Lord's Day as the memorial of the second creation, effected through the resurrection:

[19]Lord Almighty, you appointed the Sabbath ... that we might rest from our works and contemplate the work of your hand.... But we also solemnly assemble to celebrate the feast of the resurrection on the Lord's Day and rejoice on account of Him who brought home the Gentiles ... the true Israel.... This day surpasses all others ... and reveals ... the first born of the whole creation, Christ, Divine Word and true man, born of Mary alone ... crucified under Pontius Pilate ... and raised from the dead. Thus the Lord's Day commands us to offer to you, Almighty God, thanksgiving for everything that you have done ... for that grace which you have given to us and which surpasses all your other blessings.

Again:

[20]When you instruct the people, O bishop, command and exhort them to come constantly to church morning and evening, every day, and in no way to forsake it on any account, but to assemble together continually.... For it is not only spoken concerning the priests but let every one of the laity listen to it as concerning himself ... Be not careless of yourselves, neither deprive the Savior of His own members, neither divide his Body nor disperse His members ... but assemble yourselves together every day, morning and evening, singing psalms and praying in the Lord's house; in the morning saying the sixty-second psalm, and in the evening the hundred-fortieth, but principally on the Sabbath day. And on the day of our Lord's resurrection, which is the Lord's Day, meet more diligently, sending praise to God that made the universe by Jesus, and sent Him to us, and allowed Him to suffer, and

[19]Text: *ibid.* 474
[20]Cf. *ibid.* 422

raised Him from the dead. Otherwise what apology will he make to God who does not assemble on that day to hear the saving word concerning the resurrection, on which we pray three times, standing in memory of Him who arose in three days, in which is performed the reading of the prophets, the preaching of the Gospel and the oblation of the sacrifice, the gift of the holy food?

Thus the transition from the first day of the week to the Lord's Day became complete with the addition of the resurrection, the *anastasis*, which still survives in the Russian *wosskressenige*. Naming the numbered day expressed the mystery for Ephrem: "for the first day of the week, the first born of days, is worthy of reverence, for it holds many mysteries. So pay it your respect, for it has taken the right of primogeniture from the Sabbath. Blessed is he who keeps that day with holy observance."[21] Soon the name 'Lord's Day' was adopted to the Latin language in its adjectival form, and *dominica* became the ordinary name for the first day of the week in the evangelists and has remained so to our own times; in the romance languages, *dominica* in Italian, *domingo* in Spanish, *dimanche* in French, and *domnach* in Gaelic.

THE EIGHTH DAY

Exegesis in the Jewish tradition ranged from the crudest literalism to the wildest flights of allegory. Among the Hellenistic Jews at Alexandria the allegorical approach flourished, especially with exegetes like Aristobulus and Philo, for whom Pythagorean numerical symbolism was of the utmost importance. Seven and eight were sacred numbers. *Make seven or eight portions: you know not what misfortune may come upon the earth* (Eccles. 11:2). Seven was the number sanctified by the Creator, and eight was the number to signify the Redemption, and to mark the

[21]Cf. Carson, *op. cit.* 287

Covenant: *circumcise the flesh of your foreskin, and that shall be the mark of the covenant between you and me. Throughout the ages every male child shall be circumcised when he is eight days old* (Gen. 17:11-12).

Eight continued in the New Testament to be a sign of salvation and the new creation: *nor did He spare the ancient world—even though He preserved Noah as a preacher of holiness with seven others when He brought down the Flood on that godless earth. At that time, a few persons, eight in all, escaped in the ark through the waters* (1 Pet. 3:20). Hence the connection, even in the New Testament, between baptism and the symbolic number of eight.

Pliny, governor of Bithynia, in his letter to the Emperor Trajan (c.112 A.D.) tells us that the Christian communities of Bithynia assembled twice on "a fixed day" each week in the early morning for a kind of liturgy of the Word, which seems to have included baptism (or the oath), and in the evening for a meal. Hence the association from very early times of baptism and Eucharist with this fixed day, and just as the Lord's Supper of Paul (cf. 1 Cor. 11:20) may have named Pliny's "fixed day" *the Lord's Day* (Rev. 1:10), so too the symbolic number of eight of baptism may have renamed this same day the eighth day. Certainly from the middle of the second century the eighth day begins to appear in the literature with a growing significance. The *Letter of Barnabas* is our earliest witness to this designation:

[22]Furthermore He says to them: *I will not abide your new moons and your Sabbaths* (Isa. 1:13). You see what He means: the present Sabbaths are not acceptable to me, but that Sabbath which I have made, in which, after giving rest to all things, I will make the beginning of the eighth day, that is, the beginning of another world. Therefore we also celebrate with joy the eighth day on which Jesus also rose from the dead, was made manifest, and ascended into heaven.

[22]Text: SC 172.186

In this *Epistle of Barnabas* the eschatological significance of the term is certainly clear as one might expect from a convert Jew in Alexandria. His juxtaposition of eschatological Sabbath and "the eighth day, on which Jesus also rose from the dead," inclines him toward a Sabbath view of a day already numbered symbolically.

Justin Martyr around the same time and in faraway Rome, although in dialogue with a Jew, preserved and developed the baptismal symbolism of the new name:

[23]Thus, as I already stated, God speaks through Malachi, one of the twelve prophets, concerning the sacrifices you then offered up to Him: *I have no pleasure in you, said the Lord, and I will not receive your sacrifices at your hands. For from the rising of the sun even to its going down my name is great among the Gentiles, said the Lord, but you profane it* (Mal. 1:10-12). By making reference to the sacrifices that we Gentiles offer to Him everywhere, the Eucharistic bread and the Eucharistic chalice, He predicted that we should glorify His name, but that you should profane it. Furthermore, the precept of circumcision, obliging you without fail to circumcise your sons on the eighth day, was a type of the true circumcision by which we are circumcised from error and wickedness through our Lord Jesus Christ who arose from the dead on the first day of the week. For the first day of the week, while it remains the first of all days, yet is called the eighth, according to the number of all the days of the cycle, and still it remains the first.

In both Barnabas and Justin there is this clear notion of a new beginning and at the same time a renewal of the cycle as symbolized in music by the octave: in keeping with the mysterious significance of cyclical time this new beginning is the first day of the week but in as much as it recurs and renews itself, it may also be called the octave or the eighth day. However, the eighth day should not lead us to the conclusion that this is the final day of a new Christian week

[23]Text: PG 6.564

to replace the Jewish week which ended with its Sabbath: on the contrary, the eighth day leaves behind the old week proper to the first creation, and marks the beginning of a new creation—*therefore if anyone is in Christ, he is a new creation* (2 Cor. 5:17). Such is the mystery of the Ogdoad, or of the Octava in Latin, which is first and eighth at the same time.

Irenaeus (c.202) wrote a whole treatise, now lost, on the Ogdoad, in order to distinguish his orthodox opinion on the point from that of the Gnostics, who in some way personified the Ogdoad:

[24]This mother they also call Ogdoad, Sophia, Terra, Jerusalem, Holy Spirit, and with a masculine reference, Lord. Her place of habitation is an intermediate one, above the Demiurge indeed, but below and outside of the Pleroma, even to the end.

The Gnostic idea of the Ogdoad had its origins in Hellenistic astrology, in which the seven planetary spheres, the realm of change and corruption, are contrasted with the heaven above, the eighth sphere of the fixed stars, the realm of incorruption and repose. The soul ascends through the seven heavens shedding its corporality, and finds its resting place in the Ogdoad, the sphere of the divine. Thus Thomas prays to the Holy Spirit: "Come, Mother of the seven houses that thy rest may be in the eighth house."[25] Christian gnosticism could therefore very readily reconcile this type of cosmological symbolism with the eschatological symbolism of the Judaic Sabbath and the Christian eighth day, for the rest of the Ogdoad and the rest of the soul were ultimately one and the same: "The repose of the spiritual ones is on the Lord's Day, that is, on the Ogdoad, which is called the Lord's Day ... the other faithful souls are with the Demiurge in the Hebdomad."[26]

[24]Text: SC 264.32
[25]Quoted in Carson, *op. cit.*, 274
[26]*ibid.*

In Valentinian Gnosticism, according to Irenaeus *(Adv.h.* 1:11) the seventh heaven, the Hebdomad, was the sphere of the Demiurge, while the Ogdoad above was the sphere of the Holy Spirit, the mother. Thus spiritual men are reunited with the mother in the Ogdoad, while psychic men are with the Demiurge in the Hebdomad. At the consummation the latter ascend into the Ogdoad while the former, leaving behind their souls, ascend into the Pleroma:

[27]I have become to Him a thing . . . completed according to the type; I have come into being on the eighth day which is the Day of the Lord. But the whole completion of the completion you will see through the redemption that has happened to me and you will see me.

Eschatological Sabbath rest and the rest of the soul in the Ogdoad were thus easily combined and found expression, especially in Alexandria, with Clement at the beginning of the third century:

[28]By the meadow (cf. Plato, *Republic* X. 616B) is to be understood the fixed sphere as being a peaceful and congenial spot and the place of the saints; and by the seven days the motions of the seven planets, and every art and operation which strives to attain its true end in rest. But after the wandering world the journey leads to heaven, that is to the eighth motion and the eighth day.

Clement of Alexandria (150-215) was the first to introduce the gnostic cosmological notion of rest into the mainstream of Christian thought. For him the primary reference of the concepts of Sabbath and eighth day was to the Gnostic's ascent through the seven heavens to the Ogdoad:

[27]Text: SC 264.170
[28]Text: GCS.397

²⁹Those who have advanced to Gnostic perfection are at rest in the holy will of God, in the celestial church in which are gathered the philosophers of God who do not remain in the rest of the Hebdomad, but by the active beneficence of assimilation to God are promoted to the heritage of beneficence of the Ogdoad, and thereby are devoted to the pure vision of insatiable contemplation.

> In his exposition of the Sabbath commandment Clement draws on the allegorical exegesis of Philo, the Alexandrian Jew, and Aristobulus, and their Pythagorean number symbolism so dear to the gnostics. He adapts this happy series of connections to the Christian symbolism of the first and eighth days. The Sabbath rest of the seventh day is mere preparation for the true rest of the eighth day. For the eighth day is the first day, and the first day is Christ, the beginning (or *archē*) of creation, and the eighth of men:

³⁰And the third word is the one which indicates that the world was created by God, and that He gave us the seventh day for rest, because of life's troubles. For God is incapable of weariness and suffering and want. But we who bear flesh need rest. Therefore the seventh day is proclaimed a day of rest— separation from evils—preparing for the primal day, our true rest, which, in truth, is the first creation of light, in which all things are seen and possessed. From this day we are illuminated by wisdom and knowledge.... For the light of truth, a true light casting no shadow, is the Spirit of God invisibly apportioned to all who are sanctified by faith, holding the place of a luminary as a guide to the knowledge of real existence. By following him through our whole lives we become impassible, and this is to rest.... Having reached this point we must mention these things incidentally, since the discourse has turned on 'the seventh' and 'the eighth'. For the eighth may turn out to be properly the seventh, and the seventh manifestly the sixth, and this latter properly the Sabbath, and

²⁹Text: *ibid.*433
³⁰Text: GCS 2.501

the seventh a day of work. For the creation of the world was concluded in six days. For the motion of the sun from solstice to solstice is completed in six months, in the course of which, at one time the leaves fall, and at another plants bud and seeds come to maturity.... The Pythagoreans reckon six the perfect number from the creation of the world: ... just as marriage generates from male and female, so six is generated from the odd number three, which is called the masculine number, and the even number two, which is considered the feminine, for twice three are six.... Rightly, then, the number seven is reckoned to be motherless and childless, for figuratively it expresses the nature of Sabbath rest, in which *they neither marry nor are given in marriage* (Mk. 12:25). And they call eight a cube, counting the fixed sphere along with the seven revolving ones, by which is produced 'the great year,' as a kind of period of recompense of what has been promised.... Thus, man is said to have been made on the sixth day ... so as straightway to receive the rest of the Lord's inheritance. Some such thing also is indicated by the sixth hour in the scheme of salvation, in which man was perfected: for just as there are seven intervals in eight and seven thereby glorifies eight, so too the *heavens declare the glory of God* (Ps. 19:1)....

God's resting is not, then, as some conceive, that God ceased from doing. For, being good, if He should ever cease from doing too, then would He cease from being God, which it is sacrilege even to say. The resting is, therefore, the ordering that the order of created things should be preserved inviolate, and that each of the creatures should cease from the ancient disorder. For the creations on the different days followed in a most important succession; so that all things brought into existence might have honor from priority, created together in thought, but not being of equal worth.

The same identity of Sabbath rest and the soul's contemplation of divine things in the Sabbath of eternity appears in Origen's *Against Celsus*:

[31]Again, not understanding the meaning of the words, *And God ended on the sixth day His works which He had made, and ceased on the seventh day from all the works which He had made; and God blessed the seventh day and hallowed it, because on it He had ceased from all His works which He had begun to make* (Gen. 2:2-3) ... and imagining the expression *He ceased on the seventh day* to be the same as *He rested on the seventh day* Celsus makes the remark, 'After this He is weary, indeed, like a very bad workman who is in need of rest to refresh himself.' For Celsus knows nothing of the day of the Sabbath and God's rest which follows the completion of the creation of the world, and which lasts during the duration of the world, and in which all those who will keep festival with God who have in turn done all their works in their six days and who, because they have omitted none of their duties will ascend to the contemplation (of heavenly things) and to the assembly of righteous and blessed things.

Thus Origen understands the Sabbath in terms of contemplation rather than abstention from work, and he speaks of Christian life in this world as "the six days of ascending the mountain of the transfiguration before the Sabbath of beholding the transfigured Christ" *Comm. in Mt.* 12:36)[32] and elsewhere as "the six days of gathering the manna that we shall enjoy in the Sabbath of eternity" (*Hom. in Exod.* 7:5).[33] Here Origen is following Clement's idea of the perfect Christian hastening through the holy Hebdomad to the Ogdoad: "the seventh day is the rest which prepares by the cessation of sin the primordial day which is truly our repose, which is also the creation of the true light and the knowledge that shines upon us" (*Stromata* 6. 138:1).

Basil the Great (d.379) in his *On the Holy Spirit* further elaborated this transition of the seventh into the eighth day with his emphasis on the light of the first and the eighth day:

[31]Text: SC 147.330
[32]Text: PG 13.1068
[33]Text: PG 12.346

[34]Thus we all look to the East when we pray but few of us know that we are seeking our old country, Paradise, which *God planted in Eden in the East* (Gen. 2:8). We pray standing, on the first day of the week, but we do not all know the reason. On the day of the resurrection, rising up we remind ourselves of the grace given to us by standing at prayer, not only because we rose with Christ and are bound to *seek those things which are above* (Col. 3:1), but because the day seems to us to be somehow an image of the age which we await wherefore, though it is 'the beginning of days' it is not called by Moses 'first', but 'one'. For he says, *there was evening and there was morning, one day* (Gen. 1:5.), as though the same day often recurred. Now 'one' and 'eight' are the same, in itself distinctly indicating that really 'one' and 'eight' of which the Psalmist makes mention in certain titles of the psalms, the state which follows after this present time, the day which knows no waning or eventide, and no successor, that age which ends not or grows old. Of necessity, then, the Church teaches her foster-children to offer their prayers on that day standing so that through a continual reminder of the endless life we may not neglect to make provision for our passing on to that place.

> Gregory of Nazianzus, a fellow Cappadocian, shared Basil's fascination with numbers. For him seven was a number sacred among the Hebrews and eight was no less sacred among the Greeks of the fourth century. His friend and colleague, Gregory of Nyssa, wrote a homily on the sixth Psalm, entitled, *The Eighth Day*, in which his allegorical interpretation permits him to find a consistent plan of ascetical and mystical precepts in the entire arrangement of the Psalter:

[35]The title, 'For the secret' proposes accurate diligence to us in our knowledge of God. For the worst fate of the soul is false and erring perceptions about God (for what use does one derive from any good if one does not have goodness itself?).

[34]Text: SC 17bis.484
[35]Text: PG 44.504

Accordingly the title proffers you a torch to illuminate the secrets of the knowledge of God, the sum total of which is faith in the Son. For the title says 'for the secrets of the Son', for that is truly a secret, and is impervious to thought or sight, in that it far transcends human comprehension but the one who approaches with faith will be the first to reach the goal of victory. The meaning of the title, "For the Inheritor" is obvious. For the prophet pours forth to God this prayer for the soul which has departed from its inheritance when the sun has been allowed to go down on its transgression of God's commandment, that the morning sun will again dispel the darkness and that he shall deserve to hear those sweet words addressed to those on the right, *Come, you blessed of my father, receive the kingdom prepared for you from the constitution of the world* (Mt. 25:34). . . . And one would not err if one attached the same meaning to the title, 'For the morning undertaking'. For Scripture is in the habit of calling the dawn 'morning'. Dawn is the boundary of night and day, ending one and beginning the other. Scripture often enigmatically calls evil 'darkness,' so that when through the help of divine grace we undertake the life of virtue we then come to victory, *laying aside the works of darkness and walking honorably as in the daytime* as the Apostle says (Rom. 13:13). The title 'for the Octave' is close in meaning to what we have explained. For all the care shown in the life that is cultivating virtue is directed to the future life. Its beginning is called the Ogdoad, and is the successor of this earthly time which is enclosed in the Hebdomad. The title, 'For the Octave,' then, urges us not to look to this present time, but rather to look forward to the Ogdoad. For when this fluid and mutable state of time ceases, in which one thing is born and another perishes, and there will be no further need for things to be born or to perish, the hope of resurrection will change our nature into another order of life and the passing nature of time will cease together with the activities of birth and decay. Then Hebdomad will completely cease as a measurement of time and the Ogdoad will succeed which is the future age comprehending a single day, as one of the prophets says, who has named the life we hope for *the great day* (Joel 2:11). That day will not be illumined by this visible sun of ours, but rather by the true light, the sun of justice, who is called *the Rising Sun* by the prophet (Zech. 6:12) for the reason that it will never be veiled in settings.

> In the fourth-century Latin church in the West numerical symbolism was no less important for Jerome, Ambrose and Augustine. The Lord's Day as an eternal octave, consecrated by the resurrection of Christ, prefigured, at least for Augustine, that eternal rest, our end, which is the Kingdom without end:

[36]However, the Lord's Day was not made known to Jews but to Christians by the resurrection of the Lord, and from that event it began to acquire its solemnity. Doubtless, the souls of all the saints prior to the resurrection of the body enjoy repose, but they do not possess that activity which gives power to risen bodies.

It is the eighth day which symbolizes that activity, which is also the first, because it does not destroy that rest but glorifies it. The limitations of the body do not rise with the body, which is free from corruption; *for this corruptible body must put on incorruption and this mortal body must put on immortality* (1 Cor. 15:53). And so, before the resurrection of the Lord, although this mystery of the eighth day by which the resurrection is symbolized was not concealed from the holy Patriarchs, filled as they were with the spirit of prophecy, it was locked up, and hidden, and taught only as the Sabbath observance. As example we have the psalm written *for the octave* (Ps. 6) and children circumcised on the eighth day. In Ecclesiastes it is used to signify the two Testaments: *Give a portion to seven and also to eight* (Eccles. 11:2).

Before the Lord's resurrection there was rest for the departed but resurrection for none: *Rising from the dead He dies no more; death has no more dominion over Him* (Rom. 6:9). But after such resurrection had taken place in the Lord's body, so that the head of the Church might foreshadow what

[36]Text: PL 33.215

the body of the Church hopes for at the end, then the Lord's Day—that is the eighth which is also the first—began to be observed. The reason also is understood why, in observing the Pasch, they were ordered to kill and eat a sheep, since it plainly prefigured the Passion of the Lord, but they were not commanded to see that a sabbath coincided with the month of new corn and with the third week of the moon: so that the Lord might signalize that same day by His Passion, who had also come to announce the Lord's Day, the eighth, which is also the first.

> Later, at the end of the patristic age, Gregory the Great, bishop of Rome (c.600), after identifying the sixth day with our life of pain and sorrow, sees in the seventh day our repose in death, and in the eighth day our resurrection in the image of Jesus Christ. For Gregory the eighth day, the Lord's Day, the day of the resurrection and the Sabbath day are one and the same:

[37]We therefore accept spiritually and hold spiritually what has been written about the Sabbath which simply means rest; but we already have our rest, our true Sabbath in Jesus Christ, our Lord and Redeemer ... our Sabbath. Therefore ... on the Lord's Day there should be a ceasing from earthly toil and attention given in every way to prayer and contemplation ... on the day of the resurrection.

> Isidore of Seville (c. 636) sounds very similar in his *On Ecclesiastical Offices*:

[38]Seven multiplied by seven gives fifty, if you add one, which, according to the tradition coming from the authority of the ancients, prefigures the future age; this day is itself always the eighth and the first, nay rather it is always unique, that is the Lord's Day.

[37]Text: PL 77.1255 =NPNF 13.92
[38]Text: PL 83.769

2. A Pagan Name for the New Day

Sunday, the *hēmera Hēliou* of the Greeks in the century before Christ, or the *dies Solis* of the Romans in the centuries after Christ, can be seen to this day as a name for the first day of the Jewish week on a wall painting in Herculaneum, the city destroyed with Pompeii in the eruption of Vesuvius in 79 A.D. Under the caption "*theon hemerai*," or days of the Gods, the days of the week were listed in the following order: Kronos (Saturn); Helios (Sun); Selene (Moon); Ares (Mars); Hermes (Mercury); Zeus (Jupiter); and Aphrodite (Venus).

This custom of naming the different days in honor of the different planet gods was, according to some, an ancestral practice derived from Egypt and unknown to the Greeks, or, according to others, a Babylonian practice, which was already known to the Greeks of the century before Christ. The Ptolemaic picture of the universe (c.140 B.C.) with the earth as central and surrounded by the seven planets of Saturn, Jupiter, Mars, the Sun, Venus, Mercury and the Moon, may indeed be the ultimate source of the planet week, but it does not explain the order in which the names appear.

Dio Cassius, a pagan writer of the Christian era, proposed two theories to explain the method of this order of naming. In the first of his theories he applied to the planets the principle of the musical tertrachord in much the same way as the musical octave was employed elsewhere (as we shall see in the section on the mystery of the Ogdoad), to express the identity in reality of the first and eighth. Accordingly his planetary universe was divided into regular musical intervals of four. Thus if one begins with the planet Saturn, the outer orbit in the Ptolemaic universe, by virtue of the tetrachordal interval one comes to the Sun, or god of the fourth orbit: similarly by an equally clear tetrachordal interval the orbit of the Moon is reached from the orbit of the Sun: then by returning from the Moon through the outer orbit of Saturn and then Jupiter Mars is reached: Mars to Mercury is once more a clear tetrachordal interval, which is continued in the movement through the moon and Saturn to Jupiter—a movement that is concluded by a final clear tetrachordal interval between Jupiter and Venus. The result of this method, according to Dio Cassius, is the discovery of the musical harmony between the plan of the heavens and the days of the week.

The second theory of Dio Cassius suggests that "one begins with the first hour and counts the hours of the day and night, assigning the first to Saturn, the next to Jupiter, the third to Mars, the fourth to the Sun, the fifth to Venus, the sixth to Mercury and the seventh to the Moon, and then repeating the process covering all the twenty-four hours, one finds that the first hour of the next day is properly assigned to the Sun. By following this plan through the next twenty-four hours, in the same way as outlined above, the first hour of the third day is dedicated to the Moon, and by applying the same procedure to the rest, one is able to ascertain the appropriate god for each day. This then Dio Cassius concludes is the tradition."[39]

Though second to Saturn in the planetary week the Sun nevertheless was considered "the King and guide of all the other luminaries and therefore the master of the whole world."[40] Thus Sun worship took precedence over the worship of every other planetary deity and gained its faithful followers from every strata of pagan society. Plato, Caesar, Cicero, and the observant savant Pliny, acknowledged the place of the Sun in relation to man and his world. At the end of the first Christian century the mystery religions of the East appeared in the West, and Mithraism launched the cult of *Sol Invictus*, the Invincible Sun. Through Julia Domna, the daughter of the high priest of the Sun at Emesa, and the Mother of the Emperor Caracalla (211-217), the reign of the so-called Syrian emperors was established and the cult of the Sun secured. Thus, Caracalla's successor, the youthful Heliogabulus (218-222), attempted to merge all the existing religions of the empire, including

[39]F.A. Regan, *Dies Dominica and Dies solis*, Washington, D.C., 1961, p.19
[40]*ibid.* 8

Judaism and Christianity, with his beloved cult of the Sun: he even assumed the title of "Sacerdos Amplissimus Dei Invicti Solis Elagabuli," and thus the cult of the Sun and that of the Emperor became one and the same.

In this Roman world of Sun and Emperor worship, Christianity proclaimed its Son of God and Son of Man gospel. Judaism had already prepared the way for this divine proclamation in human words by constantly distinguishing between the message and the method—a technique which made revelation clear and culture pure: as early as 629 B.C. the reform of Josiah removed *from the temple of the Lord all the objects that had been made for Baal ... and ... put an end to the pseudo-priests who burned incense ... to the Sun, Moon and signs of the Zodiac.* (2 Kgs. 23:4-6). Hence the Old Testament use of numbers instead of the names of the planet week to clarify its revelation and to purify its culture. Yet Tacitus (c. 100 A.D.), generations later, mistakenly saw the Jewish Sabbath originating in the pagan feast of Saturn just as some in our times seek the origin of the Christian Sunday in the pagan day of the Sun.

But the message of the Fathers is clear: Ignatius of Antioch (c. 102) made no such error; for him the Risen Lord of the New Testament is "the Rising Sun" long before the Lord's Day becomes the Sunday:

[41]They no longer observe the Jewish Sabbath, but keep holy the Lord's Day on which through Him and through His death our life rose up.

While Ignatius develops the Old Testament 'Sun of Justice', and the New Testament 'true light' symbolism, and explains that "God has graciously called Him to come from the rising of the Sun to the setting thereof," Justin (c. 150), understandably in his *Apology* to the pagan Emperor is the first Christian writer to apply the pagan name of Sunday to

[41]Text: SC 10.88

the Christian Lord's Day; but he does so in a symbolic way and with a significance that is wholly new:

[42]And on the so-called day of the Sun those who live in the cities or in the country assemble in one place and the writings of the prophets are read for as long as time permits ... This Sunday is the day on which we assemble, for it is the first day on which God, when He changed darkness and matter, made the world, and the day on which Jesus Christ our Savior rose from the dead. They crucified Him on the day before the day of Saturn and on the following day which is the day of the Sun, He appeared to His apostles and disciples and taught them what I now pass on to you.

Here with his "so-called day of the Sun" Justin draws attention to the limitations of Sun worship, and in his *Dialogue with Trypho* makes more explicit the new significance of the Sun as symbol of the logos of God, who is more radiant, and whose rays of truth penetrate the minds and hearts of men:

[43]But, if all nations are blessed in Christ, and we who are from all nations believe in Him, then He is the Christ, and we are they who are blessed through Him. It is written that God once allowed the sun to be worshipped (cf. Deut. 4:19), and yet you cannot discover anyone who ever suffered death because of his faith in the sun. But you can find men of every nationality who, for the name of Jesus, have suffered, and still suffer, all kinds of torments rather than deny their faith in Him. For His word of truth and wisdom is more blazing and bright than the might of the sun, and it penetrates the very depths of the heart and mind. Thus Scripture says: *His name shall arise above the sun* (Ps. 72:17), and Zacharias affirms: *The East is His name* (Zach. 6:12).

[42]Text: PG 6.429
[43]Text: *ibid.* 757 =FOTC 6.335

Only fifty years later the wheel turned full circle, so to speak, and in North Africa, Tertullian (c. 200) had to explain the Sunday practice of Christians, which then and there was no longer symbolically significant at least for the pagans:

[44]Others, it must be admitted, suppose the sun to be the god of the Christians, for it is a well-known fact that when we pray we face the east, and that we celebrate Sunday as a day of festivity. And what about it? Do you not do the very same? Do not many of you, with an affectation of worshipping the celestial deities, also move your lips while facing toward the rising sun? After all, it is you yourselves who have introduced the sun into the calendar of the week; and you have chosen its day (Sunday) in preference to the preceding day (Saturn's-day) as the most fitting one in the entire week, for either a total abstinence from bathing, or for its postponement until the evening, or for taking a rest and for banqueting. In resorting to such customs, you consciously deviate from your own religious rites and follow those of strangers. For the Jewish feasts are the Sabbath and the Purification, and Jewish too are the ceremonies of the lamps and the fasts from unleavened bread. All these practices and rites are indeed foreign to your gods. Wherefore, returning now from this digression, you who reproach us with the sun and with Sunday should first consider your proximity to us. For we are not far removed from your Saturn and days of rest.

Somewhat later in the same church of North Africa Cyprian (c.250) developed the adaptation to culture, cautiously begun by Justin (c. 150), and later questioned by Tertullian (c.200), and sees the pagan Sunday as a symbol of Christ the true Sun:

[45]For us, dearly beloved brethren, there are in addition to the times of prayer observed by all, new times that are more

[44]Text: PL 1.579
[45]Text: CSEL IIIA.112

meaningful.... For we must pray in the morning that the resurrection of the Lord may thus be celebrated by morning prayer. The Holy Spirit proclaimed this of old, when in the psalms He spoke: *O my king and my God. For to thee will I pray: O Lord, in the morning thou shall hear my voice. In the morning I will stand before thee, and I will see thee* (Ps. 5:3). And again, through the mouth of the Prophet the Lord says: *At dawn they will be on watch for me, saying: let us go down and return to the Lord our God* (cf. Hos. 6:1). Likewise, at the setting of the sun and at the end of the day there must again be prayer. For since Christ is the True Sun and the True Day, as the sun and day of the world recede, we pray and petition for the light to come upon us again when we pray for the coming of Christ to provide us with the grace of eternal light. Moreover, the Holy Spirit in the psalms declares that Christ is called the day. He says: *This is the day which the Lord has made; let us exalt and rejoice therein* (Ps. 118:24). Likewise, Malachias the prophet gives witness that He is called the Sun, when He says: *But unto you who fear my name, the Sun of Justice shall arise, and healing is in His wings* (Mal. 4:2). Thus if in the Scriptures Christ is called the True Sun and the True Day, no hour is excepted for Christians, in which God should be adored often and always, so that we who are in Christ, that is, in the True Sun and in the True Day, should be constant throughout the entire day in our petitions and prayers; and when, by the laws of the world, the revolving night, recurring in its alternate changes, succeeds, there can be no danger from the nocturnal shades for those who pray, because to the sons of light even in the night there is day. For when is he without light, who has the light in his heart? Or when does he not have the sun and the day, to whom Christ is Sun and Day?

Alexandria at the end of the second century and the beginning of the third was the center where revelation and culture really met in the first Christian school of apologetics founded by Clement (c.150-215) and continued by Origen (185-253). At home in this cross-roads city of the world with its devotees of Isis, Attis and Mithra, Clement developed the symbolism of Christ as the true Sun:

[46]Hail, O Light! For in us who are buried in darkness, and imprisoned in the shadow of death, light has come forth from heaven, purer than that of the sun and sweeter than life here below. This light is eternal life for all those who share in it. But the night fears the light, and hiding itself in terror it makes way for the Day of the Lord. This is the light that never sleeps, the light that hovers over all, and the West has come round to the East. This Light is Christ, the Sun of Righteousness.

> Clement even applies to Christ the title of "Pantepoptes," "beholder of all,"[47] which the ancients applied to their Sun-God, and with echoes of Cyprian, sees Christ as "the today" of the Psalmist, "the never ending day of God which crosses over to eternity,"[48] nevertheless he carefully avoids in his writings any mention of the name of Sunday, but suggests that such pagan practices might have a place in the Divine Scheme of things:

[49]It is not only the believer who will be judged impartially before the tribunal of heaven. The same holds good for the heathen. For, since God knew, by means of His fore-knowledge, that the heathen would not believe, nevertheless, in order that it might redound to His own perfection, He gave him philosophy before giving him Faith. And He gave him the sun and the moon and the stars to worship, as the Law itself tells us (cf. Deut. 1.19) that the heathen would not become completely atheistic and perish in this condition. But they have taken leave of their senses and have worshipped graven images, and thus they will be judged according to this commandment, unless they repent: some of them deliberately rejected any belief in God; others though they did have the desire to believe, yet they did not take the trouble to do so. There were also those who, having worshipped the heavenly bodies first, did not return to worship the maker of them. For

[46]Text: SC 2.182
[47]Text: GCS 3.15
[48]Text: SC 2.152
[49]Text: GCS 2.487

this worship of the heavenly bodies was the road which was given to the heathen by which they could rise up to the worship of the true God. But there were those who were not content with the worship of these heavenly bodies which were assigned to them and so they went their own way and worshipped stocks and stones and thus *were counted as chaff and as a drop from the bucket*, (Isa. 40:15).

Origen (185-253) is no less careful in his avoidance of the pagan name of Sunday, although much more profuse in his development of the 'Sun of Justice' symbolism: "Christ is indeed the Sun of Justice; and if to Him is joined the moon, that is His Church, full with His light, then in truth will He celebrate a new moon."[50] Thus Justin and Tertullian, and not Clement and Origen, strangely enough, remain the only witness to the Christian use of the pagan name of Sunday before the decrees of Constantine (321), which promulgated and regulated the new day of public rest. Imperial edicts from the hand of this first Christian emperor naturally continued the Sunday name in regulating the civil aspects of the Christians' Lord's Day; nevertheless, we learn from Eusebius that Constantine ordered his soldiers to honor the Lord's Day, "the day of the True Light and the True Sun."

[51]He also ordained that one day should be set aside as a special day for prayer: I mean that which is truly the first and chief of all, the day of our Lord and Savior. The care of his entire household was entrusted to deacons and other ministers consecrated to the service of God: . . . and his body guard, . . . found in their emperor and instructor in the practice of piety, and like him held the Lord's salutary day in honor, and performed on that day the devotions which he loved. The same observance was recommended by this blessed prince to all classes of his subjects: his earnest desire being gradually to lead all mankind to the worship of God. Accordingly he enjoined on all the subjects of the Roman empire to observe the Lord's

[50]Text: PG 12.751
[51]Text: PG 20.1165

Day, as a day of rest, and also to honor the day which precedes the Sabbath, in memory, I suppose, of what the Savior of mankind is recorded to have achieved on that day. And since his desire was to teach his whole army zealously to honor the Savior's day (which derives its name from light, and from the sun), he freely granted to those among them who were partakers of the divine faith, leisure for attendance on the services of the Church of God, in order that they might be able to perform their religious worship.

According to Eusebius, Constantine also made this day a day of prayer for his troops:

[52]With regard to those who were as yet ignorant of divine truth, he provided by a second statute that they should appear on each Lord's Day on an open plain near the city, and there, at a given signal, offer to God with one accord a prayer which they had previously learnt. He admonished them that their confidence should not rest in their spears, or armor, or bodily strength, but that they should acknowledge the supreme God as the giver of every good and of victory itself; to whom they were bound to offer their prayers with due regularity, uplifting their hands toward heaven, and raising their mental vision higher still to the King of heaven, on whom they should call as the Author of victory, their Preserver, Guardian, and Helper. The emperor himself prescribed the prayer to be used by all his troops.

Eusebius follows the tradition of the Fathers in presenting Christ as the 'Sun of Justice.' Likewise he follows the same tradition in his careful and always qualified use of the Sunday name, which name, towards the end of the fourth century, began to disappear even from the civil decrees: the day of the Sun, which the majority rightly called the Lord's Day, in 386, became in 409 the Lord's Day, which is commonly called the day of the Sun, and in 425 the Lord's Day, which is the first day of the whole seven days.

[52]Text: *ibid.* 1168

This process of clarification and purificaton, occasioned by the interaction of Christian revelation and pagan culture, blossomed in the post-Constantinian age and continued into the fifth century. Jerome (c. 350) of the Vulgate and the desert offers clear evidence:

[53]The Day of the Lord, or the Day of the Resurrection, is indeed the true day of every Christian: for this reason it is called the Lord's Day, because on that day the Lord ascended triumphant to the Father. And if this day is called Sunday by the pagans, we too are most ready to confess that today the Light of the World has risen, that today the Sun of Justice has risen.

Maximus of Turin (c.410) goes much further and says that "the Lord's Day is called Sunday by the people of the world because Christ, the Sun of Justice, has risen and has filled the whole world with His light."[54] On the other hand, Philastrius, Bishop of Brescia (c.390), regards as heretical the custom of naming the days of the week after the planet gods, and claims divine approval for the biblical method of numbering. Such conflicting approaches naturally invited the voice of authority, and Pope Leo the Great spoke accordingly:

[55]From these and similar notions there arise forms of impiety in which the sun is worshipped at the break of day from some elevated place. Even Christians are not immune from such a practice; indeed they believe that they are acting in good conscience, when on arrival at the doors of St. Peter's Basilica, which is dedicated to the One, Living and True God, having ascended the steps which lead up to the open place, they turn around, face toward the rising sun, and bending their heads give honor to the shining orb with a reverential bow. For a long time we have deplored this custom and it has grieved us

[53]Text: CCL 78.550
[54]Text: PL 57.371
[55]Text: PL 54.218

greatly. It is due partly to ignorance and partly to the influence of paganism. For even if these latter venerate the Creator of this beauteous light, more than the light itself which is but a creature, yet we must abstain from even the appearance of such a rite; which should any one who has abandoned the worship of idols find among us, will he too not hold on to this part of his former belief as credible, which he observes to be common to Christian as well as to pagan.

> Somewhat before this intervention of Leo (c.450) on this question of Christian revelation and pagan culture, *Sol Justitiae* and *Sol Invictus,* Augustine (c.400) with his usual clarity explained the Christian policy of adopting and adapting pagan practices while permeating them with a new and distinctive Christian significance:

[56]Notice that we read in Proverbs: *A wise man continues as the sun, but a fool is changed as the moon* (Sir. 27:11) and who then is the wise man who continues but the Sun of Justice of whom it is said: *The Sun of Justice is risen unto me?* (Mal. 4:2). But the wicked upon whom He has not risen shall weep and say on that last day: *The light of justice has not shined upon us and the sun has not risen upon us* (Wis. 5:6). For, God has made the sun visible to fleshy eyes, *to shine upon the good and the bad,* who also, *rains upon the just and the unjust* (Mt. 5:45). But appropriate comparisons of invisible things are often drawn from visible ones. Who then is the fool who is changed as the moon but Adam, *in whom all have sinned* (Rom. 5:12)?

Nevertheless ... it should not be supposed that those luminaries are to be adored which are used as parables to symbolize divine mysteries—such comparisons are taken from all created things.... For just as we do not adore domestic animals, although He is called a *lamb* (Jn. 1:29) or a *calf* (Ezek. 43:19); nor wild beasts because He is called a *lion of the tribe of Judah* (Apoc. 5:5); nor stones because they are figures of Christ, nor Mount Sion because it is the figure of the Church,

[56]Text: PL 33. 208

so neither do we adore the sun nor the moon, although from these heavenly bodies ... we draw symbols of the mysteries and thereby increase our mystical knowledge. We make use of these things as symbols to illustrate the mysteries of the word of God. We make use of parables formulated with reverent devotion to illustrate our religion; likewise we have no hesitation in using the visible creation for the same purpose, the winds, the sea, the earth, as in the administration of the sacraments we use, with Christian liberty, but with necessary reserve, water, wheat, wine and oil. If, however, allegories are taken not only from the heavens and the stars, but also from lower creation and are adapted to the administration of the sacraments, they thus become a type of language of redemption fitted to win the affection of the hearers from the visible to the invisible, from the corporeal to the spiritual and from the temporal to the eternal.

> Scripture and not myth is the ultimate source of Christian symbolism: nevertheless, paganism had its influence, and while this influence is usually qualified in the use of the pagan name of Sunday, it is more daring and obvious in the corrollary practice of praying towards the East, the land of the rising sun. According to Irenaeus (c. 200) the sect known as the Ebionites adhered to the Old Testament ordinance of facing Jerusalem after the Christians adopted the new orientation. Tertullian (220) admits but does not explain this new practice, but Clement of Alexandria is more revealing:

[57]And just as the dawn is an image of the day ... and its light begins to dispel the darkness of the night, so too there dawns on those who sit in darkness a day of knowledge and of truth: thus in keeping with the manner of the sun's rising, prayers are offered while looking toward the sunrise in the East. It was for this reason that those very ancient temples looked toward the West so that the worshippers might turn to the East when facing the images.

[57]Text: GCS 3.32

Likewise Origen turns towards the East at times of prayer for "the direction of the Rising Sun ... symbolizes the gaze of the soul looking in that direction whence the True Light arises." Such symbolism had special appeal for the Cappadocians, Basil the Great (c.350), and Gregory of Nyssa (d.394).

Basil:

[58]Thus we all look towards the East at our hours of prayer but few of us realize that we are seeking our lost land ... Paradise, which God planted in Eden in the East. Similarly on the first day of the week we pray standing; yet few of us are aware of the reason ... on the day of the resurrection (which in Greek means standing again) we stand again in expectation of the age which is contained in this symbol for the day is an image of eternity: We do not stand simply because we rose with Christ to seek the things that are above.

Gregory:

[59]But when we turn towards the East we do so because our first homeland is in the East; we do not turn to the East as if God were only to be contemplated there, for He who is everywhere is not particularly apprehended in any part since He comprises all things equally.

In describing the death of his sister, Macrina, the same Gregory of Nyssa wrote:

[60]The day was almost done and the sun was beginning to set, but her zeal in no way declined. Rather as she approached the end and saw more clearly the beauty of the Bridegroom she seemed to rush toward the one she desired with even greater desire; no longer did she speak to those of us who were present; she spoke only to the One toward whom she gazed with

[58]Text: PG 32.192
[59]Text: PG 44. 1184
[60]Text: PG 46.984

steadfast look. She was turned towards the East and ... spoke only to Him ... then, evening came and the lamp was brought in, and Macrina turned towards the beam of light ... for the night prayer, and with the prayer her life came to an end.

Naturally such symbolism appears in the mystagogical lectures of Cyril of Jerusalem (d.386) almost as the only possible way of revealing the divine mysteries:

[61]Address him as personally present and with arm outstretched say: 'I renounce you, Satan.' Allow me to explain the reason of your facing West, for you should know it. Because the West is the region of visible darkness, Satan, who is himself darkness, has his empire in darkness—that is the significance of your looking steadily towards the West while you renounce that gloomy prince of night ... then ... God's Paradise opens before you that Eden, planted in the East, from which for his transgressions our first father was banished. Symbolic of this is your facing about from the West to the East, the place of light. It is at this point that you were told to say: 'I believe in the Father, and in the Son, and in the Holy Spirit.'

In fact the liturgical documents of this age carry the symbolism further; they move in a sense away from the cosmic symbolism of Origen and into the mere representationalism of the *Apostolic Constitutions:*

[62]When you gather the faithful together in the Church of God, act as a pilot of a great ship. With prudence and with discipline regulate the assembly, commanding the deacons like sailors, so that the faithful, embarking on this ship, may be directed to their proper place. And concerning the church itself, see to it that it is built facing in the direction of the East, and that it has vestries on both sides at the East so that it will resemble a ship.

[61]Text: PG 33.1068 =FOTC 64.155
[62]Text: Funk 1.159 =ANF 7.421

Nevertheless, the language of the Fathers remained symbolic as Christian revelation and pagan culture continued to interact until Isidore of Seville (c.600), the last of the Latin Fathers:

[63]The ecclesiastical manner of speaking for the days of the week is more fitting on Christian lips. But if habit has perhaps led anyone to let slip from his tongue, by chance, what he disapproves of in his heart, let him understand that all those, from whom the days of the week derive their names, were mere men, and because of certain benefits accruing to mortals, because they were very powerful and eminent in this world, divine honors were bestowed upon them by their followers, in such wise that these latter named the days and the heavenly bodies after them. First the heavenly bodies were called after the names of men, and the days from the heavenly bodies. The 'feriae' were so called from '*fando*,' that is, 'speaking,' because there is a time for speaking in both divine and human services. Those established for men are called 'holidays' (*dies festi*) while those for divine services are called 'holy-days' (*feriati*).

3. A Jewish Name for the New Day

The Sabbath of Israel came to be from the Jewish understanding of the week as a basic unit of time. Unlike the day of the relentless Sun, the week in origin belongs to the moon, whose cycle has always and everywhere aroused the attention and wonder of man. Mysterious in its shapes and phases it disappears for three nights on end only to be born again as a slender crescent after its meeting with the setting sun; then it increases and waxes, and seven days later becomes a semi-circle: seven days more and it is seen in all its fullness, only to wane again into another semi-circle before it finally fades away and vanishes. Small wonder, then, that the lunar cycle has always seemed sacred. Among

[63]Text: PL 82.216

the Assyrians, for example, its phases were marked by sacrifices to the different gods:

[64]At night, the King offers his sacrifices to Marduk and Ishtar; on the seventh day to Belith and Nergal; on the fourteenth to Ninib and Gula, and the nineteenth (representing a week of weeks from the first of the previous month) to Samsch, Belith-Matati, Sin and Belith-ile; on the twenty-first to Ea and on the twenty-eighth to Belith-ile; he pours out the offering of the sacrifice and his prayer is accepted by the god.

But the creation story of Genesis in opposition to this deification of heavenly bodies, and as an expression of Jewish monotheism, detached its week from the lunar month, and by that very fact established a calendar of successive uninterrupted weeks linked to the eternal God and unconnected in origin with the phases of the moon. But the week nonetheless remained a basic unit of time; each day was numbered, but the seventh day, which alone was blessed, was given the name of Sabbath in the Decalogue: *But the seventh day is the Sabbath of the Lord your God. No work may be done then either by you, or your son or daughter, or your male or female slave, or your beast, or by the alien who lives with you. In six days the Lord made the heavens and the earth, the sea and all that is in them; but on the seventh day He rested. That is why the Lord has blessed the Sabbath day and made it holy* (Ex. 20:10-11).

Gradually this day of rest became a day of worship, and in the prophet Ezekiel are found the instructions for the people's worship on the Sabbath day: *Thus says the Lord God: The gate toward the east of the inner court shall remain closed throughout the six working days, but on the Sabbath and on the day of the new moon it shall be open. The prince shall enter from outside by way of the vestibule of the gate and remain standing at the doorpost of the gate; then while the priests offer his holocausts and peace*

[64]N. Denis-Boulet, *The Christian Calendar*, 16

offerings, he shall worship at the threshold of the gate and then leave; the gate shall not be closed until evening. The people of the land shall worship before the Lord at the door of this gate on the Sabbaths and new moons. The holocausts which the prince presents to the Lord on the Sabbath shall consist of six unblemished lambs and an unblemished ram, together with a cereal offering of one ephah for the ram, whatever he pleases for the lambs, and a hin of oil for each ephah. On the day of the new moon he shall provide an unblemished young bull, also six lambs and a ram without blemish, with a cereal offering of one ephah for the bull and one for the ram, for the lambs as much as he has at hand, and for each ephah a hin of oil (Ezek. 46:1-7).

In the more detailed ritual laws, that are found in the remaining verses of this chapter of Ezekiel, can be seen the mentality that led to the extreme legislation of the Halakah about Sabbath observance. The Sabbath controversies in the Gospels certainly depict Jesus in conflict with this mentality, but the real conflict is his claim that *the Son of Man is Lord even of the Sabbath* (Mk. 2:28). Jesus' continued observance of the Sabbath, *as was His custom* (Lk. 4:16), meant that in the new age Sabbath observance was continued, while the full implications of this age were emerging.

Eusebius speaks about the Ebionites, who observed the Sabbath and other disciplines of the Jews on the one hand, and, on the other hand, celebrated the Lord's Day in commemoration of His resurrection; "in consequence of such a course they have received their epithet, the name of Ebionites, showing their poverty of mind, for it is thus that the Hebrews call a poor man."[65] But the Sabbath controversy, in all its aspects, remained an ever recurring theme in the writers of the second century, especially in the Apologists, of whom Justin (c. 150) is perhaps our best example in his *Dialogue with Trypho*:

---

[65]Text: PG 20.273

[66]'This last charge is what surprises us,' replied Trypho...
for you do not keep the feasts or Sabbaths. .... You place your
hope in a crucified man, and still expect to receive favors from
God when you disregard His commandments....'

'Trypho,' I began, 'there never will be, nor has there ever
been from eternity, any other God except Him who created
and formed the universe. Furthermore we do not claim that
our God is different from yours, for He is God who, with a
strong hand and outstretched arm, led your forefathers out of
the land of Egypt. Nor have we placed our trust in any other
(for, indeed there is no other), but only in Him whom you also
have trusted, the God of Abraham and of Isaac and of Jacob.
But, our hope is not through Moses or through the Law,
otherwise our customs would be the same as yours....'

In Christ an everlasting covenant and final law has been
given to us.... Concerning this New Covenant, God thus
spoke through Jeremias: *Behold the days shall come, saith the
Lord, and I will make a new covenant with the house of Israel,
and with the house of Juda: not according to the covenant
which I made with their fathers, in the day that I took them by
the hand to bring them out of the land of Egypt* (Jer. 31:31). If,
therefore, God predicted that He would make a new covenant,
and this for a light to the nations, and we see and are convinced
that, through the name of the crucified Jesus Christ, men have
turned to God ... and have practiced piety even unto death,
then everyone can clearly see from these deeds ... that He is
indeed the New Law, the New Covenant, and the expectation
of those who, from every nation, have awaited the blessings of
God. We have been led to God through this crucified Christ,
and we are the true spiritual Israel, and the descendants of
Judah, Jacob, Isaac, and Abraham....

The New Law demands that we observe a perpetual
Sabbath, whereas you consider yourselves pious when you
refrain from work on one day out of the week, and in doing so
you don't understand the real meaning of that precept....

We, too, would observe ... your Sabbath days, and, in a
word, all your festivals, if we were not aware of the reason why

[66]Text: PG 6. 496

they were imposed upon you....

The observance of the Sabbaths was imposed upon you by God so that you would be forced to remember Him, as He Himself said: *That you may know that I am God, your Savior* (Ex. 20:20)....

Before Moses there was no need of Sabbaths, festivals, or sacrifices: neither are they needed now, when in accordance with the will of God, Jesus Christ, His Son, has been born of the Virgin Mary, a descendant of Abraham....

Now, Trypho, tell me, was it God's desire that your high priests commit sin when they offer oblations on the Sabbaths? Or did He wish that they who received or performed circumcision on that day be guilty of sin, since it is His command that circumcision be given on the eighth day after birth, even though that day may fall on a Sabbath? If He knew it would be sinful to perform that act on a Sabbath, could He not have decreed that infants be circumcised either a day before or a day after the Sabbath? And why did He not instruct those persons who lived before the time of Moses and Abraham to observe these same precepts; men, who are called just and were pleasing to God, even though they were not circumcised in the flesh, and did not keep the Sabbaths?

Neither should you consider it dreadful if we drink hot water on the Sabbath, for God doesn't stop controlling the movement of the universe on that day, but He continues directing it then as He does on all other days. Besides, your chief priests were commanded by God to offer sacrifices on the Sabbath, as well as on other days. Then, too, there are so many just men who are approved by God Himself, yet they never performed any of your legal ceremonies.

> Irenaeus (c.200), however, and not Justin, was the first to lay down the fundamental principle of the relationship between the two testaments, for he was not content to treat figures of the Old Testament as mere prefigurations of Christ; rather he went on to elaborate a theology of history as the basis of exegesis. Hence for him the Jewish Sabbath was a prefiguration of Christ and the eschatological kingdom:

[67]And for this reason the Lord said: *When you make a dinner or a supper, do not call friends, neighbors, or kinsfolk lest they ask you in return and so repay you. But call the lame, the blind, and the poor and you shall be blessed, since they cannot repay you, but a recompense shall be made to you at the resurrection of the just* (Lk. 14:12). And again He said, *Whosoever shall have left lands, or houses, or parents, or brethren, or children because of Me, he shall receive in this world a hundredfold, and in that to come he shall inherit eternal life* (Lk. 18:29). For what are the hundred-fold rewards in this world, the entertainments given to the poor and the suppers for which a return is made? These are to take place in the times of the kingdom, that is, upon the seventh day, which has been sanctified, in which God rested from all the works which He created, which is the true Sabbath of the righteous, which they shall not be engaged in any earthly occupation; but shall have a table at hand prepared for them by God, supplying them with all sorts of dishes.

Again: (Irenaeus)

[68]Moreover, we learn from Scripture itself that God gave circumcision not as a means of rigtheousness, but rather as a sign by which the people of Abraham might be recognizable ... Ezekial, the prophet, says the very same about the Sabbath: *I also gave them my Sabbaths to be a sign between them and Me that they might know that I am the Lord who sanctifies them* (Ezek. 20:12). In Exodus God says to Moses: *And you shall observe my Sabbath; and it shall be a sign between Me and you for your generations* (Exod. 31:16). These things then were given for a sign; but the signs were not without significance, that is, neither without meaning nor to no purpose because they were given by a wise Artist: indeed the circumcision of the flesh typified that of the spirit, for, as the Apostle says, *We have been circumcised with the circumcision made without hands* (Col. 2:11); and the prophet says:

[67]Text: SC 153.408
[68]Text: SC 100.558

Circumcise the hardness of your hearts (Jer. 4:4). . . . But the Sabbaths teach that we should continue day by day in God's service. *For we have been counted*, says the apostle Paul, *all the day long as sheep for the slaughter* (Rom. 8:36); that is we have been consecrated to God and ministering continually to our faith and persevering in it, and abstaining from greed, and neither acquiring nor possessing treasures on this earth. Moreover, the Sabbath of God is that the kingdom of God was, as it were, indicated by created things: in which kingdom the man, who shall have persevered in serving God, shall in a state of rest partake of God's table. Such a man was not justified by these things: rather they were given to the people as a sign of his justification. Consider this: Abraham was without circumcision and without observance of Sabbaths; yet he believed God: thus was he justified and called 'the friend of God.'

> But Irenaeus, also, like many others of his age, made constant use of the Sabbath controversies in the Gospels to show the supremacy of the spirit over the letter of the law in the teaching and practice of Jesus:

[69] . . . He performed cures on the Sabbath, at Siloam, and afterwards, on many other occasions: for this reason many used to come to Him on the Sabbath day. The law commanded them to abstain from servile work, that is, from grasping after wealth, which is procured by trading and other worldly ways: but it also exhorted them to engage in spiritual exercises such as contemplation and charitable activities for the good of neighbor. For this reason the Lord reproved them for blaming Him because He healed upon the Sabbath day. By so doing He did not break the law; rather He fulfilled it and performed the duties of the High Priest—propitiating God for men, cleansing lepers, healing the sick. He even suffered death so that sinful man might return from His exile and re-enter His inheritance. . . .

Again . . . He said to them: *Have you not read what David*

[69] Text: SC 100.470

did when he was hungry? How he entered the house of God and ate the loaves of offering, loaves which only the priests are allowed to eat (Mt. 12:3-4). . . . The workman is worthy of his meat. . . . Therefore, those priests in the temple, who profaned the Sabbath were blameless, because in the temple they were not engaged in the affairs of the world but in the service of God, . . . fulfilling the law but not going beyond it, like the man who carried the dry wood into the camp of God and was justly stoned to death: *for every tree that brings not forth good fruit shall be cut down and cast into the fire* (Mt. 3:10).

With the end of the Sabbath disputes, which indeed dominated the Gospels, and much of early patristic literature, something of this original meaning of the Sabbath of Israel as a sign of the Mosaic Covenant (cf. Ex. 31:12-17), a sign of Yahweh's sanctification of His people (cf. Ex. 31:13), a perpetual covenant (cf. Ex. 31:16), and a sign forever (cf. Ex. 31:17), began to reappear in later Patristic literature. The origins of this approach can be seen even in the time of Irenaeus:

[70]You are blessed, O Lord, King of the Ages, who by Christ has made the whole world and in the beginning brought order to disorder by that same Christ . . . for by your Word, O Lord, heaven was fixed as an arch above us . . . the light and the sun were begotten for days and the production of fruit: likewise the stars and the moon for our comfort in darkness and the life of the seasons . . . the former you called 'day,' and the latter you called 'night.'

Later on in this same century the meaning of God's own Sabbath rest (cf. Gen. 2:3) claimed the attention of both Clement (150-215) and Origen (185-253), the Alexandrians, as it did of many other Christian and Jewish writers. Both attacked the notion, ridiculed by Celsus, that God needed to rest after the work of creation: "God is incapable of

[70]Text: SC 294.356

weariness, and suffering and want," wrote Clement,[71] and according to Origen "the sensation of fatigue is peculiar to those who are in the body."[72] Each understood God's Sabbath as the contemplation of His completed work rather than in terms of inactivity, and, consequently, applied to the observance of the Lord's Day the same critique that Christians commonly applied to the Sabbath. Yet in his treating of the Sabbath observance as such by Christians, it is unclear whether Origen has in mind the Jewish Sabbath or the Lord's Day:

[73]Leaving aside, then, the Jewish observances of the Sabbath, let us see of what kind the observance of the Sabbath should be for the Christian. *On the Sabbath day no worldly activities should be undertaken* (Ex. 31:14). So if you abstain from all secular works and do nothing worldly, but keep yourself free for spiritual works, come to church (*ecclesiam*), listen to scripture readings and sermons, have before your eyes the coming judgment, consider not the things that are present and visible but those that are invisible and future, this is the observance of the Sabbath for the Christian. But these things the Jews ought also to have observed. Even among them a blacksmith or a builder or any kind of manual worker abstains from work on Sabbath day. But the reader of the divine law or the teacher does not abstain from work and yet does not profane the Sabbath. For so the Lord said to them: *Have you not read that the priests in the temple break the Sabbath and are without reproach?* (Mt. 12:5). Therefore he who abstains from the works of the world and is free from spiritual activity, he it is who offers the sacrifice of the Sabbath and celebrates the Sabbath feast. He carries no burden on the way (cf. Jer. 17:24). For the burden is every sin, as the prophet says, *Like a heavy burden they weigh me down* (Ps. 38:4).

He does not kindle a fire (cf. Ex. 35:3), that is, that fire of

[71]Text: GCS 2.501
[72]Text: SC 147.332
[73]Text: PG 12.749

which it is said: *Go in by the light of your fire and in the flame which you have kindled* (Isa. 50:11).

On the Sabbath everyone remains seated in his place and does not leave it (cf. Ex. 16:29). So what is the spiritual place of the soul? Its place is righteousness, truth, wisdom, holiness and everything which Christ is, that is the place of rest. The soul ought not to leave this place, if it is to keep the true Sabbath and celebrate with sacrifices the feast day of the Sabbath, as the Lord said: *He who abides in me, I abide in him* (Jn. 15:5). (*In Num.* Hom. 23:4)

On the third of March 321 A.D. Constantine promulgated a law ordering the complete public rest from work "on the most honorable day of the Sun": On the third of July of that same year a second law permitted the fulfillment of vows as appropriate to Sundays, and as a result the legal actions necessary for the transfer of slaves. This legislation is the first clear reference to Sunday as a day free from work. Constantine's motives are much debated: "Service of God, contemplation, worship, detachment from worldly things, festival and fulfillment are the ideas suggested by the patristic notion of Sabbath rest; by contrast mere abstention from work is consistently and continually ruled out and condemned as idleness."[74]

Eusebius of Caesarea (c.300) in his *Commentary on Psalm 91* begins by defining Sabbath rest, both for God and for men, as a turning from the things of this physical world to contemplate heavenly realities. His is the first extant Christian work to claim that the Sabbath has been transferred to Sunday. His arguments are largely traditional: "a) True Sabbath rest is contemplation of divine things. b) Men will share this rest of God in the world to come. c) Devotion of the whole of life to the contemplation of divine things is an image (*Eikon*) of the eschatological rest. d) The Mosaic Sabbath was a shadow (*skia*) of the eschatological

[74]Carson, *op. cit.* 282

rest. e) The Christian Sunday is an image (*eikon*) of the eschatological rest."[75]

[76]It is necessary to discover what the Sabbath signifies. Scripture calls it the rest of God and places it after the creation of the sensible world. But what is the rest of God except His devoting Himself to the intelligible and supramundane realities? Indeed, when He looks at the sensible world and gives Himself to the exercise of His providence over the world, He is said to work. It is in this sense that we must understand the word of our Savior: *My Father works until now, and I work* (Jn. 5:17). But when He turns to the incorporeal and supramundane realities, in His heavenly realm, then we may understand Him to be resting and observing His Sabbath. In the same way, when men of God turn from the works that weary the soul (such are all works of the body and those which are dear to earthly flesh) and give themselves wholly to God and to the study and contemplation of divine and intelligible realities, then they observe the Sabbaths which are dear to God and rest for the Lord God. And it is of such Sabbaths that Scripture teaches: *Now there remains a Sabbath rest for the people of God* (Heb. 4:9), and again: *Let us strive to enter into that rest* (4:11). For the perfect Sabbath and the perfect and blessed Sabbath rest is found in the kingdom of God, above the work of the six days and outside all sensible realities, among the incorporeal and supramundane realities, where grief and sorrow and sighing have fled away (cf. Isa. 35:10). There, released from mortal and corruptible life, enjoying the blessed rest which pleases God, and freed from bodily activities and the slavery of the flesh, we shall celebrate the Sabbath and rest truly with God and beside Him. That is why the Apostle says: *Let us strive to enter into that rest* (Heb. 4:11). For the men of God (the patriarchs) bearing on earth the image (*Eikon*) of that Sabbath, of that perfect and blessed rest, abstained from things which turned them away from God, and giving themselves wholly to the contemplation of divine

[75]*ibid.* 284
[76]Text: PG 23.1165 =Carson, 282

realities, applying themselves day and night to meditation on the holy scriptures, they were then celebrating the holy Sabbaths and resting in the rest which pleases God. And so suitably, the law of Moses, providing shadows and signs of the things of which we have spoken, appointed a particular day for the people so that on this day at least they should leave their ordinary work and have leisure for meditation on the law of God.

So you see what the present text requires to be done on the day of the resurrection.... Also on the Sabbath the priests in the temple were employed in many other activities according to the Law. It does not prescribe idleness. It was not for the priests that the Sabbath was prescribed, but only for those who were unlike them in not devoting all their time and every day to the service of God and to the works which please Him. For these it was prescribed that intervals be made. But those who give themselves to feasting and drinking and disorder on the Sabbath, God rebukes by the prophet, saying: *They adopt false Sabbaths* (Amos 6:3), and again, *I cannot endure your new moons and Sabbaths and festivals* (Isa. 1:13).

This is why, rejecting those Sabbaths, the Word by the New Covenant has changed and transferred the feast of the Sabbath to the rising of the light. He has given to us an image (*Eikon*) of true rest, the day of salvation, the Lord's Day and the first day of the light, on which the Savior of the world, after all His deeds among men, and victorious over death, opened the gates of heaven, passing beyond the creation of the six days, and received the divine Sabbath and the blessed rest, when the Father said to Him, *Sit at my right hand, until I make your enemies your footstool* (Ps. 110:1). On that day of light, the first day and the day of the true sun, we also gather after the interval of six days, when we celebrate the holy and spiritual Sabbaths—we who have been redeemed through Him from the nations throughout the world—and what the law ordained for the priests to do on the Sabbath we fulfill according to the spiritual law. For we offer spiritual sacrifices and oblations, which are called sacrifices of praise and joy (cf. Ps. 27:6). We cause sweet-smelling incense to ascend, of which it is written, *May my prayer go up as incense in your sight* (Ps. 141:2). Also we offer the shewbread, renewing the memorial of salvation, and the blood of sprinkling, the blood of the lamb of God who takes away the sin of the world and purifies our souls. We light the lamps of the knowledge of the face of God. Furthermore we zealously devote ourselves to putting in practice on this day the things described in this Psalm.... Everything else which had to be done on the Sabbath we have transferred to the Lord's Day, as being more lordly (*kurioteras*), taking the lead (*egoumenes*), the first, and more worthy of honor than the Jewish Sabbath. For it was on this day in the creation of the world that God said, *Let there be light, and there was light* (Gen. 1:3).

> The same original sense of the Sabbath of Israel as the Sabbath of divine rest, or sheer delight in what has been created, can be felt much later in Jerome's commentary (c.400) on *the Gospel of the Hebrews*:

[77]And it came to pass that when the Lord came up out of the waters the whole fount of the Holy Spirit descended upon Him and rested upon Him and said to Him: My Son in all the prophets was I awaiting for thee that thou shouldst come and that I might have my rest in thee: for thou indeed art my rest: thou are my first begotten Son that reignest forever.

> Thus in a sense the spirit of the Sabbath of Israel as expressed in Genesis was born again with the development of the Christian week in the third and fourth centuries, although the Mosaic Sabbath remained a sort of social temptation for the Christians of the late fourth and early fifth centuries: "If any bishop, or any other of the clergy, fasts with the Jews, or keeps the festivals with them, or accepts from their festivals presents, such as unleavened bread or some such thing, let him be deposed: if he be one of the laity, let him be suspended. If any Christian carries oil into a synagogue of the Jews, or lights up lamps in their

[77]Text: PL 24.144

festivals, let him too be suspended."[78] Yet a little later Augustine of Hippo (c.400) was busily explaining what the Jewish Sabbath had in fact become in Christian faith:

[79]This psalm is entitled—A psalm to be sung on the Sabbath day. Lo, this day is the Sabbath, which the Jews at this time observe by a sort of bodily rest—languid and luxurious. They abstain from servile work but they surrender themselves to leisure; and although God ordained the Sabbath they keep it in ways that God forbids. On the other hand, our rest is from evil works whereas theirs is from good works, for it is much better to plough than to dance: they would abstain from good works but not from trivial works. To us also God proclaims His Sabbath. What kind of Sabbath? In the first place consider where it is: it is within us, in our very hearts. There are many indeed who are idle in body but are disturbed in heart and conscience ... but our Sabbath is the joy and peace of our hope. This is the subject of our praise, and of the psalm we sing, for a Christian enjoys the Sabbath of his own heart—that is, he rests in the quiet and peace of a serene and undisturbed conscience. Thus in this psalm we are told how men are wont to be disturbed, and we are taught to be at rest by keeping the Sabbath in our own hearts.

Although the seven days of Genesis were detached in Jewish consciousness from the lunar weeks of the East, they were in no way lacking in unity, for in the divine rest of the seventh day the six days of creation found their goal; they were all days of preparation for the Sabbath. This unity received ritual expression in the two days of fast that preceded the Sabbath of the Decalogue, for the fast of Monday and Thursday, the second and fifth days of the Jewish week, was a sort of axis around which the Sabbath revolved. Christianity remained within this structure of fast and Sabbath, but expressed its difference from Judaism

[78]*Apostolic Constitutions* cf. ANF 7.504
[79]Text: PL 37.1172

more quickly on the question of the fast than on that of the Sabbath:

[80]Your fasts must not be the same as those of the hypocrites, (the Jews). They observe Mondays and Thursdays; but you should fast on Wednesdays and Fridays.

> Wednesday, the fourth day, and Friday, the sixth day, were also the axes of the week for Tertullian; but they were probably Station days, or days of assembly which gradually became days of fast as well.

[81]Why do you devote to Stations the fourth and sixth days of the week, and to fasts the day of preparation? Anyhow, you sometimes continue your Station even over the Sabbath—a day never to be kept as a fast except at the Passover season.

> Third century texts, however, indicate that this fast had become obligatory and that it was justified as a commemorative penance for the betrayal of Christ on Wednesday and His death on Friday. Epiphanius (c.377) mentions an obligatory fast on Wednesdays and Fridays, which lasted until mid-afternoon; likewise Egeria: "It is always the custom at the ninth hour throughout the year on Wednesdays and Fridays to assemble for the liturgy in the Church of Sion at this hour, for in these parts on Wednesdays and Fridays they all fast." Around the same time Augustine (c.400) speaks about a Saturday fast and the variety of practice that was growing in the Church:

[82]I believe you heard this some time ago, but I am nevertheless repeating it now. My mother, who had followed me to Milan, found that the church there did not fast on Saturday. She began to be anxious and uncertain as to what she should do. I was not then concerned with such things, but

[80]Text: SC 248.172
[81]Text: PL 2.956
[82]Text: PL 33.200

for her sake I consulted on this matter that man of most blessed memory, Ambrose. He answered that he could teach me nothing but what he himself did, because, if he knew anything better, he would do it. When I thought that he wished to impose his views on us, solely by his own authority, without giving any reason, he followed up and said to me: 'When I go to Rome, I fast on Saturday, but here I do not. Do you also follow the custom of whatever church you attend, if you do not want to give or receive scandal.' When I told this to my mother, she willingly accepted it. And, recalling this advice over and over again, I have always esteemed it as something given by a heavenly oracle. For I have often experienced with grief and dismay that the weak are deeply disturbed by the aggressive obstinacy or superstitious fears of certain brethren, who stir up such controversial questions, that they think nothing is right except what they do themselves. And these are things of such sort that they are not prescribed by the authority of holy Scripture nor by the tradition of the universal Church, and they serve no good purpose of amending one's life, but they are insisted on simply because somebody thinks out a reason for them, or because a man was accustomed to do so in his own country, or because he saw things done somewhere on a pilgrimage, and he esteemed them to be more correct because they were further from his own usage.

> The unity of fast and Sabbath that was the axis of the biblical week in both Jewish and Christian practice, and which distinguishes it from mere lunar calculation, can still be seen in the Irish or Gaelic language which still calls our Wednesday, Dé Ceadaoin—the day of the first fast; our Friday Dé hAoinne—the day of the fast; our Thursday Déardaoin—the day between the fasts; and Sunday Dé Domhnaigh—the Lord's Day. The remaining three days—Monday, Tuesday and Saturday retain the pagan names of Dé Luain—day of the Moon; Dé Mairt—day of Mars; Dé Sathairn—day of Saturn.

Chapter Two

THE LORD'S NIGHT
AND SEASON

[1]This is our Passover feast,
when Christ, the true Lamb, is slain,
whose blood consecrates the hearts of the believers.

This is the night when first you saved our fathers,
you freed the people of Israel from their slavery,
and led them dry shod through the sea.

This is the night when the pillar of fire
destroyed the darkness of sin.

This is the night when Christians everywhere,
washed clean of sin
And freed from all defilment,
are restored to grace and grow together in holiness.

This is the night when Jesus Christ
broke the chains of death
and rose triumphant from the grave.

Most blessed of all nights, chosen by God
to see Christ rising from the dead.

Of this night Scripture says:
*The night will be as clear as day,
it will become my light, my joy* (Ps. 139:12).

[1] *Missale Romanum*

The power of this holy night
dispels all evil, washes guilt away,
restores lost innocence, brings mourners joy;
it casts out hatred ... and humbles earthly pride.

Night truly blessed when heaven is wedded to earth,
and man is reconciled with God! (*Exultet*)

> This night revealed the Christ of Jewish expectation and the Lord of the universe—"the man whose name is the dawn," [2]and whose day is prolonged by a week of days into the octave of Easter, and by a week of weeks into the season of Pentecost. These days, weeks and seasons will be discussed in the remaining three chapters: here there is question of the night under the following headings: 1) The Paschal Night and Season: 2) The Paschal Controversy: 3) The Greek Pasch: Christos Aneste: 4) The Latin Pasch: Pascha Nostrum Immolatus est Christus.

1. The Paschal Night and Season

[3]Come to the feast, ye heavens of heavens, which as the Spirit
exclaims *proclaim the glory of God*! (Ps. 19:1); in that
they are first to receive the paternal light of the Divine Spirit.
Come to the feast, angels and archangels of the heavens,
and all you heavenly host,
As you look upon your heavenly king
Come down in bodily form to earth.

Come to the feast, you choirs of stars
pointing out him who rises before the morning star.
Come to the feast, air, which extends over the abysses....

[2]Cf. PG 12.523
[3]Text: SC 27.121-123, ed. P. Nautin

Come to the feast, briny water of the sea,
honored by the sacred traces of the footsteps.
Come to the feast, earth, washed by the divine blood,
Come to the feast, soul of man, aroused
by the resurrection of a new birth.

This is the Pasch:

Common feast of the world:
Proclamation to the earth
of the Father's will for the universe:
divine dawning of Christ upon the earth;
invisible feast for angels and archangels
immortal life of the entire world,
fatal wound of death,
indestructible nourishment of man,
heavenly soul of the universe,
sacred initiation of heaven and earth,
prophet of mysteries old and new (Matt. 13:52),
seen by the eyes here on earth,
and contemplated by the spirit in the heavens....

Let us define the universal feast

that we may be nourished completely in the Word,
feasting not on earthly but on heavenly food;
let us eat the Pasch of the Word
with the spiritual desire with which the Lord
wished to eat when He said:
*With desire have I desired
to eat the Pasch with you* (Luke 22:15)

This second century *Homily on the Pasch* was assigned to
pseudo-Chrysostom at one stage, and at another to pseudo-
Hippolytus: more recently and more plausibly it is located
in the same milieu as Melito of Sardis, around the middle of
the second century, and renamed *An Anonymous Quartodeciman Homily.*

The *Exsultet*, quoted above and attributed by some to

Ambrose and by others to Augustine at a later date, re-echoes those Quartodeciman themes of heaven and earth, life and death, light and darkness, night and day, which were sounded and resounded in the literature of the early Paschal period.

Asterius of Amasea (d.410) illustrates the trend in his celebrated *Hymn to Night:*

[4]As a lamp on a lampstand, the cross, He was extinguished,
and as the sun He rose from the tomb.
It was possible to see a double wonder:
When Christ was crucified the day was darkened
and when He rose the night was as bright as day.
Why was the day darkened?
Because it had been written concerning Christ:
Darkness He made a veil to surround him (Ps. 18:11).
Why was the night as bright as day? Because the prophet had said to Him, *Darkness would not be darkness to you, night would be as light as day* (Ps. 139:12).
O night more splendid than day. O night more brilliant than the sun.
O night, whiter than snow.
(O night, more gleaming than lightening).
O night, more delightful than paradise.
O night, delivered from darkness.
(O night, filled with light).

The mystical understanding of this night image was well expressed by Gregory of Nyssa because "the usual reckoning of days and nights could not impede the swift action of the divine Word."

[5]The day of preparation (Friday) was divided into two days and one night because of the darkness that intervened when the sun was overshadowed. For if the Lord called the darkness night, and *for three hours there was darkness over the entire*

[4]Text: PG 40.436
[5]Text: PG 46.613

earth (Mt. 28:45) that space of time in the middle of the day was in fact night, with two days on either side of it, one from dawn until the sixth hour, the other from the ninth hour until evening.... Our remaining question is ... when, then, did Christ arise? *On the evening of the Sabbath* (Mt. 28:1), Matthew tells us clearly. This is the hour of the resurrection, according to the angel's word. This was the end of the Lord's stay in the heart of the earth. For when it was late in the evening (the evening was the beginning of that night which ended the first Sabbath day) then the earthquake occurred. Then the angel clad in gleaming garments rolled back the stone from the tomb. And the women rising early in the morning, just after dawn, when the splendor of the rising sun could be seen, and could then tell that the resurrection had already occurred. They recognized the marvellous event, but did not tell at what hour it occurred. The angel announced that the Lord had risen (cf. Mt.28:6), but did not add the detail of the precise time. The great Matthew alone of all the evangelists had indicated the time with accuracy, telling us that the evening of Saturday was the hour of the resurrection.

If these things are so, it is clear that the period of three days extends from the evening of Thursday to the evening of Saturday and that Friday had two days and two nights because of the intervening period of darkness. For it was necessary that in the Lord's dominion over time that His deeds should not be constricted by the prescribed measures of time but that new measures of time should be devised as the needs of things arose, and that the divine power should exercise itself in goodness in a shorter period by a contraction with the usual limits of time jettisoned so that the period of three days and three nights could be telescoped in this way.

> Thus night and darkness were the word and image in which the light and day of the Lord were revealed, and the Pasch of Israel became the biblical event that made clear the cosmic experience. Hence, the importance of the Old Testament Word in the New Testament world: *Christ, our Passover, has been sacrificed* (1 Cor. 5:7). Some of the early Greek Fathers, unacquainted with Hebrew, connected the

word Pasch with the Greek verb, *paschein*, to suffer. One of
the best examples is in Melito of Sardis, *Peri Pascha*:

[6]What is the Pasch? Its name is derived from what
happened, from the verb *to suffer*. Learn who it was who
suffered and who suffered along with the sufferer, and why the
Lord is present on the earth. It is so that in the vesture of one
who has suffered He may be taken up to the highest heavens.

The etymological connection with *Pasch* and *suffering* is
developed more elaborately by Melito a little later:

[7]He came on earth from the heavens on account of suffering
man; dressing Himself with humanity through a virgin's
womb, He took upon himself the sufferings of suffering man
through a body capable of suffering and destroyed the
sufferings of the flesh, and through His spirit incapable of
death He became the death of death which is destructive to
man.

This etymology is rejected, somewhat pedantically, by a
succession of Fathers beginning with Origen. In his recently
discovered *Peri Pascha* he labors the point:

[8]The majority of the brothers, perhaps all of them, believe
that the Pasch (Paskha) is so called on account of the Passion
(*pathos*, from the verb *paschein*) of the Savior. Nonetheless,
the actual word for the festival in question is not in Hebrew
paskha, but *phas*. The three letters of *phas*, plus the rough
breathing, (equivalent to the "h" in English), which is stronger
in their language, constitute the word for the festival, which
means, in translation, "passage." Because in this festival the
people pass from Egypt, it is appropriately called *phas*, which
means "passage." Because it is not possible in Greek to say the
word as it is pronounced in Hebrew, because the Greeks

[6]Text: OECT 22, ed. S. Hall
[7]Text: *ibid.* 34
[8]Text: *Origène. Sur la Pâque*, Paris, 1979, 154, edd. O. Gueraud, P. Nautin

cannot pronounce the stronger rough breathing of the Jews (the Hebrew letter *heth*), the word was Hellenized. In the translation of the prophets it is written *phasek*, then, more thoroughly Hellenized, the word becomes *paskha*. If one of our brothers, happening to be among Jews, should let it slip that he thinks the Pasch to be so called because of the Savior's Passion, they would make fun of him on account of his utter ignorance of the real etymology of the word.

> Eusebius of Caesarea, in his *De sollemnitate Paschali*, expands on this:

[9]Perhaps it would not be out of place to treat again of the Pasch and to explain that from the beginning it was handed down as a figure to the children of the Hebrews. For when the Hebrews, celebrating the shadow of things to come, first kept the festival of *phasek*, they took an animal from the flock. This was a sheep or a lamb. And this they immolated themselves. Then each anointed with its blood the lintels and his house. In this way they kept away the exterminator, with the blood on the ground and the ceilings. Then, having fed on the flesh of the sheep, and with loins girt with a cincture, and having taken unleavened bread and bitter herbs, they pass over from one place to another, from Egypt to the desert. It had been prescribed that they do these things at the same time as the slaughter and eating of the sheep. And it is from this passover to Egypt that the feast has received the name *Passover*.

> Gregory Nazianzus, who seems to be drawing from one if not both of these sources, tells us in *Oration 45 on the Holy Pasch*:

[10]This great, venerable Pasch is called *Phaska* by the Hebrews in their language. The word means *passage*, historically because of the flight and passing over from Egypt to the land of Canaan, spiritually because of the passage and ascent

[9]Text: PG 24.693
[10]Text: PG 36.636

from things below to things above, to the Promised Land. As we often find happening in the Scripture, the meaning of words changed from rather vague to rather clear. Something rather rough becomes more refined, as in the case that we are examining. For after considering the name of the Passion of the Savior, some decided to Hellenize the word, changing the letter 'ph' to 'p,' and the letter 'k' to 'ch,' and so have named the day *Pascha*. Custom adopted this name, consolidated it, and the more people heard it the more they liked its piety.

> For some of the Fathers, however, etymology was not a strong suit, and they developed their own as they went along. Chromatius of Aquileia is a case in point:

[11]For the passion of Christ is the true Pasch; it is from this that it has received the name 'Pasch.' The word of the Apostle clearly demonstrates this, saying, *For Christ, our Pasch, has been immolated* (1 Cor. 5:7). *With desire I have desired to eat this Pasch with you* (Lk. 22:15). We eat this Pasch, then, with Christ because He pastures (Pascha/pascit) those whom He saves. He is Himself the author of this Pasch, the author of this mystery. He has accomplished this feast of the Pasch so that He might refresh us with the food of His Passion, and might refresh us with the drink of salvation.

> Augustine, however, is familiar with the more erudite bilingual explanation, and elaborates it in his *Tractate on the Gospel of John*:

[12]Brethren, the word 'Pasch' is not Greek, as some think, but Hebrew, but as it happens very opportunely, there is a certain congruence here between both languages. Because the Greek word for 'suffer' is *'paschein'*, so 'Pasch' was thought to be related to the word 'passion.' But in its own language, that is in Hebrew, the word 'pasch' means 'passover.' Accordingly, for the first time the people of God celebrated the Pasch when

[11]Text: SC 154.276
[12]Text: CCL 36.463

they, fleeing from Egypt, passed over the Red Sea. Now indeed that figure in prophecy has been fulfilled in truth, when Christ *like a sheep was led to the slaughter* (Isa. 53:7) and with His blood our doorposts were smeared, that is, with our foreheads smeared with the sign of the cross, we are liberated from the destruction of this world, as from the slavery and destructiveness of Egypt. We perform a very salutary passover when we make the transition from the devil to Christ, and from this unstable age to the stable foundations of His kingdom.

Jerome says the same thing with even greater assurance and conciseness in his *Commentary on Matthew:*

[13]The Pasch, which in Hebrew is called *phase*, is not derived from the word *passio* as many think, but is named from the word for *passover* in that the exterminator, seeing the blood on the doors of the Israelites, did not strike against them, but passed over them, or rather that the Lord, in bringing help to His people, passed above. You must read the Book of Exodus for further details and we will discuss it if life is kind to us. Our passover, however, that is, our *phase*, is so celebrated if, laying aside Egypt and earthly things, we hasten to heavenly things.

Passage, then, is the meaning of Pasch and the passage of God in Jesus *making Him both Lord and Christ* (Acts 2:36) is the revelation and reality of the Paschal night—a night of passage from darkness to light, from night to day, from death to life, from flesh to spirit, from sin to grace, from figure to truth, from man to God, as the *Anonymous Quartodeciman* homily illustrates:

[14]Now is the time when the blessed light of Christ sheds its rays, the pure torches of the pure spirit arise and the heavenly treasures of divine glory are opened up. Night's darkness and obscurity have been swallowed up, and the dense blackness dispersed in the light of day; crabbed death had been totally

[13]Text: SC 259.234
[14]Text: SC 27.117

eclipsed. Life has been extended to every creature and all things are diffused in brightness. The dawn of dawn ascends over the earth, and He *who was before the morning star* (Ps. 110:3) and before the other stars, the mighty Christ, immortal and mighty, sheds light brighter than the universe.

For us, His faithful, He has initiated a bright new day, long, eternal and inextinguishable; it is the mystical Pasch, celebrated in figures under the law, but fulfilled in very truth by Christ; the marvelous Pasch, the wonder of divine virtue, truly a feast, an everlasting memorial.

Impassibility born of suffering, immortality born of death, life born in the tomb, healing born from plague, resurrection born from the fall, ascent to heaven born from descent to hell. God is the author of these wonders, from impossible beginnings to wonderful results. For He alone can accomplish all that He wills....

So the Law came first to signify in type the true reality, but type and figures are no more now that truth has come. Then a lamb was taken from the flock; today the lamb has come down from heaven; then there was the sign of blood, the small protection of all; today the word and cup of blood, filled with the Divine Spirit; then there was the sheep from the flock, today there is not just the sheep, but the shepherd in person. Will not the reality accomplish the salvation of all? Even their types were already salutary!...

The Pasch is the Pasch of the Lord.... No longer just a figure, just a narrative. No longer a shadow, but the Pasch of the Lord in truth. This is the night on which the flesh is eaten, for the light of the world has set upon the great body of Christ.

> Although the Christian Pasch is figuratively derived from the Passover of Israel, the reality was not achieved except in the death and resurrection of Jesus Christ. Consequently, the annual celebration of the sacrificial death of Christ continues in the time of the Church—the new Paschal night of Christ with its distinctive symbolism of light and life, or candle and cross.

THE CANDLE AND LIGHT

[15]Accept this Easter candle, a flame divided but undimmed, a pillar of fire that glows to the honor of God.
Let it mingle with the lights of heaven and continue bravely burning to dispel the darkness of the night.
May the morning star which never sets find the flame still burning: Christ, that Morning Star, who came back from the dead, and shed His peaceful light on all mankind, your son who lives and reigns for ever and ever. Amen. (*Exultet*)

THE CROSS AND LIFE

[16]And so He plants a new tree in place of the old one; it is no longer the old hand of wickedness which yesterday was extended in an impious gesture; it is His pure hand in a gesture of pity,—thus He shows His whole life truly stretched on the cross. But you, Israel, were unable to eat, whereas we ate with a spiritual, indestructible knowledge, and eating we shall not die.

This cross is the tree of my eternal salvation nourishing and delighting me. I take root in its roots. I am extended on its branches, I am delighted by its dew, I am fertilized by its spirit as by a delightful breeze. In my tent I am shaded by its shade and, fleeing the excessive heat, I find this refuge moist with dew. Its flowers are my flowers; I am wholly delighted by its fruits and I feast unrestrainedly on its fruits which are reserved for me always.

This is my nourishment when I am hungry, my fountain when I am thirsty, my covering when I am stripped, for my leaves are no longer fig leaves but the breath of life. This is my safeguard when I fear God, my support when I triumph. This is my narrow path, my steep way. This is the ladder of Jacob, the way of angels, at the summit of which the Lord is truly established. This is my tree, wide as the firmament, which He ascended from the earth to the heavens, with its immortal trunk established between heaven and earth; it is the pillar of

[15]*Missale Romanum*
[16]SC 27.177

the universe, the support of the whole world, the joint of the world, holding together the variety of human nature, and riveted by the invisible bolts of the Spirit, so that it may remain fastened to the divinity and impossible to detach. Its top touches the highest heavens, its roots are planted in the earth, and in the midst its giant arms embrace the ever present spirits of air. It is wholly in all things and in all places.

> The Paschal night was a celebration of the sacrificial death of Christ within the time and atmosphere of the Jewish feast of Passover with all its soteriological and eschatological significances. This single night celebration expressed the unity of the saving event, known as Pasch, which would later be fragmented, and become a triduum of the death, burial and resurrection, and ultimately develop into weeks and seasons, as we shall see, celebrating separately the death and resurrection of Christ. But in the second century this feast of Christian Pasch was a single night of prayer and fast: unlike the Jewish rite, which was an evening meal ending at midnight, the Christian rite was a vigil which began after midnight and ended with the Christian meal or Eucharist at dawn—a difference in rite and in faith from the Jewish night. Another Paschal homily, derived from Hippolytus but influenced by Origen, shows the early interiorization of the Jewish passover, or historical figure of redemption:

[17]The Jews celebrate an earthly Pasch having denied the heavenly one. But we celebrate the heavenly Pasch, having passed over the earthly one.

The Pasch which they celebrated was a figure of salvation of the firstborn of the Jews; the firstborn of the Egyptians died without the firstborn of the Jews also perishing; they were symbolically protected by the blood of the paschal victim. But the Pasch celebrated by us is a cause of salvation for all men beginning with the first-created, who is saved and given life in all.

[17]SC 36.55

Things partial and provisory are types of what is perfect and eternal; they are a shadowy prelude to the Truth which now emerges. But when the truth appears, the figure is no longer viable. Subjects no longer prostrate themselves before a king's statue when the king himself appears in person.

It is self-evident that the figure is less than the reality; the figure celebrates the fleeting existence of the firstborn of the Jews; the reality celebrates the eternal life of all mankind. For to escape death briefly is a matter of no great importance when one is going to die in any case a little later; but it is of great importance to escape death forever. That is what has happened to us; *for us Christ our pasch has been immolated* (1 Cor. 5:7).

The name of this feast only gets its full meaning when used in reference to the Truth; the Pasch means 'Passover'; the Destroyer slaying the firstborn passed over the houses of the Hebrews, but with us the passover of the Destroyer becomes a genuine reality; once and for all he passes over us whom Christ has resurrected for life everlasting.

We ought to examine the whole subject of the Pasch in a spiritual manner and believe in it as the apostles have interpreted it. The faithful one desires to understand the whole rationale of the figure and its relation to the Truth, and to see spiritual realities that affect him underlying the material things of that time. What pertains to the Law is thus interpreted by him in Christian terms and the invisible is deciphered from the visible.

> In this second century *Quartodeciman homily,* there is a
> sense of a feast that has become the common possession of
> the Church universal:

[18]O mystical choir! O feast of the Spirit! O Pasch of God, who has come down from heaven to earth, and from earth you ascend again to the heavens. O feast common to all, O universal joy and honor of the universe, its nurture and its luxury, by whom the darkness of death has been dissolved and life extended to all, by whom the gates of heaven have been

[18]SC 27.189-191

opened as God has become man and man has become God. Through him the gates of hell have been broken, the bars of iron have been loosed, the people below have been raised from the dead proclaiming the good news; an antiphonal choir has been formed on earth to respond to the choir above. O Pasch of God, no longer confined to the heavens and now united to us in spirit; through Him the great marriage chamber has been filled, and all wear wedding garments though nobody is expelled for not having one on. O Pasch, illumination of the new bright day—the brightness of the torches of the virgins, through which the lamps of souls are no longer extinguished, but the divine fire of grace burns divinely and spiritually in all, nurtured by the soul and body and oil of Christ.

We call on you, then, sovereign Lord, spiritually eternal, Christ, Lord and King, extend your wonderful hands over your holy Church and over your people ever holy; guard and conserve them, attacking, pursuing, and combating all their enemies, and subjugating all of them to your power, until their invisible forces are routed and wiped out. Raise now your standard above us and enable us to chant with Moses the canticle of triumph. For with you is the victory and the power for ever and ever. Amen.

Ultimately the origin of the Paschal night is derived from the cosmic experience of Spring, but its particular significance in Israel was further determined by the experience of history, and consequently the Pasch was a festival of redemption and not just of creation. This purification and transignification of cosmic rites made them ready to reveal the mystery of Christ, and able, so to speak, to return to nature for the purification of its mysteries and the restoration of all things in Christ. Consequently, Spring, the season surrounding the night of the Pasch, left its stamp on the festival, but did not explain its origin. Unlike Christmas and other days, as we shall see, the biblical origin of the Christian Pasch was always clear. Nevertheless, its seasonal dimension was also cosmically felt and eventually became the liturgical season of the Pasch to Pentecost, which will be the subject of another chapter.

The linking of the Pasch and Spring, *the beginning of months* (Exod. 12:1) is elaborated in many of the Fathers, and nowhere more beautifully than in this same *Homily on the Pasch*, by *An Anonymous Quartodeciman:*

[19]Beginning at the beginning let us say first why this month is the beginning of months and why the month of the Pasch is the first of the months of the year.

There is a secret tradition among the Hebrews which says that in this month God, the artist of creation and the creator of all, conceived His universe. It was among the first blooms, in the full beauty of the world, they say, that the sculptor saw his statue come to life, graceful, exactly as He had desired. They invoke the serenity of the heavens, the sweetness of the season, the regular course of the sun, the rising of the full moon, the burgeoning of fruits, the growth of plants, the blossoms on the trees, the lambs in the flocks, when the whole earth is verdant and the trees, laden down, creak under the burden of their fruits. This is the time when the farmer loosens the plough from its yoke and lets his team of oxen to breathe, when he sows the blessed seeds and awaits the fountains of heaven; when the shepherd milks the white milk of the flocks and the beekeeper shapes the sweet combs of the hive; when the mariner joyfully dares to confront the sea, braving the tumultuous waves in pursuit of gain. They think that this harmony of the world, this repose of all things, this blissful state, was not only the beginning of spring, but also for them the beginning of the year.

For my part, I do not disbelieve all this, but I feel, or rather I am certain, that this is so because of the spiritual nature of the Pasch: it is the beginning, the head and leader of all times and ages because in this month the great mystery is accomplished and celebrated. Just as the Lord is the first-engendered and firstborn of all beings intelligible and invisible, likewise this month, which celebrates the sacred solemnity, becomes the first of the year and the beginning of all ages; and the year is

[19]Text: SC 27.145-149

that which is announced in the Divine Scriptures: *Declare the acceptable year of the Lord* (Isa. 61:2).

> This season of Spring surrounding the night of the Pasch at the end of the fourth century was divided into the liturgical seasons of Lent and Pentecost—the new seasons, as we shall see, of the growing liturgical year.

2. The Paschal Controversy

> Scripture's *first day of the week*, when *Jesus came and stood before them* (Jn. 20:19), and its octave, *a week later*, when again, *Jesus came and stood before them* (Jn. 20:26), became *the Lord's Day* for the Apostolic Fathers, and *Sunday* for the Apologists. But there are no new names in either the new Scriptures or the early Fathers for the old night of the Passover, which the new day of the resurrection enlightened. Paul, however, proposed a new meaning or significance for the old feast: *Christ our passover has been sacrificed. Let us celebrate the feast, not with the old yeast, that of corruption and wickedness, but with the unleavened bread of sincerity and truth* (1 Cor. 5:8). But Sunday, in its week-by-week return, and not Easter, was the scriptural and apostolic day of worship celebrating in the Latin West and in the Greek East a completely new event—the day of the resurrection.
>
> On the other hand, Paul's Christological understanding of the Passover was indigenous to Jewish Christianity, and developed in the second century, as typology explored the mystery of intertestamental events. Melito of Sardis (c.160) and his contemporary, *the Anonymous Quartodeciman*, are our earliest witnesses for the annual celebration of the old Pasch with the new significance that came into full bloom in their world of Asia Minor:

[20]The text of the Hebrew exodus has been read and the

[20]Text: OECT, ed. Hall, 2-5

words of the mystery have been enunciated: how the sheep was immolated and the people saved. Now grasp this, beloved: how it is new and old, eternal and transient, corruptible and incorruptible, mortal and immortal, the mystery of the Pasch. It is old in regard to the Law, new in regard to the Word, transient in terms of figure, eternal in terms of grace, corruptible because of the slaughter of the sheep, incorruptible because of the life of the Lord, mortal because of burial in the earth, immortal because of the resurrection from the dead.

The Law is old, the Word new, the figure is transient, grace is eternal, the sheep is corruptible, the Lord is incorruptible: immolated as a lamb, resurrected as God. For *as a sheep He was led to the slaughter* (Isa. 53:7) but a sheep He was not, and *as a lamb without voice* (Isa. 53:7), but a lamb He was not. For the type has passed away and the truth has been realized. Now in place of the lamb God has come, and in place of the sheep, man, and in man, Christ who contains all things. For the slaughter of the sheep, and the rite of the Pasch, and the letter of the Law have issued in Jesus Christ on whose account everything took place in the Old Law and, even more, in the new dispensation.

For the Law has become Logos, and the old new, the two proceeding from Sion and Jerusalem, and the commandment grace, and the figure truth, and the Lamb the Son, and the sheep man, and man God. For born Son-like He has risen from the dead God-like, being by nature God and man. He is all things: inasmuch as He judges, Law; inasmuch as He teaches, Logos; inasmuch as He saves, grace; inasmuch as He begets, Father; inasmuch as He is begotten, Son; inasmuch as He suffers, sheep; inasmuch as He is buried, man; inasmuch as He is risen, God. This is Jesus, the Messiah to whom be glory forever and ever. Amen. Such is the mystery of the Pasch as it is written in the Law according to the reading just heard.

The earliest evidence for the Christian observance of the Pasch comes in the second century in *The Letter of the Apostles*, written c.150 AD, originally in the Greek, but surviving only in Ethiopic and Coptic translations. It clearly shows that the Pasch was originally observed on the fourteenth day of the month, Nisan, although in the later history of the Pasch Quartodeciman, or fourteenth day, observance was increasingly frowned on and was the basis of the ongoing Paschal controversy:

[21]After my return to the Father you will celebrate the memory of my death. For when the Pasch arrives then one among you will be thrown into prison because of my name and he will be in grief and apprehension because you celebrate the Pasch while he is in prison, separated from you.

But I will send my power under the form of the angel Gabriel and the prison gates will be opened and he will come to you and join in the night vigil with you, and stay near you until cockcrow. When you then have ended your Agape, the memorial of me which you make, he will be thrown back into prison for a testimony unto the day when he shall emerge to preach that which I have commanded you.

But you will demand of Him: 'Lord, is it indeed necessary that we take the chalice and drink it anew?' And He will say to you, 'Yes, it is necessary until the day when I will return with those who have been put to death with me.'

The fourteenth day of Nisan naturally remained the date of Passover for Christians observing the old feast with a new significance. Indeed the fourth Gospel had already confirmed this by identifying the hour of Christ's death with the time of slaughter in the Temple, when the lambs were prepared for the feast. Hence the Quartodecimans focused their attention and their preaching on the saving slaughter of the Lamb of God: indeed a *Quartodeciman homily* preached the Paschal Lamb of God, and, for the most part, Melito made the Hebrew word for Passover synonomous with the Greek verb to suffer:

[22]Already the Lord has proclaimed His sufferings in the patriarchs, prophets, and the whole people, sealing it through

[21]Text: cf. Cantalamessa, 30-33; Talley, 5-7; Casel, 19-22.
[22]Text: OECT ed., Hall, 30

the Law and Prophets. For what is to be new and great is prefigured beforehand: a coming event derives credence from its earlier prefiguration. Of such a kind was the mystery of the Lord, for long prefigured, this day revealed, finding credence in fulfillment although regarded by men as new.

For the mystery of the Lord is old and new, old in terms of figure, new in terms of grace. If you look at this figure you will see the truth through its fulfillment. Accordingly, if you wish to see the mystery of the Lord, look to Abel likewise slaughtered, Isaac likewise bound, Joseph likewise sold, Moses likewise exposed, David likewise persecuted, the prophets likewise persecuted on account of Christ. Look also to the sheep slaughtered in the land of Egypt, trampling on Egypt and saving Israel with His blood.

The mystery of the Lord is also proclaimed by the voice of the prophets. For Moses says to the people: *And you shall see your life hanging before your eyes night and day and you shall have no assurance of your life* (Deut. 28:66). And David says: *Why do the nations conspire and the people plot in vain. The kings of the earth and the rulers take counsel together against the Lord and against His anointed* (Ps. 2:1). And Jeremiah: *I was like a blameless lamb led to the slaughter. They devised evil schemes against me, saying: Come, let us cast wood on His bread and destroy Him from the land of the living and His name shall not be remembered* (Jer. 11:19, LXX). And Isaiah: *Like a sheep He was led to the slaughter and like a lamb dumb before His shearers this man did not open His mouth. Who shall tell His descent?* (Isa. 53:7) And many other things by many prophets were proclaimed about the mystery of the Pasch which is Christ, to whom be glory for ever and ever. Amen.

This one came from heaven to earth for suffering men clothing Himself with humanity in a virgin's womb and came forth as man: He took on Himself the sufferings of suffering man through a body capable of suffering and put an end to the sufferings of the flesh, and through His spirit incapable of death He killed death, the killer of man. This one, led like a lamb and slaughtered like a sheep, ransomed us from the service of the world as from the land of Egypt, and delivered us from the slavery of the devil as from the hand of Pharaoh, and sealed our souls with His own spirit, and the members of our body with His own blood. This is the one who draped death in shame, putting the devil in mourning garb, as Moses did Pharaoh. This is the one who trampled on lawlessness and left injustice childless, as Moses did Egypt. This is the one who rescued us from slavery to freedom, from darkness to light, from death to life, from tyranny to the kingdom of eternity, and made us a new priesthood, a people chosen, eternal. This is the one who is the Pasch of our salvation.

This is the one who suffered much in many people. This is He who in Abel was slaughtered, in Isaac was bound, in Jacob was exiled, in Joseph was sold, in Moses was exposed, in the lamb was immolated, in David was persecuted, in the prophets maltreated. This is the one who in the virgin was made incarnate, on the cross was suspended, in the earth was buried, from the dead was resurrected, to the heights of heaven was elevated. This is the lamb without voice. This is the lamb led to slaughter. This is the lamb born of Mary, the fair ewe. This is the one taken from the flock and dragged to slaughter, and at evening sacrificed, and by night buried, who on the cross was not broken, and in the earth did not dissolve, but from the dead rose again and raised up man from the depths of the tomb. This is the one who was slain. Where? In the midst of Jerusalem. Why? Because He cured their lame and cleansed their lepers and restored sight to their blind and raised to life their dead.

Justin the Apologist, around the middle of the second century, is silent about any Paschal celebration in Rome. Consequently the rapid spread of the Quartodeciman Pasch into the world of Sunday worship at this very time gave rise to certain questions: for example, the dawn Eucharist which ended the Quartodeciman fast on the morning of the fifteenth Nisan interfered with whatever fast had arisen by way of preparation for the resurrection feast. Hence the controversy that follows is more Paschal than Quartodeciman, for initially it concerned the fast, and indeed the feast itself, and not just the day or date of the Passover. In other words, the Quartodeciman practice of apostolic but local origin came into conflict with the universal practice of Sunday worship. Eusebius, the fourth century historian, who was the first to collect all the documents and facts of Christian history known to him, gives us the following account of this Paschal controversy of the second century:

[23]At that time no small controversy arose because all of the dioceses of Asia thought it right, as though by more ancient tradition, to observe for the feast of the Savior's Passover the fourteenth day of the moon, on which the Jews had been commanded to kill the lamb. Thus it was necessary to finish the fast on that day, whatever day of the week it might be. Yet it was not the custom to celebrate in this manner in the churches throughout the rest of the world, for from apostolic tradition they kept the custom which still exists that it is not right to finish the fast on any day save that of the resurrection of our Savior. Many meetings and conferences with bishops were held on this point, and all unanimously formulated in their letters the doctrine of the Church for those in every country that the mystery of the Lord's resurrection from the dead could be celebrated on no day save Sunday, and that on that day alone we should celebrate the end of the Paschal fast. There is still extant a writing of those who were convened in Palestine, over whom presided Theophilus, bishop of the diocese of Caesarea, and Narcissus, bishop of Jerusalem; and there is similarly another from those in Rome on the same controversy, which gives Victor as bishop; and there is one of the bishops of Pontus over whom Palmas presided as the oldest; and of the diocese of Gaul, of which Irenaeus was bishop; and yet others of those in Osrheone and the cities there; and particularly of Bacchyllus, the bishop and church of Corinth; and of very many more who expressed one and the same opinion and judgment and gave the same vote. These issued the single definition which was given above; but the bishops in Asia were led by Polycrates in persisting that it was necessary to keep the custom which had been handed down to them of old.

[23]Text: PG 20. 489-507

Polycrates himself, in a document which he addressed to Victor and to the church of Rome, expounds the tradition which had come to him as follows: 'Therefore we keep the day undeviatingly, neither adding nor taking away, for in Asia great luminaries sleep, and they will rise on the day of the coming of the Lord, when He shall come with glory from heaven and seek out all the saints.' Such were Philip of the twelve apostles, and two of his daughters who grew old as virgins, who sleep in Hierapolis, and another daughter of his, who lived in the Holy Spirit, rests at Ephesus. Moreover, there is also John, who lay on the Lord's breast, who was a priest wearing the breastplate, and a martyr and teacher. He sleeps at Ephesus. And there is also Polycarp at Smyrna, both bishop and martyr, and Thraseas, both bishop and martyr from Eumenaea, who sleeps in Smyrna. And should I speak of Sagaris, bishop and martyr who sleeps at Laodicaea and Pairius, too, the blessed, and Melito the eunuch, who lived entirely in the Holy Spirit, who lies in Sardis, waiting for the visitation from heaven when He will rise from the dead? All these kept the fourteenth day of the Passover according to the Gospel, never swerving, but following according to the rule of the faith. And I also, Polycrates, the least of you all, live according to the tradition of my kinsmen, and some of them have I followed. For seven of my family were bishops and I am the eighth, and my kinsmen even kept the day when the people put away the leaven. Therefore, brethren, I, who have lived sixty-five years in the Lord and conversed with brethren from every country, and have studied all holy Scripture, am not afraid of threats, for they who were greater than I have said, *It is better to obey God rather than men* (Ps. 118:8).

He continues about the bishops who when he wrote were with him and shared his opinion, and says thus: 'And I could mention the bishops who were present whom you required me to summon, and I did so. If I should write their names they would be many multitudes; and they, knowing my feeble humanity, agreed with the letter, knowing that not in vain is my head grey, but that I have ever lived in Christ Jesus.'

Upon this, Victor, who presided at Rome, immediately tried to cut off from the common unity the dioceses of all Asia,

together with the adjacent Churches, on the ground of
heterodoxy, and he indited letters announcing that all the
Christians there were absolutely excommunicated. By no
means were all pleased by this, so they issued counter-requests
to him to consider the cause of peace and unity and love
towards his neighbors. Their words are extant, sharply
rebuking Victor.

Among them, too, Irenaeus, writing in the name of the
Christians whose leader he was in Gaul, though he recommends
that the mystery of the Lord's resurrection be observed only on
the Lord's day, yet, nevertheless, exhorts Victor suitably and at
length not to excommunicate whole Churches of God for
following a tradition of ancient custom, and continues as
follows: 'For the controversy is not only about the day, but
also about the actual character of the fast; for some think that
they ought to fast one day, others two, others even more, some
count their day as forty hours, day and night. And such
variation of observance did not begin in our own time, but
much earlier, in the days of our predecessors who, it would
appear, disregarding strictness maintained a practice which is
simple and yet allows for personal preference, establishing it
for the future, and nonetheless all these lived in peace, and we
also live in peace with one another and the disagreement in the
fast confirms our agreement in the faith.

He adds to this a narrative which I may suitably quote,
running as follows: 'Among these, too, were presbyters before
Soter, who presided over the Church of which you are now the
leader. I mean Anicetus and Pius and Telesphorus and Xystus.
They did not themselves observe it, nor did they enjoin it on
those who followed them, and though they did not keep it they
were nonetheless at peace with those from the dioceses in
which it was observed when they came to them, although to
observe it was more objectionable to those who did not do so.
And no one was ever rejected for this reason, but the
presbyters before you who did not observe it sent the Eucharist
to those from other dioceses who did; and when the blessed
Polycarp was staying in Rome in the time of Anicetus, though
they disagreed a little about some other things as well, they
immediately made peace, having no wish for strife between

them on this matter.

'For neither was Anicetus able to persuade Polycarp not to observe it inasmuch as he had always done so in company with John, the disciple of our Lord, and the other apostles with whom he had associated; nor did Polycarp persuade Anicetus to observe it, for he said that he ought to keep the custom of those who were presbyters before him. And under these circumstances they communicated with each other, and in the church Anicetus yielded the celebration of the Eucharist to Polycarp, obviously out of respect, and they parted from each other in peace, for the peace of the whole Church was kept both by those who observed and by those who did not.'

And Irenaeus, who deserved his name, making an *eirenicon* in this way, gave exhortations of this kind for the peace of the Church and served as its ambassador, for in letters he discussed the various views on the issue which had been raised, not only with Victor but also with many other rulers of Churches.

> This evidence of Eusebius concerning the Paschal controversy of the late second century is interpreted by scholars in different ways: for some there is question only of the day and date of the Pasch; for others the very existence of the Pasch itself was the question under discussion. In general, most scholars agree that Easter Sunday represents an adjustment of the Quartodeciman Pasch to the more ancient and independently established weekly Sunday; at the same time the influence of the Pasch on this Sunday that followed is no less obvious: "A multitude of people attend on the day of preparation, and especially on the Sunday which commemorates the Passion, for the resurrection is celebrated every eighth day, and not just once a year."[24] While continuing this notion of the Pasch as passion, Origen was, nonetheless, the first Christian writer, as we have seen to define pasch as *diabasis*, transition, or passage and to apply that understanding to Christ's passage into the kingdom. He saw Easter as the festival of the faithful who

[24]Text: GCS 33.265

through Christ make the passage from sin to virtue and from death to life. This spiritualization of the Pasch lessened the appeal of the Quartodeciman Pasch and emphasized the Paschal dimension of Easter Sunday for Origen:

[25]After these things it is written, *In the second month after they set forth from Egypt, on the fifteenth day of the month, the people murmured against Moses saying, 'Would that we had died in the land of Egypt when we sat over kettles of flesh and ate bread to satiety, since you led us into this wilderness to kill the whole congregation with famine'* (Ex. 16:1-3). Granted, the sins of the people, that they murmured and were ungrateful for the divine benefits when they received the heavenly manna, are pointed out for the correction of the readers. But why is the day also recorded on which *the people murmured*? The text says: *In the second month on the fifteenth day of the month.* Certainly it was not written without reason. Recall what was said about the laws of the Passover and you will discover there that this is the time which is established to celebrate the second Passover for those who were *impure in soul* (Num. 9:10), or occupied with foreign business. Those, therefore, who were not *impure in soul* or not *on a long journey* (Num. 9:10), celebrated the Passover *on the fourteenth day of the first month* (Num. 9:11). Those, however, who were on a long journey and were impure celebrated a second Passover at this time, at which time also the manna descended from heaven. The manna did not descend on the day on which the first Passover occurred but at this time on which the second Passover occurred.

Let us now see, therefore, what order of mystery these words contain. The first Passover belongs to the first people; the second Passover is ours. For we were impure in soul, who *used to worship wood and stone* (Deut. 4:28), and not knowing God we used to serve those things which, by nature, were not God's. We also were those who *were on a long journey*, of whom the Apostle says that *we were strangers and foreigners to the*

[25]Text: PG 12.344 = FOTC 71.305

testaments of God, not having hope and without God in this world (Eph. 2:12). Nevertheless, the manna from heaven was not given on that day on which the second was celebrated. For *the bread which descended from heaven* (Jn. 6:41) did not come to those who celebrated the first celebration but to us who received the second. *For our Passover, Christ, has been sacrificed* (1 Cor. 5:7), who descended to us as the true *bread from heaven* (Jn. 6:32).

But nevertheless let us see what it is which is shown to have happened on this day. *On the fifteenth day of the second month*, the text says, *the people murmured* and said that it would have been better for us to die in Egypt *when we sat over kettles of flesh.* O ungrateful people! They who saw the Egyptians destroyed desire Egypt! They who saw the flesh of the Egyptians given to the fish of the sea and the birds of the sky again seek the flesh of Egypt! They raise, therefore, a murmur against Moses, nay rather against God.

> Thus in the third century the theological dimension of the Paschal controversy was the primary concern and the day and date aspect of the festival was not a polemical issue. Consequently, the Sunday Pasch spread and the Quarto-deciman Pasch survived as long as the fast was maintained until the Sunday feast. Indeed, in the *Didascalia Apostolorum* (260) fast and feast became the days of the Pasch anticipating the sacred triduum of the death, burial and resurrection, which developed in the fourth century:

[26]Brethren, it is appropriate then that you observe carefully the days of the Pasch and keep your fast diligently. You will begin at the moment when your brothers who belong to the (Hebrew) people make their Pasch since our Lord and Master, after He ate the Pasch with us, was betrayed by Judas after that hour and immediately we began to grieve because He had been taken away from us.

---

[26]Text: F.X. Funk, ed., *Didascalia Apostolorum*, 1.286 = R.H. Connolly, *Didascalia Apostolorum*, 187

Accordingly, beginning with the tenth day (of the moon), which is the second day of the week (Sabbati) you will fast on the days of the Pasch, taking only bread, salt and water, from the ninth hour to the fifth day of the week; you will fast the whole of (Good) Friday and (Holy) Saturday, tasting nothing.

Remain assembled, then, in the same place, staying awake and keeping vigil the whole night, supplicating, praying and reading the prophets, Gospel and psalms with fear and trembling, in fervent supplication until the third hour of the night (i.e. cockcrow) which follows the Sabbath and then eat, rejoice, make merry, exult, since Christ, the pledge of our resurrection, has risen, and let this be a law for you forever unto the consummation of the world.

The day and date aspect of the Paschal controversy concerned the Paschal Sunday and not this Quartodeciman Pasch, since it arose from efforts to incorporate a lunar feast into a solar calendar. In fact, by the end of the third century all the Churches had in principle adopted the Sunday following the fourteenth day Nisan, which is the full moon in the first Jewish month after the spring equinox. But Jewish calendars, based on the lunar year, and consequently eleven days short, sometimes place Passover before the equinox, whenever the additional intercalary month had not been inserted to make good the deficiency. The Syrians at Antioch followed this Jewish calendar, whereas the other Churches reckoned the Sunday after the full moon and spring equinox by their own scientific computation. Thus, in perfectly good faith, the Churches were at variance for reasons of computation: at Rome, for example, the equinox had been fixed on March 25 since the time of Caesar, whereas Alexandria from astronomical considerations had settled on March 21. The Council of Nicaea (325) urged the celebration of Easter everywhere on the same day and date, and accordingly, adopted the Alexandrian reckoning and fixed the equinox on March 21, which in the fourth century was also its true date in the Julian calendar. Thus, at Nicaea the Paschal controversy concerned uniformity of worship in theory, but astronomical computation in practice:

[27]Having examined carefully the question whether it was necessary for the universal Church to celebrate the Pasch on the same day, it was discovered that three quarters of the world were in accord with the practice of Rome and Alexandria, and that the only part out of line was the East. It was decided that all discord and disagreement should be set aside, and that the brethren in the East should follow the practice of Rome and Alexandria and elsewhere, so that each and all on the same day and with one voice should send up their prayers on the one holy day of the Pasch. All the Orientals, who had been in disagreement with the others, accepted and ratified this decision (Council of Nicaea).

> The historian, Socrates, writing after 439, and quoting Constantine's letter desiring uniformity of practice throughout the world, passes very sober comment on the controversy at Nicaea:

[28]It appears to me that neither the ancients nor the moderns had much rational foundation for their debate ... for with Christianity the obligation to observe the Mosaic Law and its ceremonial types ceased.... Neither Christ nor His apostles enjoined this feast on us by any law ... but the feast of Easter came to be observed in each place according to the customs of that place ... the Quartodecimans affirm that the observance of the fourteenth day was delivered to them by the apostle John while the Romans and those in the Western parts assure us their usage originated with the apostles Peter and Paul: but neither of these parties can produce any written testimony in confirmation of their claims. I am therefore of opinion that they who agree in faith differ according to custom and usage.

> The problem of computation remained in the fourth, fifth and sixth centuries until in 526 Dionysius Exiguus was entrusted with the revision of the Roman calendar. He made use of the golden number, the nineteen-year cycle of

---

[27]Cf. J.B. Pitra, *Spicilegium Solesmense*
[28]Text: PG 67.625 = LNPF Ser. 2,2.130

Anatolius (258) which had been in use in Egypt, and this revision became universally accepted. Something of this problem of faith and discipline during these centuries of computation difficulties can be seen in a letter attributed to Ambrose (386) written to the bishops of Aemelia:

[29] Holy Scripture and the tradition of the Fathers teach us that it requires more than ordinary wisdom to determine the day for the celebration of Easter. Those who met at the Council of Nicaea, in addition to their decrees, true and admirable, regarding the faith, using the help of men skilled in calculations, formulated for the above-mentioned celebration a scheme of nineteen years, and set up a sort of cycle on which might be patterned subsequent years. They called this the 'nineteen-years' cycle,' and, if we follow it, we should not waver amid foolish ideas regarding a celebration of this kind. Having found a true method of calculating, let everyone be of one opinion, so that the Sacrifice of the Mass for the resurrection of the Lord may be offered everywhere on one night.

Two observances are necessary in solemnizing the Passover: the fourteenth moon and the first month, called the month of new fruits. Now, that we may not seem to depart from the Old Testament, let us review the very chapter which concerns the day for celebrating the Passover. Moses tells the people to keep the month of new fruits, specifying that it be the first month, saying, *This will be the beginning of months for you, it will be the first of the months of the year* (Ex. 12:2); and *thou shalt offer the Passover to the Lord thy God on the fourteenth day of the first month* (Ex. 12:6).

Six years ago we celebrated Easter on April 21, which was the thirtieth day of the month, as we reckon it; therefore, we must not be disturbed to be soon celebrating Easter on the thirtieth day of Pharmuth. If anyone says it is in the second month, since Easter will occur three days after the completed month, which appears to end on April 21, he should realize that our concern is with the fourteenth day, which occurs on April 18, well within the month's count. The Law only requires

[29] Text: PL 16.1025 = FOTC 26.189

that the day of the Passion be celebrated within the first month of the new fruits.

This reckoning is satisfactory as far as the full month is concerned, since it still has three days remaining for its completion. Easter does not pass into a different month when it is celebrated within the same month, the first. And, too, we should not be bound to the letter if the custom of the celebration is our guide. The Apostle, too, teaches us, saying: *Christ, our passover has been sacrificed* (1 Cor. 5:7). The passage just read teaches us not to follow the letter, for you have the words: *You will perform the Pasch to the Lord your God on the fourteenth day of the first month* (Ex. 12:6). He uses the word *day* instead of *month*; consequently, those skilled in the Law compute the month by the course of the moon. Since the course of the moon, that is, its first day, may begin on more than one of the nones, you see that the nones of May can still be reckoned within the first month of new fruits. According to the judgment of the Law, therefore, this is the first month. Finally, the Greeks call the moon *mene* and so call the month *menas,* in Greek, while the natural practice of foreign peoples uses the term *month* in place of *days.*

Yet, the writings of the Old Testament show that we must celebrate the Passion one day and the resurrection another. We note, too, that the day of the Passion is appointed on a fast day because the lamb is to be slain toward evening, although we can understand the *last time* instead of *evening* according to John who says: *Children, it is the last hour* (1 Jn. 2:18). But, according to the mystery, it is certain that the slaying took place in the evening when the shadows were falling quickly, and the fast should be kept on that day, for then you will eat it with anxiety, since those fasting have anxiety.

On the day of the resurrection there is the joy of refreshment and happiness, for it appears that the people left Egypt on that day, after the first-born of the Egyptians had been slain. It is evident then that the day of the resurrection should be kept after the day of the Passion, and the former should not be on the fourteenth of the month but later, as the Old Testament says. The day of the resurrection is that on which the people departing from Egypt *were baptized in the sea and in the cloud*

(1 Cor. 10:2), as the Apostle says, and overcame death, receiving a spiritual food and drinking a spiritual drink from the rock. Again, the Lord's Passion cannot be celebrated on the Lord's Day. And, if the fourteenth day falls on the Lord's Day, another week should be added, as was done in the seventy-sixth year of the era of Diocletian. Then, with no hesitancy on the part of our predecessors, we celebrated the Lord's Day of Passover on the twenty-eighth of Pharmuth, April 23. The course of the moon and careful calculation support this plan to celebrate the next Easter on the twenty-first day, because the month is commonly extended to the twenty-first.

Since we have so much evidence of the truth, combined with the example of our predecessors, let us keep the feast of the people's salvation with joy and gladness, and color our doorposts where is hung the door of the Word.

> Until the eighth century, the Irish and the Bretons retained the solar cycle of twenty-eight years, authoritative at Rome at the time of the conversion: in other words, they refused to accept the revision made in Rome in 526 by Dionysius Exiguus of the cycle of Anatolius which had been the table of computation at Nicaea. Hence the letter of Columbanus to Pope Gregory (c.600) on the Paschal question to justify the Celtic usage.
>
> Columbanus rested his case on two main arguments. First, there was the authority of Anatolius whose tables were preserved by the Irish and whose learning had been praised by Jerome: "I tell you candidly," wrote the monk to the Pope, "that whoever denies the authority of Jerome will be accounted a heretic and contemptuously rejected by the Churches of the West, for in everything that regards the Scriptures they believe implicitly in Jerome."[30] Secondly, Easter, being the festival of light, should be celebrated on a night during the greater part of which the moon is shining. But if the celebration was deferred until the twenty-first or

[30]Text: cf. PL 80.259

twenty-second day, when the moon entered on her last quarter, darkness would dominate the light, and the victory of Satan over Church rather than of Christ over Satan would be symbolized: they who say that Easter can be celebrated at the age of the moon canot confirm their assertion by the authority of Scripture; nay, they are incurring the charge of sacrilege and contumacy, and are endangering their souls (Ep. 1).

3. The Greek Pasch

The light of this night lit up the Christian world of Constantine, Greek East and Latin West, after the Council of Nicaea.

[31]The emperor himself, as a sharer in the holy mysteries of our religion, would seclude himself daily at a stated hour in the innermost chambers of his palace; and there, in solitary converse with his God, would kneel in humble supplication, and entreat the blessings of which he stood in need. But especially at the salutary feast of Easter, his religious diligence was redoubled; he fulfilled, as it were, the duties of a hierophant with every energy of his mind and body, and outvied all others in the zealous celebration of this feast. He changed, too, the holy night vigil into brightness like that of day, by causing waxen tapers of great length to be lighted throughout the city: besides which, torches everywhere diffused their light, so as to impart to this mystic vigil a brilliant splendor beyond that of day. As soon as day itself returned, in imitation of our Savior's gracious acts, he opened a liberal hand to his subjects of every nation, province, and people, and lavished abundant bounties on all. (Eusebius)

Quartodeciman Pasch and Paschal Sunday became one celebration in the *sacratissimum triduum crucifixi, sepulti, resuscitati* of the fourth century, and the evening Pasch of

[31]Text: PG 20.1168 = LNPF 1.545

Christ began the Paschal vigil of the Church. The world was at one, and in Jerusalem and *at home*, according to Egeria, the Passover of the Church was celebrated in the same manner:

[32]On the next day, Saturday, the customary service is held at the third and sixth hours, but the ninth hour is not observed on this Saturday but preparations for the Paschal vigils take place in the Great Church, in the Martyrium. The Paschal vigils are performed the same here as at home; the only additional feature here is that the newly-baptized, once they are baptized and dressed in white garments, when they emerge from the font are conducted at the same time as the bishop first to the Anastasis. The bishop enters within the rails of the Anastasis, a hymn is chanted, then the bishop offers a prayer for them, and then goes to the Great Church with them where, according to custom, the whole people celebrate the vigil. There the customary things are done just as we do them, and after the oblation there is the dismissal. And after the dismissal of the vigil in the Great Church, immediately there is a procession with hymns to the Anastasis; there is read a passage from the Gospel on the resurrection, a prayer is said, and the bishop again performs the oblation. But everything is done rapidly because of the people, lest they be delayed too long, and then the people are dismissed. The hour of the dismissal of the vigil on this day is the same as with us at home.

The *Little Trumpets* of Pseudo-Chrysostom are a collection of Paschal homilies that possibly belong to the late third century for in them there is concern for the day and date of the Pasch, and also fidelity to the exegesis of the Exodus text. But the exegesis is done in the spiritual style of Origen (d. 254), which enabled the Greek Fathers of the fourth century to move from the Quartodeciman Pasch of Christ to the Sunday Pasch, first of the Church, later of man, and, finally, of the creation:

[32]Text: SC 296.290

[33]The lamb for you is Christ on your exodus from this life and He takes you with Him to heaven when He ascends there. He also leads you to everlasting life. In leading the man who is born from David He also brings along His followers ... who no longer fear the Pharaoh, and are no longer immersed in servility and earthly difficulties, on account of a brief ... pleasure which was typified by Israel eating the meats ... in Egypt.

Such is earthly pleasure which has a train of bitterness and is plagued with cares. It has a carnal, animal maw. For you leaving this earthly life is the beginning of true life, just as for them the symbolic Pasch was the beginning of months. Now the beginning of life is when you renounce the life of this world and this earth. Now you find what is the true life—life in the spirit.

Christ is sacrificed, so you know His sacrifice was offered for you. Then for you is fulfilled the words of the Scripture, *Like a sheep He was led to the slaughter and like a lamb dumb before His shearer* (Isa. 53:7). Christ's gentleness preserves the prototype of the sheep. His ascent on high without a descent to the depths preserves the ascent of the kid to the heights. Goats jump and ascend to lofty, inaccessible places. Heaven was lofty and inaccesible to man from the day when man sinned against the divine commandment, became a slave to the flesh and was estranged from the Holy Spirit. But the divine victim sacrificed for you ascends and brings you with Him. He died with you in order that you might live with Him.

The blood of the lamb brings salvation to you if you approach the blood with faith, if you anoint with faith as with blood those senses and thoughts through which death enters, bringing sin with it, just as Israel anointed their doors with blood. If concupiscence does not enter through your eyes, your ears, your smell, your taste, your touch, and afterwards through your thoughts, death will have no power over you, but, carrying in your body the death of Jesus, you will have obvious life in your body and so the death of the first-born

[33]Text: PG 59.733

Adam will pass over you, as the destruction of the first-born passed over the Hebrew homes.

And so the name of this feast is called the Pasch of the Jews, signifying the passing over. *Your lamb shall be without blemish* (Exod. 12:5): Jesus was also without blemish for you; Scripture says, *He had committed no sin and there was no deceit in His mouth* (Isa. 53:9).

A perfect male (Ex. 12:5). The perfection of justice is only found in the true king. *The sheep one-year-old* (Ex. 12:5) is a type of Christ the eternal. A year is a symbol of an age, which often revolves itself the same in every age, and it contains all the revolutions in itself, a type of the new man, in which the old is changed into the newness of our human nature: *Put on the new man*, Scripture tells us (Eph. 4:24). When you put on the blamelessness and perfection of the sheep you will be a lamb of God and when you present *your own body a living, holy sacrifice pleasing to God* as the Apostle says, *you will be transferred to eternal life* (Rom. 12:1).

Do you see that your Pasch bears no comparison with the Jewish Pasch, but merely a shadowy resemblance? Infant Israel, at the sacrifice of the sheep thought that God was concerned about the sacrifice and that it had obtained salvation through it, and did not see it as a type of sacrifice that really brought salvation. Accordingly, it was said to them by God through Jeremiah: *I did not command you concerning sacrifices* (Jer. 7:22). There is no lie with God that He would order you and say that He did not order you. The focus of the thing is shown from the fact that the sacrifice was accomplished in a prophetic manner and was a presignification of the sacrifice of Christ.

When God ordered them to sacrifice a sheep He showed that Christ was to be sacrificed, and everything pertaining to the sheep prefigured what concerned Christ, some of which you have already considered, others consider now to the best of your ability.

At Nazianzus in the Spring of 362, Gregory, in his first sermon, relived in existential tones, the sufferings of Jesus Christ, sacrificed, as he felt he was, like Isaac, by his own bishop father, who called him from his retreat in Pontus to rule the local Church,—the Pasch of Gregory with Christ from Pontus to Nazianzus:

[34]Yesterday, the lamb was immolated; the doorposts were anointed with its blood; Egypt bewailed its firstborn; the destroying angel passed us over in fear and respect for this seal; the precious blood protected us. Today, we have fled purified from Egypt, from the Pharaoh, the cruel sovereign, and those pitiless rulers. We are freed from the mud and brick and not one will prevent us from celebrating it, not with the old leaven of malice and injustice but with the unleavened bread of purity and truth (cf. 1 Cor. 5, 8), with no admixture of the impious yeast of Egypt. Yesterday I was crucified with Christ; today I will be glorified with Him. Yesterday I died with Christ; today I will return to life with Him. Yesterday I was buried with Christ; today I will rise with Him from the tomb.

Let us, then, carry our first fruits to Him who has suffered and risen for us. Do you think, perhaps, that I am talking of gold, silver, garments, or precious stones? Insubstantial earthly goods, transitory, tied to earth, owned for the most part by the wicked, the slaves of materialism and the prince of this world? No, let us offer ourselves: it is the most precious and dearest gift in the eyes of God. Give to His image what resembles it most. Recognizing our greatness, honor our model, understanding the force of this mystery and the reasons for Christ's death.

Become like Christ, since Christ has become like us. Become gods for Him since He became man for us. He has become inferior to make us superior; He has become poor to enrich us by His poverty; He has taken the condition of a slave to procure freedom for us; He has come on earth to bring us to heaven.

For Gregory the Pasch of Christ was the Pasch of his own life and that of his Church, as he, and his flock, suffer with Christ, die with Him and rise with Him. This most sensitive

[34]Text: PG 35.397

and eloquent of all the Greek Fathers follows in his preaching the classical structure of exordium, encomium and conclusion, in oration 45, *On the Holy Pasch*:

Exordium:

[35]Today salvation has come upon the world....
Christ is risen ... rise with Him.
Christ is freed from the tomb ... be freed from the bond of sin.
The old Adam is dead ... the new is risen.
Rise in Christ ... be *a new creation* (2 Cor. 5:17).
This is the Lord's Passover, the Passover; again, I say Passover:
The Passover of the Father :
The Passover of the Holy Spirit—
Feast of feasts and solemnity of solemnities.

In the Encomium he praises God for the salvation of man, and traces the history of that salvation from "the God who always is ... to the being ... who forgot the commandment,... was banished from the tree of life, from Paradise and from God." After the fall the sinful condition of man "required the Word of God Himself, source of life and immortality.... He came forth ... as God, and one person in two natures, flesh and spirit, and the latter deified the former.... He was a perfect victim on account of that which He assumed, having been anointed with deity, and made equal with God."[36]

Afterwards, there follows the sacred night of Passover when primeval darkness was dissolved, chaos reduced to order, and man took flight from the Egypt of sin:

[37]*Towards evening* we feed on the lamb; *In haste* ... lest we delay our return to sin; *With bitter herbs* ... for life according

[35]Text: PG 36.624
[36]Text: *ibid.* 633-637
[37]Text: *ibid.* 645

to the will of God is bitter and arduous; *Loins girded* . . . by the girdle of continence, light and contemplation; *Shoes on feet* . . . for safety, lest we walk in the darkness of sin; And *leaning on staves* . . . the words about the flesh and about the Passion.

> The Christian Pasch is plainer than that of old for we now partake of the Law in the light of the Gospel: "Therefore, let us sacrifice ourselves to God . . . every day, and at every moment; let us accept everything for the sake of the Word. By sufferings let us imitate His Passion; let us gladly mount upon the cross, . . . for to suffer with Christ, and for Christ, is better than a life of ease with others":[38]

[39]Conclusion:

> O Pasch, great and holy, redeemer of the world;
> I will speak to you as to a living person.
> O Word of God, light and life, wisdom and might,
> I rejoice in all your names.
> O Procession and Expression of Divine Thought;
> O Word conceived to conceive man;
> Receive, O Word of power, this my discourse—
> The completion of my offering, not with first fruits;
> A song of praise and a prayer of petition
> That we may not suffer what we cannot endure,
> Just the sacred cares of our passage and pasch
> into the heavenly tabernacle and to your altar;
> That we may offer there the acceptable sacrifice
> to the Father, Word, and Holy Spirit, glory, honor,
> might, world without end. Amen.

> Gregory of Nyssa (d. 394) is a theologian with a faith vision of the universe: for him the Pasch of Christ inaugurates, not only the Pasch of the Church, but also the Pasch of man, which will restore all creation to the creator. "The kingdom announced by the Pasch is the triumph of order and of the unity of creation where all men are

[38]Text: *ibid.* 653
[39]Text: *ibid.* 664

assembled in an adoration without reserve." The tableau of eternity etched by Gregory in his first homily is characteristic of his approach:

[40]In the words of David, then, which we have just heard and have repeated with him, *Praise the Lord all ye nations; praise Him all ye peoples* (Ps. 117:1). He invites without exception all men born of Adam to this chant; those from the West, the East, and in between, North and South, he invites each and every one in this psalm. Elsewhere he invites some men specifically, calling them saints or sons (cf. Ps. 149:1; 8:3), exhorting them to sing a hymn. In this instance he leads in unison the nations and peoples in the psalm.

When, then, as the apostle says, *the figure of this world has passed* (1 Cor. 7:31) and Christ has appeared as king and God to all, and every unbelieving soul is led to the fullness of faith and certainty of knowledge, and malicious tongues are restrained and bridled, He shall check the vanity of the Greeks, and the errors of the Jews, and the uncontrolled tongue-wagging of heretics. Then at last all the nations and peoples from the beginning of time will prostrate themselves and join in harmonious praise of God, the saints singing their usual praises, the impious making supplication by necessity. And then in truth the song of victory will be sung in harmony by all, victors and vanquished; then even that slave, the author of disorder who has assumed and arrogated to himself the dignity of his master, will be seen admonishing everybody while he is being drawn to punishment by the angels, and all the ministers and allies of this wickedness will be afflicted by suitable punishment and judgments. The one king and judge will appear whom all confess to be the Lord of all. There will be a quiet and silence as the praetor takes his seat on the tribunal, and the people, all ears and eyes, wait attentively on the words of his proclamation. *Therefore, praise the Lord, all ye nations, praise Him, all ye peoples* (Ps. 117:1). Praise Him as powerful, praise Him as benign, since He has restored to life those who have fallen and are dead; He has repaired the broken vase, and

[40]Text: PG 46.653

in His bounty He has changed into incorruptible living beings the dread remains in the sepulcher. As after a long voyage He has led back to its proper domicile the soul which had left the body (four) thousand years before, in no way alienated through time and forgetfulness from its own organism, but returning to it more quickly than bird to its nest.

The Creator of the universe, when He decided to create man, made him not as a worthless being, but as the most precious of all beings and named Him king of the entire earthly creation. With this in mind He made him wise and in God's image, adorning him with every grace. Now surely He did not give him such precedence in nature if He intended him to be born and die and suffer complete extinction? But it is vain and foolish to attribute to God such a plan, such a proposition, such an intention. For it is the way of children to build with care and quickly scatter the building, revealing a mind with no fixed and final purpose. Our teaching points to the other extreme, that God's first creation was fashioned immortal but that, after the fall and the first sin, man was deprived of immortality as a penalty for transgression. Then the fountain of goodness outflowed with kindness and, inclining to the work of His own hands, God adorned it with wisdom and knowledge until He thought good to renew us in our former state.

In another homily *On the Pasch,* Gregory draws out the joyful implications of the liturgical celebration of the Paschal Vigil, with its invitation to exultation and joy:

THE PASCHAL LITURGY; AN INVITATION TO JOY:

[41]The true Sabbath rest, that which has received God's blessing, in which the Lord has rested from His works on behalf of the world's salvation, spending the Sabbath in the inactivity of death is now at an end. It has manifested its grace to our eyes, our ears, and our heart through all these things

[41]Text: PG 46.681

which the feast has accomplished in us—in our eyes, our ears, and our joyful heart.

What have we seen? A light like a cloud of fire of the candles burning during the night. All night our ears have resounded with psalms, hymns and spiritual chants. It was like a river of joy running through our ears to our soul and filling us with blessed hopes. And our heart, delighted by what we heard and saw, was marked with ineffable joy, conducting us by means of the visible to the invisible. These blessings, *which eye has not seen, nor ear heard, nor have entered into the heart of man* (1 Cor. 2:9), are shown to us in replica by the blessings of this day of rest. They are a guarantee to us of the ineffable blessing we hope for.

Since, then, this night is aglow with lights, since it mingles the brightness of its lights and the first rays of dawn, making one day with no interval of darkness, let us reflect, brethren, on the prophecy that says: *This is the day which the Lord has made* (Ps. 118:24). This proposes to us nothing difficult or hard, but joy, happiness, rejoicing, as it goes on to say, *let us be glad and rejoice in it* (Ps. 118:24). O wonderful instructions! O sweet order! Who can be slow in carrying out such instructions? Who does not feel guilty even at a slight postponement of carrying out these orders? Joy is our task and rejoicing is our instruction. By this the judgment pronounced on sin is effaced and grief is turned into joy.

THE PASCHAL MYSTERY, PROMISE OF REDEMPTION

It is said in Jewish Wisdom that *evils are forgotten on the day of joy* (cf. Sir. 11:25). This day makes us forget the first sentence pronounced against us; or rather it eliminates its very existence and not just its memory. For it has completely erased the memory of our condemnation. At that time birth took place in travail; now our (re) birth is painless. At that time we were flesh born of the flesh; now it is a spirit that is born of spirit. At that time we were sons of men; now we are born children of God. At that time we were relegated from heaven to earth; now the one in heaven has made us sharers of heaven with Him. At that time death reigned because of sin; now, thanks to Life, it is justice which has taken over the power. At that time one man opened the gates of death; now through one man the gate of life is opened in its place. At that time we fell from life to death; now death is abolished by life. At that time we were hidden under the fig leaf by shame; now by glory we approach the tree of life. At that time through disobedience we were expelled from Paradise; now through faith we are admitted into Paradise.

> For Chrysostom (d. 407) everything about the Paschal celebration is spiritual—the preaching of the Word, the hallowed prayers, the priests' blessings, participation in the divine mysteries, peace and concord, and finally all the spiritual gifts worthy of the generosity of God. This is the Pasch of the neophytes into the life of grace and the virtues:

[42]Coming to the end of my exhortation I turn to those who in this blessed night are having the grace of baptism conferred on them: I address myself to those fair offshoots of the Church, those spiritual flowers, those new recruits of Jesus Christ: Two days ago the Lord died on the cross. Today He has risen from the dead. In the same way two days ago these neophytes were held in the bondage of sin. But today they rise along with Christ. He died in the flesh and rose in the flesh. They likewise were dead in sin and have risen from sin. The earth in the present season of spring produces for us roses, violets, and every type of flower. Today the waters of baptism show us a field much more pleasant than the earth. And do not wonder, beloved, if the waters produce fields bedecked with flowers. For the earth did not spontaneously produce growths of herbs from the beginning but rather in obedience to the orders of the Lord. *And the waters produced living creatures when they heard the words, let the waters produce creeping creatures having life* (Gen. 1:20). And it was so done. This inanimate substance has produced living beings. So also the divine

[42]Text: PG 52.769

command can effect everything. For then it was said, Let the waters produce creeping creatures having life. But today it is not creeping things but spiritual charisms that are produced. Then the waters produced irrational fish. Now they produce rational, spiritual fish for us, thanks to the fishermen, the apostles. *Come, follow me, He said, and I will make you fishers of men* (Matt. 4:19). An absolutely new method of fishing! For fishermen normally take the fish out of the water and kill what they catch. But we cast the fish into the water and that catch is given life.

Brethren, you see how great this gift is. Pay particular attention, you who this night have been received among the citizens of the heavenly Jerusalem. Show vigilance in proportion to the excellence of the graces which you have received so that they may ever abound; for the Lord increases His liberality to those who show gratitude for His gifts. He does not allow you, dear brethren, to live haphazardly; you should direct your lives according to His laws and rules so as to live correctly, paying the closest attention even to what seem to be the most unimportant details. This life is an unending struggle and it is necessary that those who once enter this arena of virtue should always maintain a scrupulous temperance. *Every athlete that strives for the prize practices great self-control* (1 Cor. 9:25). In athletic contests you see how the athletes take care of themselves although their contest is only with fellow human beings. Notice how austere is their discipline in training their body. We should imitate them, all the more since our contest is not with mere men but with spirits of wickedness. Our discipline and our exercises ought to be spiritual since the arms we have received from the Lord are spiritual. Our eyes ought to be restrained and regulated to avoid lighting indiscriminately on every object. Our tongue should be guarded to prevent speaking without prior reflection. Our teeth and lips should be placed as guards on our tongue, keeping it from violating these barriers and confining it to sounds which are regulated and timely, speaking with discretion only such words as would instruct and edify the audience. Immoderate laughter should be completely avoided; our walk should be peaceable and orderly, and our clothes decent and respectable. Whatever is prescribed for the arena cannot be too detailed or too correct in matters relating to exterior modesty, for bodily decorum is an index of the sentiments of the soul.

If we quickly contract these good habits we will walk without effort in the path of virtue and reach the end of our journey without mishap. The ways will be made more and more level before us and we will obtain great help from above. So we will be able to weather the storms of this life without fear, triumph over all the wiles of the devil and attain to eternal blessings by the grace and bounty of our Lord Jesus Christ with whom is glory, honor and power with the Father and Holy Spirit, today and always, for ever and ever. Amen.

> This spiritual understanding of the Pasch continued and was further developed by the Fathers of the fifth century. By this time the newly developed liturgy of Good Friday, as we shall see, replaced the Quartodeciman Pasch, and the Paschal Vigil became a celebration of baptism in expectation of the resurrection.
>
> Proclus of Constantinople (d. 446) in his Paschal homilies exalts the miracle of the resurrection, the mystery of baptism, and the renewal of nature:

[43]How beautiful is the Paschal celebration! Beautiful too is the present assembly. The mysteries contained so much that is both old and new! Our week of feast or rather of joy contains so much community that it is not just men on earth that rejoice but also the powers above join in our activities and celebrate with us because of the resurrection of Christ. For now the angels join in the feast, and the hosts of archangels celebrate the king of heaven, Christ our God, received as victor returned from earth to heaven. The choirs of saints keep festival too: They proclaim Christ *risen before the dawn* (Ps. 110:3). The earth celebrates the feast; it has been washed in the divine blood. The sea celebrates; it has been honored by Christ's footsteps. And let every man celebrate, born again of the water

[43]Text: PG 65.796

and the Holy Spirit. Let our first parent, Adam, celebrate, made free of his first transgression.

Such is the joyous grace with which Christ has filled us by His resurrection. He not only provides us with a festival but also grants us salvation from suffering, immortality from death, healing from wounds, and resurrection from a fall. Formerly, dearly beloved, the mystery of the Pasch was mystically accomplished in Egypt through the Law, and symbolically revealed through the slaughter of the Lamb. But now through the Gospel we spiritually celebrate the solemn Paschal day of the resurrection. Formerly, the Lamb from the flock was sacrificed according to the Law. But now Christ himself, the Lamb of God, is led forth. Formerly, a sheep from the fold was taken, now, in place of a sheep, it is the Shepherd himself, the good shepherd who lays down his life for his sheep! Formerly, it was the sign of the sprinkled blood of an irrational animal that provided protection for the new people. Now the precious blood of Christ is poured out for the salvation of the world that we may receive the remission of sins. Formerly, the firstborn of the Egyptians were put to death. Now the numerous offspring of sinners are purified by confession. Formerly, Pharaoh and his fearful host were submerged; now the spiritual Pharaoh with all his force is submerged by baptism. Formerly, the Hebrews after crossing the Red Sea sang the hymn of victory to their benefactor, crying let us *sing to the Lord, for He is gloriously magnified* (Exod. 15:1). Now those initiated in baptism mystically sing the hymn of victory, saying, 'There is one who is holy, one Lord Jesus Christ, to the glory of God the Father' (Liturgy of John Chrysostom).

> For Proclus the renewal of nature is not just the rule of spring, but the cosmic effect of the resurrection—*the restoration of all things in Christ* (Eph. 1:10).

[44]The blessed Paul has well said: *the former things have passed away, behold they are made new* (2 Cor. 5:17). The

---

[44]Text: PG 65.792

heavens are made new, for He who came down from them consecrated them by His ascension. The earth is made new, for it was sanctified by His human birth in the stable. The sea is made new, since it kept afloat on its surface the footsteps of Him whom neither flesh conceived nor sin had rendered heavy. The earth is made new, since He freed it from war and filled it with a great calm. Mankind is made new, since it was washed by Him in water and molded in the fire of the spirit. The worship of God is made new, since sacrificial fumes and circumcision have disappeared and now faith is resplendent, praising and adoring three persons in one substance.

> This same spiritual understanding of the Pasch is continued by a contemporary of Proclus, Basil (d. 468), Metropolitan of Seleucia:

[45]Christ's loving concern for us is inexpressible: it has enriched His Church with many blessings. Great in His designs and powerful in His works, He has redeemed our nature from the curse of the law; He has cancelled the decree of the old debt. He has triumphed on the cross of wood over Him who had waylaid Adam by means of a tree. He has blunted the sting of fearful death. He has rejuvenated those who have grown old in sin, not by fire but by water. He has shown that the tomb of three days was a gate leading to resurrection. Those who had not been citizens of Israel He has proclaimed fellow-citizens and intimates of the saints. To those who were strangers to the covenants of the promise He has delivered the heavenly mysteries. To those who have no hope He has graciously given a pledge, the spirit of salvation. For those who were without God in the world He has completed temples of the Trinity.

Those who were afar off He has made near—afar off, not in terms of place but in terms of conduct, not by distance but by intention, not by space but by cult—He has brought them near through the saving cross, embracing those who had showed themselves restive.

Truly as the prophet said, *Who has heard such things and*

[45]Text: SC 187.206

who has seen them? (Isa. 66:8). All the angels are terrified by the mystery. All the heavenly powers tremble before the wonder. The throne has not been left vacant, yet the world has been saved. He has not departed from the heavens and yet He has liberated the earth.

There is still proclaimed in the Byzantine liturgy of the Paschal Vigil a homily usually attributed, and with good reason, to Chrysostom: it is an appeal, in his rhetorical style, to all those invited by God, and sings of the hope of a universal resurrection. Suitably, it concludes this section on the Pasch, as preached by the Greek Fathers:

[46]If anyone is pious and loves his God, let him enjoy this beautiful feast. If anyone is a faithful slave let him enter with joy into the joy of his Lord. If anyone has endured the hardships of fasting, let him now receive his penny reward. If anyone has labored from the first hour, let him receive today his just recompense. If anyone has come at the third hour, let him join with gratitude in the feast. If anyone has come after the sixth hour, let him not be upset, he will not be penalized. If anyone was delayed until the ninth hour, let him come without hesitation. If anyone has come just at the eleventh hour, let him not be perturbed at the lateness of the hour. for the Lord is liberal and receives the last as the first. He gives to the one coming at the eleventh hour just as to the one working from dawn. He takes pity on the last to arrive just as on the first; the latter receives in justice, the former in charity. He rewards both good actions and good intentions. Let all, then, enter into the joy of the Lord. Let first and last receive their reward. Let rich and poor sing in unison. Let the abstemious and the careless celebrate today's feast. Whether you have observed the fast or not, rejoice today!

The festive board is laden; let you all feast yourselves. The fatted calf is served; let no one go away hungry. Let all of you enjoy the wealth of His kindness. Let no one bewail His poverty; the kingdom is opened to all. Let no one deplore His

[46]Text: PG 59.721

offenses, pardon has come from the tomb. Let no one fear death. He has been overcome by death and thereby has in turn overcome it. He has descended into hell and rebuked it. He has cast down in terror those who touched His flesh and Isaiah has forseen this, exclaiming, *Hell below was in an uproar at the coming* (Isa. 14:9). When it ran to you below it was made bitter. It was dejected for it was overturned. It took flesh and received God. It seized earth and found heaven. It received that which was visible and fell into that which was invisible. *O death where is your victory? O death, where is your sting?* (1 Cor. 15:55).

Christ has risen and death has been cast down. Christ has risen and devils have fallen. Christ has risen and the angels rejoice. Christ has risen and there are no corpses left in the sepulcher. For Christ in rising from the dead is the first-fruits of those that sleep. To Him be glory and power for ever and ever. Amen.

CHRISTOS ANESTE

4. The Latin Pasch

The significance of the Pasch in Western faith is certainly acknowledged by Justin, the Apologist (c.150), in his *Dialogue with Trypho*, the Jew, which took place in Ephesus about 135, and was composed afterwards in Rome, between 155 and 161.

[47]The mystery of the lamb which God ordered you to sacrifice as the Passover was truly a type of Christ, with whose blood the believers, in proportion to the strength of their faith, anoint their homes, that is, themselves. You are all aware that Adam, the result of God's creative act, was the abode of His inspiration. In the following fashion I can show that God's precept concerning the Paschal lamb was only temporary.

[47]Text: PG 6.561 = 6.208

God does not allow the Paschal lamb to be sacrificed in any other place than where His name is invoked (that is, in the Temple at Jerusalem), for He knew that there would come a time, after Christ's Passion, when the place in Jerusalem (where you sacrificed the paschal lamb) would be taken from you by your enemies, and then all sacrifices would be stopped. Moreover, that lamb which you were ordered to roast whole was a symbol of Christ's Passion on the cross. Indeed, the lamb, while being roasted, resembles the figure of the cross, for one spit transfixes it horizontally from the lower parts up to the head, and another pierces it across the back, and holds up its forelegs. Likewise, the two identical goats which had to be offered during the fast (one of which was to be the scapegoat, and the other the sacrificial goat) were an announcement of the two advents of Christ, of the first Advent, in which your priests and elders sent Him away as a scapegoat, seizing Him and putting Him to death; of the second Advent, because in that same place of Jerusalem you shall recognize Him whom you had subjected to shame, and who was a sacrificial offering for all sinners who are willing to repent.

Nevertheless, *in his First Apology,* written to the Emperor, Antoninus Pius, in explanation of Christian faith and worship, there is no mention of any Paschal celebration in the Rome of his day. Soter (166-74), Eleutherus (174-89), and Victor (189-98) were the popes of Paschal discipline; but Hippolylus (d. 235), anti-pope and martyr, is our first Paschal preacher at Rome, announcing "a Pasch that would spread to the Gentiles and would be understood by faith, and will be observed literally."[48]

In North Africa, early in the third century, the Paschal celebration already existed as a night-long vigil of fast and prayer, including the baptism of neophytes and the celebration of the Eucharist at the dawn of the Lord's Day. Tertullian (d.220) wrote no complete treatise on the Paschal celebration, but from the many brief references to it,

[48]Text: GCS 26.237

scattered throughout his works, the picture can be easily pieced together.

[49]If Christ is a new creation then the solemnities we keep in His honor must be likewise new; otherwise, when we celebrate the Pasch each year in the first month, we violate the Apostolic prohibition *of seasons, and days, and months, and years!* (Gal. 4:10). . . . Similarly, when we fast on the Sabbath of the Pasch, we are fasting on a day when fast was forbidden by the Law (*On Fasting*).

[50]The celebration of the Pasch is the most solemn and suitable time for baptism, for the Lord's Passion, into which we are baptized, has been just completed. Nor will it be incongruous to interpret figuratively the words of the Lord— *You will meet a man bearing water* (Mk. 14:13): He points out the place for the celebration of the Pasch by the sign of water (*On Baptism*).

[51]The wife of an unbelieving husband is unable to give to the Lord satisfaction in matters of religious discipline . . . for what husband, if he does not believe, will without anxiety allow his wife to be absent at the Paschal solemnities the whole night long (*To His Wife*)!

[52]We take also in congregations before day-break, and from the hand of none but the presidents, the sacrament of the Eucharist, which the Lord has commanded (*On Prayer*).

In the Roman world of the third century the Paschal practice of the Church of Rome spread rapidly and widely: this can be seen in the observation made by the historian, Socrates, on Nicaea and the Paschal controversy:

[53]But all other Christians in the Western parts, and as far as the ocean itself, are found to have celebrated Easter after the

[49]Text: PL 2.975
[50]PL 1.1222
[51]Text: *ibid.* 1294
[52]Text: CSEL 70.158
[53]Text: PG 67.629-632

equinox, from a very ancient tradition. And in fact these acting in this manner have never disagreed on this subject. It is not true, as some have pretended, that the synod under Constantine altered this festival: for Constantine himself, writing to those who differed respecting it, recommended that as they were few in number, they could agree with the majority of their brethren. His letter will be found at length in the third book of the *Life of Constantine* by Eusebius; but the passage in it relative to Easter runs thus:

'It is a becoming order which all the Churches in the Western, Southern, and Northern parts of the world observe, and some places in the East also. Wherefore all on the present occasion have judged it right, and I have pledged myself that it will have the acquiescence of your prudence, that what is unanimously observed in the city of Rome, throughout Italy, Africa, and the whole of Egypt, in Spain, France, Britain, Libya, and all Greece, the diocese of Asia and Pontus, and Cilicia, your wisdom also will readily embrace; considering not only that the number of Churches in the aforesaid places is greater, but also that while there should be a universal concurrence in what is most reasonable, it becomes us to have nothing in common with the perfidious Jews.'

Lactantius is one of our main Latin sources for knowledge of this period—the first quarter of the fourth century. His *Divine Institutes* is in seven books and was dedicated to the emperor, Constantine. It has a couple of references to the Paschal lamb that are relevant here:

[54]Lastly, the immolation of the animal called by those very people who carry to the feast (*apo tou paschein*) is because it is a figure of suffering, the Passion of our Lord. God in His foreknowledge of the future gave this feast through Moses to be celebrated by His people.

Then the middle of the heavens will be opened, though the night be stormy and dark, so that the light of the descending God might shine as a flame in the whole world. The Sibyl

[54]Text: CSEL 19.384 = FOTC 49.314,521

spoke of this in these verses: 'When He shall come—there will be brilliant fire in the midst of darksome night.' This is the night which is celebrated by us with a vigil on account of the coming of the king, our God. The significance of this night is twofold because in it He recovered life after He had suffered, and afterwards He will receive the kingdom of the world.

> After Nicaea (325) there arose the triduum *crucifixi, sepulti et resuscitati*, especially at Milan where Ambrose (339-397) was bishop, and Augustine (387) was baptized: in this way Quartodeciman Pasch and Paschal Sunday were united in a single celebration—the Sacratissimum triduum:

[55]To be sure, *the Law was given through Moses; grace and truth came through Jesus Christ* (Jn. 1:17). He who spoke the Law, coming later Himself through a virgin in later times, accomplished the fulfillment of the Law, because *He came not to destroy the Law but to fulfill it* (Mt. 5:17).

He celebrated the Passover in a week when the fourteenth of the month fell on the fifth day [of the new moon]. In fact, on that very day, as the above indicates, He ate the Passover with His disciples; on the following day, that is, the sixth day [of the new moon] and the fifteenth day [of the month] He was crucified; the sixteenth was on the great Sabbath, and therefore He arose from the dead on the seventeenth.

We must keep the law regarding Easter in such a way that we do not observe the fourteenth as the day of the resurrection; that day or one very close to it is the day of the Passion, because the feast of the resurrection is kept on the Lord's Day. Moreover, we cannot fast on the Lord's day; fasting on this day is what we criticize in the Manichaeans. One shows disbelief in the resurrection of Christ if he proposes a law of fast on the day of the resurrection, since the Law says that the Passover should be eaten with bitterness, that is, with sorrow because the Author of our salvation was slain by mankind's great sacrilege. On the Lord's Day the prophet bids us rejoice,

[55]Text: PL 16.130-131

saying: *This is the day which the Lord has made; let us be glad and rejoice in it* (Ps. 118:24).

Consequently, we must observe both the day of the Passion and of the resurrection, to have a day of bitterness and one of joy, fasting on one day, being refreshed on the other. If it happens, however, as will occur next time, that the fourteenth day of the first month is the Lord's Day, since we should not fast on that day nor break our fast on the thirteenth which falls on the Sabbath, for it is a day of special observance as the day of the Passion, the celebration of Easter should be postponed to the following week. Otherwise, it happens that the fifteenth when Christ suffered will be on the second day of the week, the third day will be the sixteenth, when the Lord's body rested in the tomb, and the fourth day will be on the seventeenth when the Lord arose.

Therefore, when, as will happen next time, the three holy days run into the following week, the three days within which He suffered, lay in the tomb, and arose, the three days of which He said: *Destroy this temple and in three days I will raise it up* (Jn. 2:19), what can cause troublesome doubt in us? If we scruple because we do not celebrate the day of the Passion or the resurrection on the fourteenth, recall that the Lord Himself suffered, not on the fourteenth, but on the fifteenth, and arose on the seventeenth. If our difficulty is in our failing to observe the fourteenth of the month which falls on the Lord's Day, that is, April eighteenth, and we tell you to celebrate the following Lord's Day, there is authority for this practice, too.

A short while ago, when the fourteenth of the first month fell on the Lord's Day, the solemnity was observed on the following Lord's Day. And in the eighty-ninth year of the era of Diocletian when the fourteenth day of the first month fell on March twenty-fourth, we celebrated Easter on the last day of March. So, too, did the people of Alexandria and Egypt. They wrote to say that when the fourteenth fell on the twenty-eighth day of the month of Phamenoth they celebrated Easter on the fifth day of Pharmuth, which is the last day of March. Thus, they agreed perfectly with us. Again, in the ninety-third year of the era of Diocletian when the fourteenth fell on the fourteenth of Pharmuth, which is April ninth and happened to be the

Lord's Day, they celebrated Easter on the Lord's day, the twenty-first of Pharmuth, or, according to us, April sixteenth. Since we are supplied with a method of calculating as well as precedent, we should have no more trouble on this point.

Many of Zeno (363-371) of Verona's sermons, which are the oldest surviving from the Latin Fathers, concern the Pasch and its celebration, and are often called prefaces on account of their brevity in some of the manuscripts: the length of the liturgy probably determined their length:

1. [56]After the devout completion of your chaste fasts for the purpose of holy expiation, after the sweet vigils of a night resplendent with its own sun (i.e., Christ), after your souls have blossomed to hope of immortality in the life-giving bath of the milky font, from which you, so differing in age and social status, have suddenly emerged like children of one birth, I exhort you to celebrate the feast of so great a birth with happy festivity ... in a heavenly banquet, honorable, pure, salvific, and eternal, which in your hunger you can attend so as to be always full and happy.

2. The head of the house grants you from his stores precious bread and wine from his own table. First, three boys bring in together the vegetables, upon which, to make them more flavorful, they sprinkle the salt of wisdom (cf. Dan. 1:12-17). Christ pours the oil (cf. Lk. 10:34). Moses has quickly procured the mature lamb (cf. Exod. 12:4) and Abraham the fatted calf—(cf. Gen. 18:17) faithfully prepared. Isaac innocently carries the pot and the wood (cf. Gen. 22:6). Jacob patiently picks out the speckled beasts (cf. Gen. 30:32). Joseph, in charge of measuring, allocates a grain ration to all (cf. Gen. 42:6).

3. If anyone lacks for anything, Noah, who built the ark to store up everything, will not deny it to him (cf. Gen. 6:21). Peter, the fisherman, lays out an abundance of seafood along with the marvellous fish (cf. Mt. 4:18; 17:24-27). Tobit, the wanderer, carefully cleans the freshwater fish and roasts it (cf.

[56]Text: CCL 22.71

Tob. 6:6). John, the devoted precursor, in camel's hair, brings honey and locusts from the desert (cf. Mt. 3:4). Paul with his invitation warns lest anyone reproach another who eats (cf. Rom. 14:3). David, the royal shepherd, supplies silver white milk and cheese at all times (cf. 1 Sam. 17:18).

4. Zacchaeus puts out fourfold gifts without delay (cf. Lk. 19:8). Our Lord and God, Jesus Christ, the Son of God, who was fed on this banquet before us, speaks sweet words. How sweet to my lips are your words. *Sweeter than honey from the comb to my palate* (Ps. 119:103). Brethren, whoever believes these words shall find still more bountiful food. If he takes care of it he shall fill forever both himself and others with all blessings, through our Lord, Jesus Christ.

Elsewhere Zeno likes to emphasize the rhythmical return of the Pasch; in its end is its beginning:

[57]Wreathed round with multiform grace in its established course, the day of salvation has arrived through the windings of the seasons in its customary tracks. The same day is its own successor and predecessor. Ever new although of great age, both parent and child of the year it precedes and follows the seasons and infinite centuries. It gives birth to a beginning for itself from its end and yet does not depart from the cradle of its birth. Assuredly, it bears the image of the mystery of the Lord, for by its setting it celebrates His Passion and by its rising it celebrates the resurrection:

Among the great writers of the fourth century Latin West, Chromatius of Aquileia (d.407) in Italy has received little recognition; yet he is among the foremost of the Latin Fathers and was closely linked with the defeat of Arianism, the vindication of Chrysostom and the settlement of the Origenist controversies. His *sermon on the Universal Vigil* is at once a song of recognition and a prayer, a proclamation of the divine power rejoicing at the three stages of creation, heaven, earth and hell. This trinitarian Pasch is celebrated

[57]Text: *ibid.* 132

by Christians, Jews and pagans, almost in spite of themselves:

[58] All the vigils which are celebrated in honor of the Lord by the universal Church are certainly pleasing and acceptable to Him. But this day in particular is called and believed to be *the Day of the Lord* beyond all others. For about today it has been written: *This was a night of vigil for all the Israelites* (Exod. 12:42). And the night preceding this day is rightly called 'the vigil of the Lord' because He kept vigil on this night during His lifetime so that we should not sleep through it in death. The Lord undertook for us the sleep of death through the Passion of the cross. But, behold, that sleep of the Lord has become the vigil of the whole world, because the death of the Lord has driven far from us the sleep of that eternal death to which we were all subject. This He Himself declares through His prophet saying: *When I lie down in sleep, I wake again, and my sleep has been sweet* (Ps. 3:6). Clearly that sleep has become sweet for Christ the Lord because He has recalled us from the bitter death to sweet life. Therefore, this night is called the Lord's vigil, because in it He also has awakened from the slumber of His Passion and death in which He has clearly declared the mystery of His own divinity and of our humanity. For in the sleep of His Passion He slept in the flesh, but in His divinity He journeyed to the depths of hell to lead out forcibly mankind therein detained. Therefore our Savior wished to come from heaven to earth to visit the world; and to descend from earth into hell to illuminate it. He visits all places with His works of mercy to show mercy to all. Rightly, therefore, this night is called the Lord's vigil because it illuminates hell as well as earth.

There is a further reason why Father, Son and Holy Spirit should celebrate the vigil of the Son of God. According to the will of Father and Holy Spirit, the Son died for us that by rising from the dead He might confer life on us. This day, then, is not just the celebration of angels and of men. It is also sacred in virtue of Father, Son and Holy Spirit because the whole

[58] Text: SC 154.258

Trinity collaborated in the redemption of the world and the liberation from captivity causes joy to all three divine persons. Therefore, we should solemnize with all devotion the celebration of such an important night, because on this night the world was redeemed. On this day, death was vanquished and life became victorious. Today the captives of the world are set free.

The angels rejoice in heaven in celebrating the most glorious expectation of this holy night. Men rejoice on earth, redeemed by the precious blood of Christ celebrating the resurrection of the same Lord Jesus Christ. Even the infernal powers rejoice, because today a light has risen for them, because they, too, have been reached by the glorious celebration of this holy night. And even though Jews and Gentiles seem estranged from the celebration of this holy day they are nonetheless not without joy because they are somehow inspired by the mysterious grace and blessing of the name of Christ—he who is blessed in Him on earth will be blessed in Him in heaven. Amen—for He is the Lord of all. Finally, not a few of the Jews and even Gentiles celebrate as their own the solemnity of our vigil, at least in joy of heart, if not liturgically.

> In his lifetime, Jerome (d.420) compared the obscurity of his own monastic sermons with the widespread fame of Augustine's. Preaching daily to the monks he was more concerned to instruct than to move: always he explains the text; yet the preacher breaks through the exegete:

[59]I cannot put in words the thoughts of my mind, and my tongue cannot express the joy of my heart. And I am not alone in my suffering, this longing to communicate my sentiments, but you suffer, too, with me, for your joy is more in your inner souls than in outward expression. This day seems brighter than others to me. The sun shines brighter on the world, the stars and all the elements rejoice. At the death of Christ they had ceased to shed their light and had gone into hiding. They could not look on their Creator crucified. But now that this

[59]Text: CCL 78.545

day is His day of victory, after His resurrection from the dead, they perform their proper task, attending upon Him by their own brightness (if one can call it that). Heaven believes, earth believes. And the net let down for the whole world cannot contain the Jews.

This is the day the Lord has made; let us be glad and rejoice in it (Ps. 118:24). Just as the Virgin Mary, Mother of God, holds first place among all women, so among all other days this day is mother of all. A novel thought, perhaps, but one confirmed by Scripture. This day is one of seven and one outside of seven. This is the day called the octave, and that is why certain psalms are entitled *For the Octave.* This is the day the synagogue ended and the Church began. This is the day, the octave day, the souls were saved in Noah's ark. Likewise, says Peter, *the Church also saves you* (1 Pet. 3:21). But why go on *ad infinitum*? It would take the whole day to list everything significant in regard to this day.

For all these reasons, dearly beloved, let us chant in unison, *This is the day the Lord has made; let us be glad and rejoice in it* (Ps. 118:24). Today Christ with the thief has set aside the sword of fire and opened the gate of paradise which had remained unyielding to all. Today Christ has said to the angels: *Open to me the gates of justice; I will enter and speak to the Lord* (Ps. 118:19). And once opened they never more close to believers . . . for the gate of the Church opens for us the gate of Paradise.

> Here, Augustine (d.430) gets a lion's share for he preached a lion's share: some seventy-four Paschal homilies survive and are considered authentic, while there are countless imitations. Let us begin in Milan, Easter 387, at the vigil of his baptism and that of his son Adeodatus:

[60]The Church in Milan had not long before begun to worship with this form of consolation and exhortation, wherein with great fervor the brethren sing together in voice and heart. For it was only a year, or not much more, since

[60]Text: PL 32.770

Justina, the mother of the boy king, Valentinian, had persecuted your man, Ambrose, in favor of her heresy, to which she had been seduced by the Arians. A devout people, who were prepared to suffer death together with their bishop, your servant, kept watch in the church. Therein, living in prayer, my mother, your handmaid, held a first place amid these cares and watchings. Ourselves, still cold to the warmth of your Spirit, were nevertheless stirred by the astonished and disturbed city. At that time it was established that, after the custom of the Eastern lands, hymns and canticles should be sung, so that the people would not become weak through the tedium and sorrow. From then up to the present day that custom has been maintained, with many, or almost all, of your congregations taking it up throughout other parts of the world.

> For Augustine the vigil is not just a watch; it is truly a preparation for eternity,—a symbolic preparation in refusing to sleep, and a mystical preparation in searching for God: just as sleep is an image of death, so this vigil of the Pasch is an image of eternity, which in time has many and different names:

THE WORLD KEEPS VIGIL

[61]On this night all the world keeps vigil, the hostile and the reconciled worlds. The reconciled one does it to praise the Healer; the hostile one to pour insult on the judge who had passed the unfavorable verdict. The one keeps vigil all vibrant and resplendent in tenderness; the other's vigil is with trembling and gnashing of teeth. Love inflames the one, injustice the other. Love keeps the one from falling asleep, diabolical jealousy the other, on this feast. So our very enemies teach us in spite of themselves how we ought to keep watch since it is in envy of us that they keep watch. Many of those who in no way are sealed with the name of Christ keep vigil this night because of pain; many, too, because of shame, and some,

[61]Text: PL 38.1088

already close to the faith, because of fear of God. Thus various reasons inspire man to keep this vigil.

Ought not the friend of Christ watch in joy when the pagan watches in pain? Ought not the Christian be fervent in observing the vigil when even the pagan is ashamed to sleep? Ought not he keep vigil who has already entered this great house (the Church) when the one who is only preparing to enter it keeps vigil?

Watch, I tell you, and pray. Let us celebrate this vigil internally and externally. Let God speak to us in these readings. Let us speak to Him in our prayers. If we hear His words obediently, He whom we pray to will dwell in us.

THE VIGIL OF VIGILS

[62]This is our annual feast, and our Pasch, not in prefigure by the sacrifice of a lamb as for the people of the Old Law, but for us, the new people, fulfilled by the death of our Savior. *For Christ, our Passover, has been sacrificed* (1 Cor. 5:7) and *the former things have passed away; behold, they are made new* (2 Cor. 5:17) .

Let us keep vigil, then, dearly beloved, because Christ's burial was prolonged until this night; so that on this very night the resurrection of the body should take place, a body which on the cross was a butt of derision but is now adored in heaven and on earth. This night, of course, is understood to be part of tomorrow which we call the Lord's Day. And His resurrection had to take place at night because by His resurrection He also enlightened our darkness. Nor was it in vain that the psalmist of old sang to Him: *Thou shalt enkindle my lamp, O Lord, my God; thou shalt enlighten my darkness* (Ps. 18:29).

Accordingly, our piety confronts us with this great mystery, so that just as our faith fortified by the resurrection continues to keep vigil, so also this night, enlightened by our vigil, may shine forth in splendor so that we may worthily think with the Church spread throughout the world today lest we be found in

[62]Text: SC 116.210-211

the night. For all these people—and what people!—congregated in the name of Christ on all sides for this solemn festival the sun has set, but day has not ended since it has been succeeded by an earth resplendent with the light of the heavens. He who has granted us the glory of His name has illuminated this night: He to whom we say *Thou shalt enlighten my darkness* (Ps. 18:29) enlightens our hearts, so that just as our eyes rejoice at this splendor of lighted candles so our mind may be enlightened and shed light on the meaning of this resplendent night.

GOD THE CREATOR

[63]We have been listening to many readings from Sacred Scripture. Their length will prevent our speaking at our usual length, and even if we could you would not be able to keep the thread. With God's help, then, we wish to speak to you, beloved brethren, on the first verse of the Bible in the reading you have heard: *in the beginning God created heaven and earth.* (Gen. 1:1). Consider attentively the creator. I am well aware that you cannot consider Him in Himself. So at least consider His works and praise the Creator.

In the beginning God created heaven and earth. Yes, His works are visible, but the creator is hidden; the object of our view is visible, but the object of our love is invisible. So when we behold the world and love its creator our love transcends our view. We see with our eyes, but love with our souls.

THE DEATH OF DEATH

[64]Where is death? Seek it in Jesus Christ, for it exists no longer. It was in Him but it exists no longer. O life, the death of death! Take courage and it will die also in you. What has begun in our Head will continue in His members. Death will die also in us. When? At the end of the world. At the

[63]Text: PL 46.821
[64]Text: PL 38.1114

resurrection of the dead in which we believe without the slightest doubt. *He who believes and is baptized will be saved* (Mk. 16:16).

Read what follows—it is formidable: *He who does not believe shall be condemned* (Mk. 16:16). Death will die in us but it will be victorious in those who are condemned. There will be everlasting death where death itself does not die because the torments will be everlasting. In us, however, death will die and will exist no more.

SURVIVAL AND LIFE

[65]How many years does he live or, better, how many should he? Eighty years, for example, was his life expectancy, fifty of which are gone and thirty remain. He lives one: that makes fifty-one lived, and twenty-nine left to live. One is added to what is lived, one taken away from what is left to live. But when you add, you do not keep what has been taken away. In fear a second year is lived; there remain twenty-eight. A third year is added; that leaves twenty-seven. In living we draw on the span of life, and life is shortened in the process and finally is no more. For there is no way of avoiding the last day.

But our Lord Jesus Christ came to tell us in some such words: 'O men, what are you afraid of; I have created you and have not abandoned you. O men, ruin is from you, creation from me; O men, why did you fear death? Behold, I die; behold, I suffer. Behold, you should not fear what you do, because I show you reason for hope.' Behold, He did so; He showed us resurrection for eternity. The evangelists have described it in their Scriptures; the apostles have preached it throughout the world.

[65]Text: PLS 2.570

BELIEVE AND TOUCH

[66]*Do not touch me*, He said, *for I am not yet ascended to my Father* (Jn. 20:17). Should you touch me prior to my ascent to the Father then you only see the man in me. What has this faith given you? Let me ascend to my Father. I have never left Him but for you I will ascend to Him if you believe me to be equal to the Father.

Our Lord Jesus Christ has never left His Father when He descended from Him. No more has He abandoned us in returning to His Father. For in the moment of departing and sitting at the right hand of the Father He said to His disciples: *I am with you even unto the consummation of the world* (Mt. 28:20).

THE PRESENCE OF CHRIST

[67]Have faith and He whom you do not see is present with you. But these two, when the Lord spoke with them, because they had not faith, they did not believe that He had arisen, and they had no hope that He could rise. They had lost faith and lost hope. They were dead men walking with a man alive, they were dead men walking with life itself. Life was walking with them but in their hearts there was no life yet.

And you, if you wish to have life, do what they did to recognize the Lord. They offered Him hospitality. The Lord looked bent on continuing His journey but detained Him. When they reached the end of their journey they said: *Stay with us here for the day has turned to evening* (Lk. 24:29). Take in the stranger if you wish to recognize the Savior. Hospitality restored to them what lack of faith had taken away; the Lord manifested Himself in the breaking of bread. Learn where to seek the Lord, where to get Him, where to recognize Him, in eating bread. For the faithful know something that gives them a better insight than the uninitiated into this text.

[66]Text: PLS 2.573
[67]Text: PL 38.1119

THE ONE SHEPHERD

[68]We believe all this without seeing it. We are bidden to love Christ, the Lord, without seeing Him. And we all exclaim: I love Christ. *How can he who does not love his brother, whom he sees, love God, whom he does not see?* (1 Jn. 4:20). In your love for the sheep testify to your love of the shepherd. For the sheep are the shepherd's members. He condescended to become a sheep so that the sheep might be His members. That the sheep might be His members, *like a sheep He was led to the slaughter* (Isa. 53:7). That the sheep might be His members it was said of Him: *Behold the lamb of God who takes away the sins of the world* (Jn. 1:29). But this lamb has great strength. Would you like to know what strength appeared in that lamb? The lamb was crucified and the lion was vanquished. See and consider with what strength Christ the Lord governs the universe, when by His death He has vanquished the devil.

THE DAY THAT THE LORD HAS MADE

[69]Our hymn, then, exalts the good life. When we all exclaim in harmony, with joy of spirit and heartfelt accord: *This is the day which the Lord has made* (Ps. 118:24); let us be in harmony lest our lips testify against our conduct.

See what joy, brethren; the joy in your assembly, the joy in chanting psalms and hymns, the joy of evoking Christ's Passion and resurrection, the joy of hope in life everlasting. And if mere hope causes such joy, how great will be the joy of realization? These are the days when we hear 'Alleluia' and our spirit is somehow transformed.

THE NEW CHANT

[70]We are admonished to sing a new chant to the Lord. The

[68]Text: PLS 2.580
[69]Text: *ibid.* 557
[70]Text: PL 38.210

new man knows this new chant. The chant is the expression of joy, and on reflection it is also an expression of love. The one, then, who knows how to love the new life knows how to sing this new song. We must learn what the new life is to learn what the new song is. All things belong to the one realm: the new man, the new song, the New Testament. Therefore the new man will both know the new chant and belong to the New Testament.

O brothers. O sons. O Catholic offshoots. O holy, celestial plants. O you who are regenerated in Jesus Christ and born in heaven, listen to me, or rather hear from me the words: *Sing to the Lord a new chant* (Ps. 96:1). Good, you say. I am singing. Yes, you are singing. I hear you. But let not your life belie your words. Sing with the voice, sing with the heart, sing with the mouth, but sing with your whole life: sing to the Lord a new chant. But how should you sing of that which you love? Doubtless it is what you love that you wish to sing of. You would like to know His glory to sing of it. You want to know what is His glory? *His glory is the assembly of the saints* (Ps. 149:1). The glory of Him who is sung about is nothing other than the one who sings about it. Become yourself the glory that you sing of. You are His glory if you lead the good life. For His glory is not in the synagogue of the Jews.

ALLELUIA

[71]Since it has pleased the Lord our God to allow me to be physically present here, let us join in your charity, let us join with you in singing Alleluia, which in Latin means 'Praise the Lord.' Brethren, let us praise the Lord, in our life and on our lips, in heart and on mouth, by word and deed. God wants our 'Praise the Lord' to be said without any lack of harmony in the one who praises: let what is in our life and on our lips then be harmonized in ourselves first; let our inner conscience square with our outer protestations, let our deeds, I say, match our words, lest our fine words be belied by evil conduct.

[71]Text: PL 38.1190

O blessed 'Alleluia' in heaven where the angels are the temple of God. There, agreement is perfect among those who chant; they have not to contend with the conflict between the law in the members; they have no struggle of concupiscence, in which the victory of charity is at stake. Here and now let us chant 'Alleluia' with concern so that there we may chant it with complete freedom from care.

Let us chant 'Alleluia' here in the midst of dangers and temptations, we and others. God is faithful, says the Apostle, *He will not allow us to be tempted above our ability* (1 Cor. 10:13). Let us then chant 'Alleluia.' Man is blameworthy but God is faithful. He does not say *He will not permit you to be tempted* but *He will not permit you to be tempted above your ability* (1 Cor. 10:13). With the temptation He will also give you a way out that you may be able to bear it. Preaching molds you like the potter's vase; the temptation hardens you. In entering think of the way out, for God is faithful: *the Lord guards your going in and your coming out* (Ps. 121:8).

O Blessed Alleluia of heaven! No more anguish, no more adversary. No more enemy. No more love of destruction. God is praised there and here, but mingled with fear here, but without disturbance above. Here, are those who are going to die; there, those who will be triumphing forever. Here the one who chants in hope, there, in possession; here it is Alleluia *en route*, there it is Alleluia on arriving home.

Today let us chant, brethren, no longer to entice repose, but to lighten our burden. Chant as a man on a journey, but keep time. Chant to sustain your effort, do not cultivate laziness. Chant and march. What do I mean, 'March?' Progress, make progress in good. For there are those, as the Apostle tells us (cf. 2 Tim. 3:13), who make progress in evil.

As for you, march to make progress, to advance in goodness, to progress in integrity of faith, and in purity of life. Chant and march, without straying, without going back, without marking time.

Maximus of Turin (d.420), a lively popular preacher, sacrificed theological reflection for ancient symbolism;

nevertheless, as a poet and mystic his Paschal vision is enriched by the requirements of an ardent sensibility:

[72]Great indeed is the mystery of the cross. And, properly understood, even the world itself is saved by this sign. For when sailors cleave their way through the sea they first raise a mast and spread the sails. Likewise our sins, like the unbridled, unrestrained waves of the sea, are destroyed by the Lord's cross. Those who are protected by the sign of the Lord seek the harbor of salvation and escape the danger of death. For the sail hanging on the mast is a sort of figure of the mystery. It is, what I might call, the Christ suspended upon the cross.... Just as the Church cannot stand without the cross, so, too, a ship without the mast is powerless. For the wind immediately disturbs it and the winds toss it to and fro. Wherever the sign of the cross, however, is raised the devil's wickedness is immediately banished and the gusts of wind are lulled.

Similarly the good farmer, when he prepares to till the soil of his land in his quest for staple provisions attempts this only through the sign of the cross. For when he attaches the share-beam to the plough share, attaches the lugs and inserts the plough handle, he imitates the cross; the very composition of the implement resembles in some way the Lord's Passion.

The sky also is arranged so as to be a figure of this sign. For since it is divided into four parts, that is, east, west, south, and north, it embraces four angles like a cross. Even man's gait, when he stretches out his arms, is cruciform, and that is why we are commanded to stretch out our hands when we pray....

Again:

[73]Brethren, it is not by chance that we read today this psalm in which the prophet bids us *rejoice and be glad* (Ps. 118:24). For holy David invites all of creation to today's festivity. Today by Christ's resurrection the gates of hell are opened, the

[72]Text: CCL 23.149

[73]Text: *ibid.* 214

earth is renewed by the Church's neophytes, heaven is reached by the Holy Spirit. Hell, once opened up, yields up its dead, the renewed earth raises up the dead, heaven made blessed receives those ascending to it.... For Christ's resurrection is life for the dead, pardon for sinners, and glory for the saints.

In the resurrection, then, all the elements get glory. For I think that the sun itself is brighter on this glorious day. The sun must needs rejoice at the resurrection of Him at whose death it was saddened, and must needs welcome Him alive at whose death it shrouded itself with a mourning veil of mist. And as it was then draped like a good servant in mourning for the burial rites so now it should shine in observing the resurrection.

Therefore, brethren, let us all rejoice on this holy day. Let no one, in his consciousness of being a sinner, withdraw himself from the common rejoicing. Let no one be held back from the public prayers by the burden of his crimes. However great a sinner one is, he must not despair of forgiveness on this day for there is no small precedent. If the thief entered paradise, why won't the sinner deserve forgiveness? And if the Lord showed mercy to the thief at his crucifixion, will He not be much more merciful at His resurrection? And if the lowliness of suffering bestowed so much on one who trusted, how much more will the glory of resurrection bestow on him who prays?

Again:

[74]Brethren, God has granted us a great and marvellous gift of faith. On the Pasch, the day of salvation, He has risen and granted resurrection to all. Raising Himself from the depths to the heights, He has raised us also on high. For all of us Christians, the Apostle says, are the body of Christ and His members. In Christ's resurrection, then, all His members are necessarily raised with Him, in passing over from death to life. The word Pasch in Hebrew means passage or progress, doubtless because through this mystery there is a passage from worse to better things. It is a good passage to pass from sin to justice, from vice to virtue, from old age to infancy, of

[74]Text: *ibid.* 218

simplicity not of years. For virtue, too, has its ages. By our previous falls we were established in the seniority of sin, but by Christ's resurrection we have been renewed in the innocence of little children.

Again:

[75]Brethren, today as yesterday let us celebrate our joy. If the shadows of night have interrupted our celebrations it is nonetheless the same day of celebration. The darkness of evening separates day and night, but the brightness which suffuses the joy of the Lord is eternal. Christ gave us illumination yesterday; today again we are in the warm glow of His presence. Jesus Christ is both yesterday and today (Heb. 13:8), says the blessed Apostle. . . .

This is called 'today' because like a living, unfailing splendor it does not cease to illuminate the world in perpetual light and because this unceasing flame seems to be one uninterrupted day.

In Leo the Great (d.461) there is no such lack of theological reflection; neither is there a poetic or mystic spirit. But there emerges a new type of Paschal homily with emphasis on doctrine, especially the incarnation and the redemption: Christ took our nature upon Himself for our salvation: again; "the cross of Christ, which was set up for the salvation of man is both a sacrament and an example—a sacrament in that divine power is released; and an example in that man's devotion is aroused."

[76]The whole of the Easter mystery, dearly-beloved, has been brought before us in the Gospel narrative, and the ears of the mind have been so reached through the ear of flesh that none of you can fail to have a picture of the events: for the text of the divinely-inspired story has clearly shown the treachery of the Lord Jesus Christ's betrayal, the judgment by which He was

[75]Text: PL 57.605
[76]Text: SC 74.128

condemned, the barbarity of His crucifixion, and glory of His resurrection . . . happy, had we not fallen from what God had made us; but happier, if we remain what He has remade. It was much to receive form from Christ; it is more to have substance in Christ.

> This approach of Leo, more doctrinal than mystagogical, continued in Rome, and in the West generally, and the Paschal Vigil became a night between the day of the crucifixion and the day of the resurrection. Deprived of neophytes, the vigil lost its baptismal quality and became a vigil of the resurrection. By the end of the Patristic Age, Gregory the Great, (d. 604) during the Paschal festivities spoke on *The Grace of God* in Mary Magdalene, the public sinner. His word is simple, direct and without affectation: it is also without the spirit of the Pasch!

[77]Jesus said to her *Mary* (Jn. 20:16), after He had called her by the common title of her sex *woman* (Jn. 20:15) and was not recognized; He calls her now by name. As if He were to say openly, recognize Him by whom you yourself have been recognized. God said the same thing to a perfect man, *I know you by name* (Exod. 33:12). *Man* is a name common to all, but *Moses* is a proper name and the Lord said to him very properly that He knew him by name; as if He were to say: I do not just know you in a general way like the others but in a more special fashion. Mary, then, because she is called by name, recognizes the One that calls her and straightway calls Him *Rabboni* (Jn. 20:16), that is, Master, because it was He who was sought without and He it was who taught her to seek for Him within. Now the evangelist does not describe what Mary did but it is suggested by the words. Jesus said to her: *Do not touch me for I have not yet ascended to my Father* (Jn. 20:17). In these words it is shown that Mary wished to embrace the feet of Him whom she had just recognized. But the Master says to her; Do not touch me. Not that the Lord rejected the touch of women after His resurrection. For we are told of the two women who

[77]Text: PL 76.1192

came to His tomb that they approached and held His feet in their embrace (cf. Mt. 28:9).

But the reason for not touching Him is added in the words, *for I have not yet ascended to my Father* (Jn. 20:17). Jesus ascends to the Father when He is regarded as equal to the Father. For whoever does not believe that He is equal to the Father, the Lord, has not yet ascended to the Father in His heart. Therefore He truly touches Jesus who believes that the Son is coeternal with the Father.

PASCHA NOSTRUM IMMOLATUS EST CHRISTUS

Chapter Three

NEW DAYS OF THE LORD

The Paschal night, of this night Scripture says: *This night will be as clear as day* (Ps. 139:12),[1] shone forth in a variety of days. Cosmic experience and biblical event combined, so to speak, to reveal and proclaim the eternal in time, as Christ became the Sol Invictus of the Magi from the East, and Christmas and Epiphany came to be—new days of the Lord of history and the universe. Even the first day of the new year of man became a new year's day of God. And forty days after His resurrection *He led them out near Bethany and with hands upraised He blessed them. As He blessed He left them and was taken up to heaven* (Lk. 24:50): Ascension Thursday is the memorial of that event. Likewise forty days after His birth, *the couple brought Him up to Jerusalem so that He could be presented to the Lord* (Lk. 2:22); and Presentation day became the memorial of this ascension, so to speak, on earth. Hence the division of this chapter into five days or different temporal experiences of the one eternal mystery: 1. Christmas Day; 2. Epiphany; 3. New Year's Day; 4. Ascension Thursday; 5. Presentation Day.

1. Christmas Day

The Latin phrase, *natalis dies,* as used in the Emperor's Court, came to mean more than an anniversary of birth: it

---

[1] *Exsultet, Missale Romanum*

signified days of great celebrations, such as the Emperor's Accession to the purple or the day of his apotheosis. In early Christian usage, as applied to the martyrs, it meant the day of earthly death or celestial birth. In reference to Christ it referred to His birth in the flesh on a certain day, and is found for the first time in the Philocalian calendar of 354, heading the list of Roman martyrs drawn up in 336—the first feast each year of the Church's annual celebration of anniversary of her martyrs:

ITEM DEPOSITIO MARTYRUM
(DEC. 25) VIII KAL. JANU. NATUS CHRISTUS IN BETHLEEM JUDEAE[2]

The origins of this Christmas feast remain obscure, both in time and in inspiration, but the earliest document that survives emphasizes the biblical events that surround the feast and not the cosmic mysteries of the solstice. This homily is entitled *On the Birthday of the Infants* and treats not just of Christ's birth, but also of the visit of the Magi and the slaughter of the Holy Innocents. It was delivered (c.360) by Optatus, bishop of Milevis, a staunch opponent of Donatism in Numidia, North Africa. This sermon was first published in 1917 by Dom Morin and re-edited by Dom Wilmart in 1922.

[3]1. Behold, this day has come on which we celebrate the mystery of Christ's Nativity with due solemnity, a day on which we know that we have mingled with divinity and have been liberated from errors. We see a hope of eternal quiet and accordingly not unwillingly we endure the labor of perseverance. For Christ the Lord is born , a man mingled with God, so that He might mingle the Church in the divinity in Himself, might show an example of virtue to His future

[2]N. Denis-Boulet, The Christian Calendar, 53
[3]Text: PLS 1.288

brothers and thus open up the reward of the heavenly kingdom for the faithful.

The Star and the Magi

2. The majestic star arose, revealing a new kingdom and a light to believers. This stirred up the Magi from faraway lands to inquire after the king of souls with devout mind. They went in haste, they sought, they found, they paid honor with mystical gifts, and, under instructions, they went back another way, no doubt lest those who had known Christ might cling to their former errors, but by another way, that is, so that they might direct their actions, their whole way of life into virtuous pursuits and rejoice that they had escaped. This made Herod insane with fury. Or rather the devil cast down in Herod grieved that the Church had been snatched from his jaws and joined to God. With subtle pretenses Herod pretended that he would adore the Lord, so that he might kill, if it could be done, the man mingled with God. But the providence of the Holy Spirit thwarted Herod's bid to eliminate Christ and in his thirst for blood he ordered the slaughter of the innocents.

3. This is the way of the heavens, the truth of the Gospels, the perpetual way of the saints. *I am the way, the truth and the life. Nobody comes to the Father except by me* (Jn. 14:6). If, then, Christ is the heavenly way which He has paved to be endured by the brothers who would follow him, if, revealing a hidden truth, He gave life to those believing in Him, let us who are sealed in the militia of the faithful follow bravely in the footsteps of Christ. If the world hates us, if the secular power persecutes us, already it hated the Lord Himself and by subtle inquiries sought to kill Him. And when he killed the infants in place of Christ he made a crowd of martyrs, but he did not find Christ whom he had badly looked for.

> The final section of the homily is devoted to the consideration of the gifts brought by the Magi. The following is a sample:

⁴8. Let us offer what we have learned that the Magi offered to the Lord: *gold, frankincense, myrrh* (Mt. 2:11). But we do not have any gold because we have left behind the goods of this world. What, then, are you going to do, you who have pre-elected poverty? In what way can you go to Christ, in what way will you adore Him when you do not bring with you a weight of gold, or the sweet aromas of incense and myrrh?

The cosmic implications of this biblical feast, arising from its proximity to the birth of *Sol Invictus*, are expressed in an anonymous homily of the fourth century, published by Bernard Botte as an appendix in his *Les Origines de la Noel et de l'Epiphanie*, entitled, *De Solstitia et Aequinoctia Conceptionis et Nativitatis Domini Nostri Jesu Christi et Johannis Baptistae*, and carefully analyzed by Thomas Talley.⁵ But the argument of this document, known in the literature as *De Solstitiis*, is from the Bible (however ill-used) and not from the pagan festivals. Christmas, be it December 25 or January 6, is computed from the date of the Passion, be it March 25 or April 6, according to the Semitic mind, which identifies the day of Christ's Passion and the day of His conception as it identified the patriarchs' days of birth and death—a sign of completion or perfection. This argument is bolstered further by the Scriptures: by identifying the festival of Tishri around the autumnal equinox (September 25) as the time of the Baptist's conception, the conception of Christ, six months later, can be placed around the spring equinox, and consequently His birth at the winter solstice (December 25), as the birth of the Baptist had to be the summer solstice (June 25)—hence the mere coincidence of the solstices and the equinoxes with the conceptions and births of the Baptist and the Christ. Therefore according to this document, *De Solstitiis*, the Scriptures give to the seasons their true significance and not *vice versa*.

---

⁴Text: *ibid.* 294

⁵Talley, *The Origins of the Liturgical Year*, 92-96

[6]Now the Lord was born in the month of December, the season of winter, eight days before the Kalends of January (i.e., 25 December), when the ripe olives are pressed to produce ointment, that is chrism, in which extract from other herbs is mingled. This is the time when bleating lambs are born, when the vine shoots are trimmed with pruning forks so that they may bear the wine of sweetness from which the apostles became inebriated with the Holy Spirit: for, He says, *I am the vine and my father is the vinedresser. Every branch in me that does not bear fruit will be cut down and cast into the fire* (Jn. 15:1-2; Mt. 3:10). But they also call it the birthday of the Unconquered One, who, to be sure, is so unconquered as our Lord who was the vanquisher of vanquished death. Or what they call the Sun's birthday is Himself the Sun of Justice concerning whom Malachi the prophet says, *But for you who fear my name the sun of righteousness will shine out with healing in its rays* (Mal. 4:2). He too was circumcised according to God's testimony because he had been brought to Abraham on the eighth day, that is, on January 1 on which day was the departure (cf. Gen. 17:9-12; Mt. 1:2).

> This blending of biblical event and cosmic experience continued and can be seen especially in the Latin Fathers at the end of the fourth century, and throughout the fifth as the Christmas feast is developed in the West. Maximus of Turin is a good example: "Common folk do well to call this birthday of our Lord the new sun, and make the assertion emphatically that Jew and Gentile find themselves in agreement on this appellation. Let us willingly make this custom our own, for at the Savior's birth the radiance of the sun itself is renewed, and not just the salvation of the human race."[7]
>
> Elsewhere he continues:

[6]Cf. Talley, 156, n. 27
[7]Text: CCL 23.261

[8]Even if I were to remain silent, brethren, the very season itself would bring to our notice the fact that the nativity of Christ is at hand. In fact, the period of preparation in reaching its end has pre-empted my preaching: by its groanings the world itself announces the imminence of something that will restore things to a better situation, and in impatient waiting this same world anticipates the brightness of a more resplendent sun that will illuminate the darkness. While it feared that its course would be ended by the shortness of its hours, it also indicated hopefully that its annual circuit would be renewed. This expectation of creation then persuades us to expect that Christ, the new Sun, when He rises, will illuminate our sinful darkness and that the sun of justice will by the vigor of His nativity disperse the lengthy fog of our crimes.

Again:

[9]When the whole world had been oppressed by the darkness of the devil and a fog thick with crimes possessed the age, the sun thought fit to shed forth the beginning of His birth at the last time, that is when the night was still incumbent.

Again:

[10]For if the sun was obscured when Christ was suffering it is all the more necessary therefore that it should shine forth with greater splendor than usual when He is born; and if it poured out its darkness on the Jews when they perpetrated death why should it not show its brightness on Mary giving birth to life? Or why should we not believe that at the birth of Christ the sun came with greater luster to pay its respects, when a brighter star preceded the Magi to lead the way? And if a star performed a function of night in the daytime why do we not believe that the sun also might steal some nocturnal time by an earlier rising than usual? From this, in a word, I think it came

[8]Text: *ibid.* 249
[9]Text: *ibid.* 262
[10]Text: *ibid.* 261

about that the night shrunk, while the sun in haste brought forth its light prematurely in obeisance to Christ's nativity: nay, rather, I do not say that it was night, or had any darkness, when the shepherds kept watch and the angels rejoiced ... for the angels and shepherds expressed their joy in their own voice or words, but the elements express theirs by their functions, since they cannot do so in words.

> Here one can see the transformation of *Natalis Solis Invicti* into the sacramental experience of the birth of Christ, at least in the Roman world. On the other hand, Augustine, in North Africa, where Christmas may have existed as a biblical feast before its cosmic transformation in Rome, is in no way sacramental in his approach: "You must know, first of all, that the day of the Lord's birth does not possess a sacramental character, but is only a recalling of the fact that He was born, and so it was only necessary to mark the day of the year on which that event occurred, by devout festivity. But there is a sacrament in any celebration when the commemoration of the event is so made that it is understood to indicate something which must be reverently received: Easter, we celebrate in this sacramental manner, but not Christmas." [11] Thus his thirteen Christmas Day sermons, which survive, are more symbolical than sacramental, more lyrical than liturgical:

[12] The Day who has made all days has made this day holy for us. The psalm sings about Him: *Sing ye to the Lord a new canticle, sing to the Lord, all the earth. Sing ye to the Lord and bless His name, bring the good tidings of the Day of Day, of His salvation* (Ps. 96:1-2). What is this Day of Day if not the Son of the Father, Light of Light? But that Day which begot this Day, who was born of the Virgin today—that Day has no sunrise, has no sunset. I am speaking of God the Father as Day. For Jesus would not be *Day of Day*, if the Father were not also Day.

[11] Text: PL 33. 205
[12] Text: PL 38.1005 = ACW 15.96

What is Day but Light? Not light of eyes bound to flesh, not light common to man and beast, but the Light which shines upon the angels, the Light to see which our hearts are purified. Indeed, the night in which we are now living, in which the lamps of the Scriptures are lit for us, passes away; and there will come that which is foretold in another Psalm: *In the morning I will stand before Thee, and will contemplate Thee* (Ps. 59:17).

Consequently Augustine, remaining within the African tradition, emphasized the scriptural dimension of the feast, more than the cosmic or pagan aspects:

[13]Our Lord Jesus, who was with His Father before He was born of His mother, chose not only the virgin from whom He was to be born, but also the day on which He was to be born. Misguided men very frequently go by certain dates. One man chooses a day for setting out new vines; another, a day for building; another, a day for starting on a journey; and sometimes, too, a man takes a special day for getting married. When they do this, they have this in mind, that anything undertaken may for that reason thrive and prosper. But noone is able to choose the day of his own birth; whereas the Lord, who was able to create both, was also able to choose both.

Moreover, He did not make His choice of day after the manner of those ... people who think that the fates of men are bound up with the position of the stars. Obviously, He was not made happy by the day on which He was born; but the day on which He deigned to be born was made a happy one by Him. For indeed, the day of His birth also shows the mystery of His light. The Apostle indicates this when he says: *The night is past, and the day is at hand. Let us ... cast off the works of darkness, and put on the armor of light. Let us walk honestly, as in the day* (Rom. 13:12-13). Let us recognize that it is day, let us be day ourselves. When we were living without faith, we were night. And, because this same lack of faith, which covered the whole world like the night, had to be lessened by

[13]Text: PL 38.1007 = ACW 15.101

the growth of faith, so on the birthday of our Lord Jesus Christ the nights began to be shorter, while the days became longer.

Let us, therefore, brethren, keep this day with due solemnity; not, like those who are without faith, on account of the sun, but because of Him who made the sun. For He who was the Word, *was made flesh* (Jn. 1:14), that for our sakes He might be under the sun. Under the sun, to be sure, in His flesh; but in His majesty, over the whole universe in which He made the sun. And now, too, He, incarnate, stands above that sun which is worshipped as god by those who, intellectually blind, do not see the true Sun of Justice.

The image of the day, as the symbol of light, runs through all these Christmas day sermons:

[14]Today *Truth is sprung out of the earth* (Ps. 85:12). Christ is born of flesh. Rejoice on this solemn occasion. On this day be reminded also of the Eternal Day and think of it, and with a profound hope desire the eternal gifts. Since you have received the power to be made *the sons of God* (Jn. 1:12), presume that you are such. For your sakes has the Maker of time been made in time. For your sakes has the Maker of the world appeared in flesh. For your sakes has the Creator been born.

Again:

[15]So this is the day on which the Maker of the world came into the world, the day on which He who had never been absent in His power, became present in flesh; because He was in this world, and He came unto His own. *He was in the world, but the world knew Him not* (Jn. 1:10), because the light shone in darkness, and *the darkness did not comprehend it* (Jn. 1:5). He came, therefore, in the flesh to cleanse the vices of the flesh. He came born of the earth, a Physician to heal our inner eyes which this our outer world had made blind; thus, when He has

[14]Text: *ibid.* 1011 = ACW 15.112
[15]Text: *ibid.* 1018 = ACW 15.128

healed them, *we who were heretofore darkness are made light in the Lord* (Eph. 5:8), and the light will no longer shine in darkness as a light present for such as are absent, but will become visible to seers of the truth.

Again:

[16]Today we are celebrating an anniversary, so you should expect a sermon proper for the occasion. Christ has been born: as God of the Father, as man of His mother; of the immortality of His Father, of the virginity of His mother; of His Father without a mother, of His mother without a father; of His Father without time, of His mother without seed; of His Father as the beginning of life, of His mother as the end of death; of His Father as the Ruler of all days, of His mother as the Sanctifier of this day.

Finally:

[17]Today, a festive day for us, has dawned as the birthday of our Lord Jesus Christ. It is His birthday, the day on which He was born. And this is today, because beginning with today the day begins to grow. Our Lord Jesus Christ had two births, the one divine, the other human. Both were miraculous. The first was without woman for a mother, the other, without man for a father. What the holy prophet Isaiah says, *Who shall declare His generation?* (Isa. 53:8) can be referred to both beginnings. Who could find the proper words to explain God's act of begetting? Who could properly explain the childbearing of the Virgin? The former was without day; the latter, on a definite day. Both transcend human estimation, both strike us with great awe.

For Leo, (c. 450) the feast of the nativity was no mere festival or commemoration: "as the year rolls round there recurs for us the sacramental day of our salvation, which

[16]Text: *ibid.* 1015 = ACW 15.121
[17]Text: *ibid.* 1019 = ACW 15.129

was promised in prophecy, accomplished in the fullness of time, and will endure for ever."[18] His many homilies that survive on the feast of the Nativity all reflect this sacramental understanding of the feast of "present redemption, of past prophecy and future bliss," and express it in a language that is no less sacramental or real:

Birthday of Life

[19]Rightly, then, did the birth of our salvation impart no corruption to the Virgin's purity, for the birth of truth was the preservation of honor. Such was the nativity which became the power of God and the wisdom of God ... Christ ... whereby He might be one with us in manhood, and surpass us in Godhead: unless He were true God He would not bring us a remedy; unless He were true man, He would not give us an example. . . . Let us give thanks ... that we might be in Him a new creation and a new production. Let us put off the old man of sin, and having shared in this new birth of Christ let us renounce the works of the flesh. Christian, acknowledge your dignity—you have become a partner in the divine nature: remember the head and the body of which you are now a member. . . .

He Came in the Flesh

[20]His incorrupt nature preserved the virginity of the Mother ... and His divine spirit respected the holiness ... of the sanctuary He had chosen for himself ... that He might raise the fallen, restore the broken and bestow on us the power of chastity ... that we might recover in this our second birth the virginity that was lost in our first. . . . In this nativity of Christ, according to David the prophet, *truth sprang out of the earth and righteousness looked down from heaven* (Ps. 85:12); in this nativity also is fulfilled the prophecy of Isaiah—*let the*

[18]Text: PL 54.104
[19]Text: *ibid.* 192
[20]Text: *ibid.* 196

earth produce and bring forth salvation, and let righteousness cover the earth: (Isa. 45:8) in the first transgressor the earth of human flesh was cursed, but in the flesh of the Virgin there is produced a seed that is blessed and free from the fault of its stock; each one of us becomes a sharer of this new flesh through regeneration... This new birth of flesh, that is the birth of our Lord and Savior from the virgin mother, occurs to the thoughts of the faithful on all days and at all times but is suggested to us by no day more than this, when with the new-born light still shedding its rays on nature there is borne in upon our senses the brightness of this wondrous mystery. For the angels converse with the astonished Virgin, and her conception by the power of the Holy Spirit seems to recur not only to the memory but indeed to one's very eyes as well today ... today ... Today the Word of God appears clothed in flesh, and that which was never visible to human eyes begins to be tangible to our hands as well. Today the shepherds learn from angels' voices that the Savior is born in the flesh of our flesh, and today, too, we join with the whole army of heavenly hosts and say: *Glory to God in the highest and peace to His people on earth* (Lk. 2:14).... This birthday of the Lord is the source of life for His faithful ones, because the birthday of the head is the birthday of the body ... just as the entire body of the faithful is crucified with Christ in His passion, raised with Him in His resurrrection, placed at the Father's right hand in His ascension, so with Him are we born in each generation through this nativity....

Wisdom in Darkness

[21] ... Let not the frailty of earthly thoughts raise itself against the loftiness of God's grace ... for the mystery of this bounty is great and this gift exceeds all gifts ... that God should call man son, and man should call God his Father ... peace-loving sons of our Father ... all the members of adoption must meet in the first-begotten of the new creation, who came not to do His own will but the will of Him that sent Him ... for they that

---

[21]Text: *ibid.* 213

are reborn after one pattern must have a spirit like that of the model: indeed the birthday of the Lord is the birthday of peace.... When, therefore, we try to understand the mystery of Christ's birth ... let all the clouds of earthly reasoning be put aside ... for the authority on which we trust is divine ... our inward ear tells us that that is true which the blessed John, full of the Holy Spirit, uttered with his voice of thunder: *in the beginning was the Word* (Jn. 1:1) ... *the word was made flesh* (Jn. 1:14). Therefore, in both natures ... it is the same Son of God ... renewing man in his manhood, but enduring unchangeable in Himself ... because the supreme and eternal Essence, which lowered itself for the salvation of mankind, transferred us into its divine glory, but did not cease to be in itself what it always was and is and will be.... What mind can grasp this mystery ... the old nature becomes new: strangers receive adoption and outsiders are given an inheritance—the ungodly are made righteous the miserly benevolent, the incontinent chaste, the earthly heavenly....

Although Scripture tells us *to rejoice in the Lord always* (Phil. 4:4), nevertheless this day arouses in us the deepest spiritual joy, because the mystery of the Lord's nativity is shining brightly upon us.

> The solar symbolism that infused the celebration of this feast in the fourth century to express, on the one hand, the teaching of Nicaea on the divinity of Christ and, on the other hand, to satisfy the desires of Constantine, the syncretist, or Christian emperor of a pagan empire, continued into the time of Leo. Nevertheless, Leo warned:

[22]Lest the tempter win you back again with any of his wiles, and mar even the joys of the present festival by his deceitful art, misleading simpler souls with the pestilential notion of some to whom this our solemn feast day seems to derive its honor, not so much from the nativity of Christ as, according to them, from the rising of the new sun. Such men's hearts are wrapped

---

[22]Text: *ibid.* 198

in total darkness, and have no growing perception of the true Light: for they are still drawn away by the foolish errors of heathendom, and because they cannot lift the eyes of their mind above that which their carnal sight beholds, they pay divine honor to the luminaries that minister to the world. Let not Christian souls entertain any such wicked superstition and portentous lie. Beyond all measure are things temporal removed from the Eternal, things corporeal from the Incorporeal, things governed from the Governor. For though they possess a wondrous beauty, yet they have no Godhead to be worshipped. That power then, that wisdom, that majesty is to be adored which created the universe out of nothing, and framed by His almighty methods the substance of the earth and sky into what forms and dimensions He willed. Sun, moon, and stars may be most useful to us, most fair to look upon; but only if we render thanks to their Maker for them and worship God who made them, not the creation which does Him service. Then praise God, dearly beloved, in all His works and jugdments. Cherish an undoubting belief in the Virgin's pure conception. Honor the sacred and divine mystery of man's restoration with holy and sincere service. Embrace Christ born in our flesh, that you may deserve to see Him also as the God of glory.

Again:

[23]From such a system of teaching proceeds also the ungodly practice of certain foolish folk who worship the sun as it rises at the beginning of daylight from elevated positions: even some Christians think it is so proper to do this that, before entering the blessed apostle Peter's basilica, which is dedicated to the one living and true God, when they have mounted the steps which lead to the raised platform, they turn around and bow themselves towards the rising sun and with bent neck do homage to its brilliant orb. We are full of grief and vexation that this should happen, which is partly due to the fault of ignorance and partly to the spirit of heathenism: because

[23]Text: *ibid.* 218

although some of them do perhaps worship the Creator of that fair light rather than the light itself, which is His creature, yet we must abstain even from the appearance of this observance: for if one who has abandoned the worship of gods finds it in our own worship, will he not hark back again to this fragment of his old superstition, as if it were allowable, when he sees it to be common both to Christians and to infidels?

> The association in the West, in a symbolic way, of the birth of Christ and the birth of the Sun, especially after Nicaea, probably explains the spread in the East of the Christmas feast, for Epiphany, as we shall see, developed its own significance on account of the particular mythology of its probable place of origin. In a sermon preached at Antioch on Christmas Day 386, John Chrysostom states: "It is scarcely ten years, in fact, since this day has been made manifest and known to us. At present the feast is not everywhere kept, for I know that even now many are still discussing it among themselves."[24] The purpose of this sermon was to establish December 25th as the real birthday of the Lord. Like the argument of the *De Solstitiis* tractate he follows the literal exegesis of Antioch and, beginning with Zechariah entering the Holy of Holies on the Day of Atonement, the September equinox, he establishes March 25 as the day of Christ's conception and December 25 as the day of His birth. Again the biblical events are uppermost in his mind and not the cosmic influence of the *Natalis Solis Invicti.* In fact the records of the census taken, "while Quirinius was governor of Syria" (Lk. 2:2), and preserved in the Tabularium of Rome, were for Chrysostom the explanation of the feast that originated there on December 25:

[25]That for which patriarchs painfully labored, which prophets foretold, and just men longed to see, this has happened and today been fulfilled: God has appeared on earth

[24]Cf. PG 49.351
[25]Text: *ibid.* 353

in the flesh and walked with men. Let us rejoice, therefore, and exult, brethren. For if John leaped in his mother's womb at the coming of Mary to Elizabeth much more ought we, who have seen, not Mary, but our Savior born this day, to leap and exult, to marvel and stand amazed over the magnitude of God's dispensation, which exceeds all thought (cf. Lk. 1:41). For consider how great a thing it would be to behold the sun descended from heaven and running about the earth, emitting hence its rays to all. But if in the case of a body of light this would strike all beholders, reflect with me and consider what it is to see the Sun of Justice emitting His rays from our flesh and illuminating our souls. For a long time I have desired to see this day and not merely to see it but to see it observed by such a large congregation. And I have prayed continually that this place of assembly might be filled as you can see it filled now. This, then, has come to pass and been realized.

> Five days previously, in celebrating the anniversary of Philogonius, bishop of Antioch, Chrysostom cut short his homily—Homily VI in the series known as *On the Incomprehensible Nature of God*—to give us precious reflections on the forthcoming Feast of the Nativity on 25 December, 386:

[26]So now I shall proceed to another path of preaching, for a feast day is about to arrive and it is the most holy, august and awesome of all feasts; it would be no mistake to call it the chief and mother of all holy days. What feast is that?

The day of Christ's birth in the flesh.

It is from this day that the feasts of the Theophany (i.e. Epiphany), the sacred Pasch, the Ascension, and Pentecost had their source and foundation. Had Christ not been born in the flesh, He would not have been baptized, which is the Theophany or Manifestation; nor would He have been crucified, which is the Pasch; nor would He have sent down the Spirit, which is Pentecost. So it is that, just as different rivers arise from a source, these other feasts have their beginnings from the birth of Christ.

[26]Text: PG 48.752 = FOTC 72.174

Not only for this reason is it right that the day of Christ's birth should enjoy the principal place but also because what occurred on this day provides a much stronger reason for us to experience a holy fear and trembling than all the others do. For the fact that Christ who became man also died was a consequence of His birth. Even though He was free from any sin, He did take upon Himself a mortal body and that should make us all marvel. That He who is God was willing to become man . . . makes us shudder with the deepest holy fear; it fills us with terror and trembling.

This is what amazed Paul when he said, *Wonderful indeed is the mystery of our religion.* How wonderful? *God was manifested in the flesh* (1 Tim. 3:16). . . . This is why I especially greet and love this day. . . . And this is why I ask and beg all of you to be here in church for that feast with all zeal and alacrity. Let each of us leave his house empty so that we may see our master wrapped in swaddling clothes and lying in a manger (cf. Lk. 2:7). This is a sight which is filled with holy fear and trembling. It is incredible and beyond our every expectation.

> The biblical nature of this feast is further expressed by Chrysostom's inclusion of the Magi's visit: but he interprets this biblical event in a moral manner and links the moral dispositions of the Christian worshipper to the sacramental birth of Christ on the Christian altar. The result is a homily that seems closer in kind to our times than to the times of the Fathers:

[27]Can you, a Christian, not bear to give a brief measure of time to enjoy this blessed sight? If we shall present ourselves in a spirit of faith, there is no doubt but that we shall truly see Him as He lies in the manger. For the table of this altar takes the place of the manger.

And surely the master's body will be lying on this altar, not wrapped in swaddling clothes, as it was after His birth, but clothed all about by the Holy Spirit. Those who have been

[27]Text: *ibid.* 753 = FOTC 72.177

initiated understand what I am saying. The Magi adored Him, but that was all. If your conscience is without stain when you come forward, we shall allow you even to receive that body and then to go off to your home. Do you, therefore, come forward and bring your gifts, not such gifts as the Magi brought, but gifts which are far holier and more august. The Magi brought gold; you bring a temperate and virtuous spirit. They brought incense; you must offer pure prayers, which are the incense of the soul. They brought myrrh; you must bring a humble and contrite heart along with alms.

If you come forward with these gifts, you will enjoy and share in this sacred table with great trust and confidence. Why do I speak these words at this time? I know for sure that on that day many will come forward and lay hostile hands on that spiritual sacrifice. We must not do this to the harm and condemnation of our souls. We must approach the altar to win salvation for ourselves. That is why, now, before that day, I beg and beseech you, only after you have cleansed yourselves in every way are you to approach these mysteries. Let no one say to me: 'I am so ashamed. I have a conscience filled with sins. I am carrying the heaviest of burdens.' The period of five days is time enough to cut away the multitude of your sins if you are sober and watchful and if you pray. Do not look to the shortness of the time but consider the loving kindness of the master. The people of Nineveh drove off God's great wrath in three days (cf. Mt. 12:41). The narrow span of time did not deter them, but after their eager souls won for them the master's loving kindness, they were able to accomplish the whole task...

Do you not know that this table is filled with a spiritual fire? Therefore... if you have any wickedness, drive it out and banish it from your soul. Does one of you have an enemy who has treated him with the greatest injustice? Let that man do away with his hostility; let him keep in check his soul, which is burning and swollen with hate, so that there may be no tumult or commotion in his heart.

You are going to receive your king in communion. And when your king comes into your soul, it must be very tranquil and still. Your thoughts must be marked with the deepest peace. But you were treated most unjustly and you cannot bear to put aside your anger. Why, then, do you do even greater wrong and more serious harm to yourself? Whatever your enemy may do to you, he will not treat you as badly as you treat yourself if you refuse to be reconciled to him and if you keep trampling underfoot the laws of God.

> Gregory Nazianzus in Constantinople (379-81), some five or six years before Chrysostom in Antioch, preached on the *Theophany, or Birthday of Christ.* Scholars for the most part agree that his sermon was preached on December 25, 380, although some, on account of the word theophany or epiphany in the title, favor January 6, 381: in either case it remains a nativity oration—one of the famous forty-five orations of Gregory, delivered during his episcopacy in Constantinople with the special purpose of protecting and preaching the Nicaean faith of his congregation. These orations soon became famous in the schools of rhetoric and followed the classical structure and style of 1. Exordium, 2. Encomium and 3. Conclusion.

Exordium:

[28]Christ is born! Glorify you Him. Christ comes from Heaven! Go you out to meet Him. Christ comes to earth! Be you exalted.... Let the heavens rejoice and let the earth be glad ... He is from heaven and He is on earth. Christ in the flesh ... Christ of a Virgin.... Again darkness is past; again light is present ... let the people that sat in the darkness of ignorance now see the Great Light of full knowledge.... Gone is the shadow ... here is the truth ... clap your hands together, all you people ... *unto us a child is born* (Isa. 9:15).... A Son is given ... Let John cry his cry: *prepare you the way of the Lord* (Mt. 3:3): I too will cry my cry; I will cry the power of this day—the Son of God is the Son of Man.... This is the festival of the Theophany ... the day of birth ... two names for the same day ... for truly is it both ... for ...

[28]Text: PG 36.312

by birth God was made manifest to man: the name Theophany is given on account of the manifestation; and that of Birthday in respect of His birth. Theophany and Birthday—this is the festival we are celebrating today.... Therefore, let us keep this feast, not after the manner of a heathen festival, but in the way of divine things—not the way of the world ... but a way above the world.... Let us not adorn our porches, arrange dances or decorate our streets: let us not feast the eye, enchant the ear, prostitute the taste ... or indulge the touch: let us not be effeminate in silks and satins ... nor adorned with silver or gold ... let us not appraise the bouquet of wines, nor the dainties of cooks ... let not sea nor land tempt me with their precious waste ... thus have I been trained to look upon the luxuries of this world.... Let us leave all these things to the pomps and festivals of the Greeks ... and if we must in some way have luxury, let us seek it in the Word and the Law of God, that our delight may be in Him who has called us together.... I am your host today: you are my guests for this feast.... I shall feed you a discourse on God and on divine things as abundantly and as nobly as I can ... that when you depart, you may have had the enjoyment of delights that never really fade away.

Encomium:

God always was, always is, always will be. More correctly God always is, for *was* and *will be* belong to time and are subject to change, but *is* is eternal—eternal being—the name He revealed to Moses ... in Himself He sums up and contains all being ... like some great sea of being, limitless and unbounded, transcending all conception of time and place ... only adumbrated by the mind ... and very darkly at that ... one image from this ... and another from that combining to give us some sort of momentary glimpse of the truth ... which escapes before conceptions of mind are formed, and remains as an object of wonder, of desire, of purification, of salvation ... so that when we are thus made or remade in His image, He may, to use a bold expression, hold converse with us as God's.... Some conception!... The divine nature is therefore boundless and hard to understand.... And when infinity is considered from the two points of view—beginning and end, the mind finds in one the unoriginate ... and in the other ... the imperishable, and thus the Eternal is grasped by way of conclusion ... for eternity is neither time nor part of time and cannot be measured.... This is all I shall say of God for the subject of this feast is not the doctrine of God but rather that of the incarnation....

When I speak of God ... I mean Father, Son, and Holy Spirit ... a movement of self-contemplation ... going forth beyond itself to conceive the heavenly and angelic powers. This conception was a work fulfilled by His Word, and perfected by His Spirit—secondary splendors ... illumined with the first rays of God ... the World of Spirit ... before.... A second world, material and visible ... A compound of earth and sky ... to show that He could call into being ... a Nature ... alien to Himself.... But perhaps someone of you, who are in the festive mood, may say: Spur your horse to the goal; talk to us about the festival and the reasons why we're here; yes, that I am about to do....

Spirit and Matter remained within their own boundaries ... then the Creator-Word produced a single living being out of both creations, the visible and invisible, and man was fashioned—a new angel, a mingled worshipper, fully initiated into the visible creation and only partially into the invisible ... earthly and heavenly; temporal and yet immortal; visible and yet intellectual; spirit and flesh in one person ... a living creature, trained here and moved elsewhere; and to complete the mystery, deified by its inclination towards God....

This being He placed in Paradise ... and gave him a law ... a commandment ... this commandment he forgot ... and for his sin he was banished ... from the tree of life, and from Paradise, and from God; and put on the coat of skins ... that is, perhaps, the coarser flesh, mortal and contradictory ... shame ... and he hid himself from God;—death, and his punishment, was his only mercy! He needed a stronger remedy, for his diseases were growing worse—mutual slaughters, adulteries, perjuries, idolatries. As these required a greater medicine, a greater medicine was given—the Word of

God; the Invisible, Incomprehensible, Bodiless, Beginning of Beginning, Light of Light, Source of Life and Immortality, Image of Archetypal Beauty, Immovable Seal, Father's Revelation. This Word put on flesh for the sake of our flesh, and mingled Himself with an intelligent soul for my soul's sake, purifying like by like ... and was made man. Conceived by the Virgin.... He came forth then as God with that which he had assumed, one person in two natures, flesh and spirit, and the latter deified the former....

Oh mysterious union.... Existence comes into being; the uncreated is created; the uncontained contained....

What is this mystery?...

I had a share in the image; I did not keep it. He protects of my flesh that He may save the image and make the flesh immortal. He communicates a second communion more marvelous than the first—now God becomes man and man is made God....

Will you deem Him little because He humbled Himself for you?... Because He lit the candle of His own flesh ... and swept the house in search of the coin—the divine image that was lost in human passion. Do you reproach God ... because He gives himself with a towel to wash the feet of His disciples and to show that humiliation is the road to exaltation?... Even now the Word must suffer ... by one group He is honored as God but confused with the Father; by another He is dishonored as mere flesh and severed from the Godhead....

But soon you will see Him in the Jordan river ... and behold the Spirit ... that is of one nature with Him: you shall see Him tempted but conquering and served by angels ... betrayed and crucified ... offered as a Lamb and offering as a priest; as a man buried in the grave, as God rising again, and ascending ... to come again in His own glory. What a multitude of festivals in all the mysteries of Christ—my redemption and my return to the Paradise of Adam.

Conclusion:

Now then I beg you: adore this birth which loosed you from the pangs of your birth ... honor Bethlehem ... the road to

Paradise: worship the manger ... which fed you the Word; bear gifts with the Magi ... to the one who died for you; come with shepherds and sing with angels ... let this festival be common to the powers in heaven and the powers on earth. ... I am persuaded that the heavenly hosts join in our exultation and keep with us this day of High Fesitival. ...

Be born with Christ this day ... if He flees into Egypt ... be an exile with Him; live every minute of the life of Christ ... teach in the temple and drive out the traders; before Herod ... keep silence for the most part ... put on the purple, take the reed in hand, and be mocked by those who mock the truth ... be crucified with Him ... rise with Him and be glorified with Him and reign with Him. Behold and be beheld by the great God—in trinity worshipped and glorified, and preached as clearly as the chains of my flesh will allow me to confess Jesus Christ, our Lord. Amen.

> By defining the divinity of Christ and the humanity of Christ, the Councils of Nicaea (325) and Chalcedon (451) made more clear the nature of the Christmas feast, or birthday. Consequently, in the less controversial atmosphere of the fifth and sixth centuries other aspects of the feast developed in both the East and the West: for example, in the East, especially after the Council of Ephesus (431), which defined the divine maternity, many of the Greek Fathers extol the role of Mary in the nativity, none perhaps more eloquently than John Damascene (650) at the end of the patristic age:

[29]Today the Creator of all things, God the Word, has composed a new book (cf. Isa. 8:1) which surged forth from the heart of the Father to be written, as with a pen, by the Holy Spirit, the language of God. It was given to a man who knew letters but did not read it. For Joseph did not know Mary nor the mystery itself.

Daughter all holy of Joachim and Anne, who escaped the principalities and powers and *the burning arrows of the evil*

[29]Text: PG 96.672

one (Eph. 6:16), you who lived in the bridal chamber of the Spirit and was preserved intact to be the bride of God and the mother of God by nature. Daughter all holy, appearing in the arms of her mother but a source of terror to the rebellious forces. Daughter all holy, nourished on her mother's milk but surrounded by troops of angels. Daughter beloved of God, glory of your parents. Generations of generations will call you blessed, as you asserted with truth. Daughter worthy of God, beauty of human nature, rehabilitation of Eve, our first mother.

Likewise in the West, the human figure of Joseph appears at an early stage, especially in the homilies of Peter Chrysologus (c.450), Archbishop of Ravenna:

[30]His holy mind, shocked at the novel situation, was in turmoil. His spouse stood, pregnant yet a virgin. She stood large with the child she carried, yet not free from the cause for blame. She stood in concern about her pregnancy, but free from fear about her integrity. She stood dressed as a mother, yet not excluded from the honor of virginity. What was the husband to do in such a case? Was he to accuse her of sin? But he himself was the guardian of her purity. Was he to press a charge of adultery? But he was the herald of her virginity. What was he to do in such circumstances? He thought of putting her away, since he could neither reveal outside what had happened, nor keep it inside. He thought of putting her away, and he told it all to God, because he had nothing to tell to men.

2. Epiphany

The origin of Epiphany in the East is as obscure as Christmas in the West, for January 6 in Egypt and Arabia had the same significance as December 25 in Rome and North Africa. Hence the strong possibility, too, of Epiphany

[30]Text: PL 52.588 = FOTC 17.233

being a biblical feast computed from April 6, the other solar equivalent of the lunar Passover date (14 Nisan), and consequently, according to the Semitic mind, the day of Christ's death and conception. Thus the day of Christ's birth coincided with January 6, the date of the Solstice in the East, as it did with December 25, the date of the solstice in the West. In the East, however, the homage paid to the triumphant sun was accompanied by mythological reminiscenses of far greater anitiquity than the Western Aurelian festivities of *Natalis Solis Invicti,* as Dionysus, out of sheer natural delight, made the rivers of the East run red with wine. Sometime in the early second century a Gnostic sect, according to Clement of Alexandria (c.200) tried to Christianize this belief: "The followers of Basilides celebrate the baptism of Jesus . . . on the eleventh day of the month of Tubi (January 6), for in their view the Word became incarnate only at the baptism of Jesus."[31] In these circumstances the baptism of Jesus and the miracle of Cana gave a new significance to the river and the changing of its waters into wine. Biblical event and cosmic experience are once again at work in the emergence of a Christian feast: Epiphanius, bishop of Salamis in Cyprus (367-403), gives us, in his work (*On Heresies* (51, 22) a fascinating account of a vigil celebrated in Alexandria in Egypt to Aion on the night of January 5/6.

[32]For the leaders in the cult of idols are forced to recognize some part of truth and, being liars, to deceive the idolaters who rely on them. In numerous places they observe a very great feast on this same night of the Epiphany in order that those who believe in error should not seek out the truth. This first occurred in Alexandria in what is called the Koreion, that is, a very large temple, the sanctuary of Kore. They keep vigil all night, celebrating their idol in songs, and to the sound of flutes, and at the end of the vigil after cockcrow they descend, carrying torches to a subterranean location and from there

[31]Cf. SC 30.150

[32]Text: GCS 31.285 = Talley, *op. cit.* 105

carry a wooden statue seated nude on a stretcher, having a golden mark in the shape of a cross on the forehead, and two similar marks on the hands, and two on the knees, the five marks being all of gold.

They carry the statue seven times around the temple in a circle to the sound of flutes and a tambourine and hymns, and then after their festivities they go down again to the subterranean location. And when they are asked what is this mystery, they respond: today at this hour Kore, that is, the virgin, has given birth to Aion. This practice also takes place at Petra, the metropolis of Arabia, the scriptural Edom, and they chant the virgin in the Arabic language—her name in Arabic is Chaaman—that is to say, young maiden or virgin, and her son is called Dousares, that is to say, the only son of the Lord. This also takes place at Elousa on the same night as at Alexandria or at Petra.

Epiphanius, besides this description of the birth of Aion on Janury 6, has a description of a further feast on the same occasion involving drawing water from the Nile:

[33] ... That is why, in many places down to our own day, the divine prodigy which took place then is reproduced as a testimony for unbelievers. So they testify in many places to springs and rivers changed into wine. So the spring in Cibyra, in the town of Caria, at the hour when the servants drew and he said, *give to the steward* (Jn. 2:8). And the spring in Gerasa renders the same testimony. We have drunk from the spring of Cibyra and our brothers from the spring located in Gerasa at the martyrium. And many in Egypt render the same testimony about the Nile. So, on the eleventh of the month Tubi in the Egyptian calendar, all draw water and set it aside, in Egypt and in many countries.

Epiphany is certainly an older feast than Christmas and was from its origin, according to Cassian, a celebration of Christ's nativity and events connected with it, especially His

[33]Text: *ibid.*; cf. Talley, 112

baptism: "in Egypt custom observes the ancient tradition of Epiphany; a time when the Lord's baptism and the birth in the flesh are commemorated and celebrated on a single festival day, unlike the practice of the West which separates the festival and divides the mystery."[34] The Western practice prevailed in the East in the fourth century, as we have seen with the spread of the Christmas feast; consequently, Epiphany remained the feast of the baptism, and was called *Ta Phota*, the Lights, because enlightenment or illumination was a synonym in Greek for baptism.

The following *Oration on the Holy Lights* was preached by Gregory Nazianzus at Constantinople on the festival of the Epiphany, January 6, 381, once again following the classical structure of Exordium, Encomium, Conclusion.

Exordium:

[35]My friends, once again Christ and His Mystery . . . this holy day of lights has arrived. . . . The baptism of Christ is celebrated. . . . My Christ, the real light, which gives light to every man . . . my purification . . . from the darkness and confusion of my sin. . . . Listen to the Voice of God . . . *I am the Light of the World* (Jn. 8:12). Therefore approach Him . . . be enlightened by Him . . . It is a season of new birth . . . let us be born again; it is a time of reformation . . . let us be made again in His image. . . .

Let us not remain what we are . . . let us become again what we once were. . . . The light shines in darkness in this life . . . in this flesh . . . and is chased by darkness, but not overcome by it. . . . Behold the mystery of this day and feel the power of this mystery . . . you will be raised higher than my words can raise you, when the power of the Word multiplies the power of my words.

[34]Cf. PL 49.821
[35]Text: PG 36.336

Encomium:

Now having purified the theatre, let us discourse a little about the festival.... God is the subject of this festival.... Therefore, let us call God to mind.... When I speak to you of God, you should be enlightened immediately by one flash of light and by three at the same time ... of Whom ... by Whom ... in Whom ... These words—*of, by, in*—do not denote a difference of nature ... but characterize the personalities of a nature which is one and unconfused.... And the Son of God deigns to become and be called the Son of Man.... At His birth we duly kept festival ... with the star we ran ... with the Magi we worshipped ... with the shepherds we were enlightened ... with the angels we were glorified.... Now we come to another action of Christ and another mystery ... I cannot restrain my pleasure; I am rapt into God ... Christ is made manifest.... Let us shine forth with Him ... Christ is baptized ... let us descend with Him and ascend with Him.... Our festival is of baptism ... let us speak about the different kinds of baptism ... Moses baptized, but it was in water: before that in the cloud and in the sea. This was by way of type or symbol—the sea of water and the cloud of the Spirit as the manna of the bread of life and drink of the divine cup. John also baptized ... not just like the Jews in water, but unto repentance ... Jesus, too, baptized, but in the Spirit—this is the perfect baptism. (How then is He not God by whom you, too, are made God!) I know also of a fourth baptism—that by martyrdom and blood, which Christ Himself also underwent.... Yes and I also know of a fifth baptism—that of penance—a baptism of tears, much more laborious, and received by him *who washes his bed every night with tears of repentance* (Ps. 6:7); who imitates the repentance of Manasseh, and the humiliation of the Ninevites; who utters the words of the Publican in the temple, and is more justified than the stiffnecked Pharisee; who bends down like the Canaanite woman and asks for mercy and crumbs—the food of a dog, who is very hungry.

Conclusion:

Come now; let us venerate this day the baptism of Christ: let us keep the feast ... not by pampering the flesh, but ... rejoicing in the Spirit.... Be like lights in the world ... a quickening force to all other men.... Stand up tall—perfect lights beside that One Great Light. Learn the mystery of the illumination of heaven: be enlightened about the Trinity—see more clearly and more purely ... even now you are receiving the One Ray from the one Godhead in Christ Jesus, our Lord, our might and our glory for ever and ever. Amen.

> In the East, the Epiphany naturally became a day for catechesis. Again Gregory Nazianzus is a good example of the preacher working the two days into one:

[36]Yesterday we kept high festival on the illustrious day of the Holy Lights; for it was fitting that rejoicings should be kept for our salvation; and that far more than on weddings, birthdays, namedays, housewarmings, children's registrations, anniversaries, and all other days that people celebrate for their earthly friends.

And now today let us discourse briefly concerning baptism. The Sacred Scripture recognizes three births for us, namely our natural birth, baptism, and that of the resurrection.... Let us discourse about the second, which is now necessary for us and which gives its name to the Feast of Lights. Enlightenment (i.e., baptism) is the splendor of souls, the conversion of life, the question put to the Godward conscience. It is the aid to our weakness, the renunciation of the flesh, the following of the Spirit, the fellowship of the Word, the improvement of the creature, the overwhelming of sin, participation in light, the dissolution of darkness....

> In a remarkable development of the text, God is light (1 Jn. 1:5) in the same homily Gregory continues:

[36]Text: *ibid.* 361

[37]God is light (1 Jn. 1:5): the highest, the unapproachable, the ineffable, that can neither be conceived in the mind nor uttered by the lips, that gives life to every reasoning creature. He is to the world of thought what the sun is to the world of sense, presenting Himself to our minds in proportion as we are cleansed, and loved in proportion as He is presented to our mind.... That light, I mean, which is contemplated in the Father, and Son, and Holy Spirit, whose riches is their unity of nature and the sole outleaping of their brightness. A second light is the angel, a kind of outflow or communication of that first light, drawing its illumination from its inclination and obedience thereto.... A third light is man, a light which is visible to external objects. For they call man light because of the faculty of speech in us....

After reviewing many episodes from the Old Testament associated with light, Gregory comes to the New:

[38]It was light that shone around the shepherds when the eternal light was mingled with the temporal. It was light that was the beauty of the star that preceded to Bethlehem to guide the way of the wise men, and to the escort of the light that is above us, when He came amongst us. Light was Godhead when He was shown on the mountain to His disciples—and a little too strong for their eyes. Light was that vision which blazed forth upon St. Paul, and by wounding whose eyes it healed the darkness of his soul. Light is also the brilliancy of heaven to those who have been purified here, when the righteousness shall shine forth as the Sun. In a special sense, Light is the illumination of baptism ... the great and marvelous sacrament of our salvation.

We get a rare glimpse of an actual Epiphany liturgy in Gregory of Nazianzus' *Panegyric on St. Basil*. The Roman emperor Valens (364-378) was a champion of Arianism, and had resorted to exiles, banishments, confiscations and other

[37]Text: *ibid.* 363
[38]Text: *ibid.* 365

kinds of violence against the Orthodox Church. He rightly
saw Basil as one of the strongest champions of orthodoxy
and moved against him, but more than met his match, as
Gregory tells it:

[39] But when, after having invaded all places, he launched his
attack upon this unshakeable and invulnerable mother of the
Churches, the only spark of truth still remaining unquenched,
with the purpose of enslaving her, then for the first time he
realized that he had planned badly.

> Gregory then relates an incident where Basil proved
> immune to the threats of the emperor's praetorian prefect,
> Modestus, who had to report to Valens that Basil was
> superior to all threats and deaf to all arguments and
> attempts at persuasion, and that the only recourse left was
> the use of force.

[40] At these words, the emperor, condemning his own
conduct and overcome by the praises of Basil, for even an
enemy can admire a man's courage, forbade the employment
of force. . . . Although his threats had changed to admiration
he did not enter into communion with Basil, being ashamed to
make the change, but he sought the most expedient means to
justify himself.

For the emperor entered the Church with all his retinue. It
was the day of Epiphany (in 372 or 373) and the Church was
thronged. He took his place among the people and thus gave
the appearance of professing unity. Once he was inside, the
singing of the psalms struck his ears like thunder, and he
observed the sea of people and the orderly behavior, more
angelical than human, prevailing in the sanctuary and its
precincts. He saw Basil posted, facing his people, *standing
erect*, as the Scripture describes Samuel (1 Sm. 19:20) with
body, and eyes, and mind undisturbed, as though nothing
unusual had happened, but like a pillar, if I may say so,

[39]Text: PG 36.557
[40]Text: *ibid.* 561

attached to God and the altar, while those about him stood in fear and reverence....

At this sight dimness and dizziness enveloped the emperor's eyes.... But when the time came for him to present at the divine table the gifts which had to be offered with his own hands, and no one, as was the custom, assisted him, since it was not clear that Basil would receive them, then his feelings were clearly manifested. For he began to stagger, and if one of the ministers of the sanctuary had not lent his hand to support his wavering steps, he would have suffered a lamentable fall. But let this suffice.

> Gregory of Nyssa also gives us a picture of the popularity of the feast of Epiphany, in a sermon preached on January 6, probably in 383. This sermon, called *On the Feastday of Lights*, is devoted to an exposition of the sacrament of baptism, and the day was obviously a commemoration of Christ's baptism by John: Again, the classical structure is followed:

Exordium:

[41]Now I recognize my own flock. Today I see the familiar figure of my Church turning from the cares of the flesh, and ... crowding within the sacred sanctuary ... like bees: some are busy within, while others outside hum around the hive. My children, never abandon this zeal ... I feel a shepherd's affection ... I am filled with happiness, and work with pleasure at my sermon.... Now is the time to remember our holy mysteries ... which purge from our souls and bodies that sin which is hard to cleanse: for my part I rejoice ... over you that are already initiated, and over you that are still uninitiated.... Therefore, let us leave the other matters of the scriptures for other occasions, and abide by the topic set before us and explain as far as possible the gifts and graces that belong particularly to today's feast for each festival has its own grace and demands its own treatment.

[41]Text: PG 46.577

Encomium:

Now then ... a few days ago Christ was born ... Today, He is baptized by John ... that He might bring the Spirit down from above and raise man up to heaven.... Baptism, then, is a purification and remission of sin, and a cause of renovation and regeneration.... Water does not bestow this gift; it is bestowed by the command of God and the visitation of the Spirit that comes sacramentally through the water to set us free.... Therefore, do not despise this divine washing ... on account of the use of water, for the Spirit that operates through the water is mighty, and wonderful deeds are wrought by the Spirit over material things.... This holy altar by which I stand is stone ... but by the benediction it is made a holy table ... no longer touched by the hands of all, but by the priest alone. This common bread, when the sacramental action consecrates it, becomes the Body of Christ. So with the oil; so with the wine ... before the benediction they are of little value, after the sanctification bestowed by the Spirit, each has its own operation.... The same power of the Word makes the priest venerable and honorable, separated by the new blessing bestowed upon him from community with the rest of men. Yesterday, he was one of the people; today he is suddenly rendered a guide, a president, a teacher of righteousness, an instructor in hidden mysteries.... Water likewise renews the man to spiritual regeneration, when the grace from above hallows it ... then it cleanses and illuminates man ... how? how? how? How heaven? How earth? How sea? How every single thing?... Reason, when perplexed, falls back upon this syllable 'how,' like those who cannot walk fall back upon a seat.... Fire, air, earth and water ... we conceal ourselves in water, as Christ did in the earth; and by doing this three times we represent the grace of the resurrection, which was wrought in three days; and this we do while the names of the Three Sacred persons are spoken over us.... Everywhere the ancient Scriptures prefigured the sacrament of regeneration in dark sayings and actions.... Let us recall its types ... for this festival season of necessity demands their recollection: Hagar

... wandering in desolation ... is shown by an angel a well of living water, and saves Ishmael: Rebekah, mother of Jacob, is found at the well: Rachel is found at the well ... a great stone lay upon it ... and none rolled away the stone save Israel, who is mind seeing God. He gave water to the sheep of Rachel; that is he reveals the hidden mystery, and gives living water to the flock of the church ... Moses ... from the water; and the Red Sea proclaimed the good tidings of salvation by water...; and Elijah clearly proclaimed the sacramental rite of baptism ... for the fire was kindled by water thrice poured out upon it, so that it is clearly shown that wherever the mystic water is, there, too, is the warm, fiery Spirit burning up the ungodly and warming the faithful. Elisha, too, washes the sick man in the Jordan ... for Jordan alone of rivers receiving in itself the first fruits of sanctification and benediction, conveyed in its banks, as in its own very type, the grace of baptism to the whole world.

These are indications in deeds and acts of regeneration, but there are also prophecies in words and language: Isaiah— *Wash away the evil from your souls* (Isa. 1:16): David— *Draw nigh and be enlightened* (Ps. 33:6): Ezekiel— *I will sprinkle clean water upon you, and you will be cleansed ... and a new spirit will I give you* (Ezek. 36:25-27). . . . And the beauty of Carmel is bestowed upon the soul, which resembles the desert. . . . For Elijah dwelt in Carmel and the mountain became famous because of him, and since John the Baptist, illustrious in the spirit of Elijah, sanctified the Jordan, therefore, the prophet foretold that the beauty of Carmel would be given to the river; and the glory of Lebanon from the similitude of its lofty trees, he, too, transfers to the river: for as great Lebanon presents a sufficient cause of wonder in the very trees it brings forth and nourishes, so is the Jordan glorified by regenerating men and planting them in the Paradise of God— leaves that will not wither ... and like a good planter, God will rejoice in His own works. . . . Here we must stop. But you ... must show me the new life that must follow your regeneration ... we must see in you signs of the new-born man ... you must become sober, content ... charitable, truthful, courteous, and affable.

Conclusion:

I have finished ... spoken enough on this subject of the festival which the yearly circle brings around.... Let us conclude with a few words of praise: truly, O Lord, are you the pure and eternal font of happiness ... you cursed us but blessed us; banished us ... but recalled us; stripped away our fig leaves but placed upon us a costly robe; sprinkled us with clean water and cleansed us...; no longer shall Adam in us be confounded by your call nor convicted by his conscience to hide in the thicket of Paradise; nor shall the entrance be inaccessible to those who draw near—Paradise and heaven itself can be walked by man ... now we sing the angel's song ... then let us sing ... let my soul be joyful in the Lord, *for He has clothed me with the garment of salvation and has placed upon me a robe of gladness* (Isa. 61:10).

> Two manuscripts in the Bodleian Library, Oxford, contain an unedited homily, *De Epiphania*, ascribed to Chrysostom. The baptism of Christ is the subject of this homily, which was obviously preached on the actual feast: the opening line sounds the keynote at once of the homily and of the feast of the Epiphany in the East:

[42]Christ has been made manifest to the world. Let all of us believers celebrate the festival together in harmony. Christ is a name that is many names at once: *for He is at the same time God and Lord* (Jn. 20:28), and *Word* (Jn. 1:14), and *only begotten Son* (Jn. 1:18), and *king of kings* (Rev. 17:14), and *power and wisdom* (Dan. 2:20), and *truly the vine* (Jn. 15:1) and *cornerstone* (Eph. 2:20), and *heavenly bread* (Jn. 6:51), and *fountain of life* (Ps. 36:10), and *true light* (Jn. 1:9), and *prince of peace* (Isa. 9:5), and *father of the age to come* (Isa. 9:5).

Come, then, beloved brethren, let us celebrate the feast in a spiritual fashion...

[42]Oxford, Bodleian, Barocci 147, ff. 254v—257v; Holkham gr 22 (olim 69), ff. 361v—365v. Published by permission.

The ineffable grace has been manifested to the world and all obscurity has been dissolved...

What are you doing, Lord? Why do you conceal your divinity through your humanity?...

The Jordan, seeing you, grew frightened and retreated, unable to endure the likeness of divine fire, and does John dare to render service to you? The sea, seeing your divinity, fled into retreat, and does John dare to lay his right hand on your head? Do not, Lord, do not you approach your servant, but rather, Lord, baptize me—a sinner and one who has need of cleansing...

Enlighten the eye of my mind. Regenerate my soul and make me wholly clean and baptized, I who have need of baptism.... Your flawless and exceedingly holy body does not need the washing by which you are baptized by me ... *I have need to be baptized by you and do you come to me* (Mt. 3:14), you, the undefiled, the stainless, the sinless, the blameless one, *who enlightens every man who comes into the world* (Jn. 1:9).

I know who you are, for I recognized your glory and divinity before ever I saw the light of day. While still confined in my mother's womb I recognized your greatness when my mother became my mouthpiece and she who gave me birth proclaimed you in song in the words of David ... and I leaped in my mother's womb and spoke the following words to your mother: *Blessed are you among women and blessed is the fruit of your womb. And whence is this to me that the mother of my Lord should come to me?* (Lk. 1:42).

Whence is this to me that the master comes to the servant? Whence is this to me that the sun comes to the dust? Whence is this to me that the Creator runs to the object of His creation?....

When John had said such words Jesus replied to him, *Let it be so now* (Mt. 3:15).... Do not noise abroad the mystery enacted today in the Jordan....

If you do not wash my body in the running waters of the Jordan, the mystery of the Trinity will not be manifested. If I do not descend into the Jordan, the Spirit will not be enkindled. If you do not sanctify the water of the Jordan, the head of the dragon will not be crushed. If you do not immerse my body in the river Jordan, the water of the sea will not be sanctified. *Let it be so now* (Mt. 3:15).

But John said to him, What are you doing, Lord? The Jordan, seeing you, the sun of the sun, shrank back, and does John, mere clay,... dare to become a sharer in such a mystery? No, master, do not force me to perform what I am unable to do. My eye twitches. The joints of my limbs are in dissolution. My heart is in a flutter. My mind is beside itself. My hand is powerless. I am all fearful and trembling. How can you force me to do what I cannot do?

Jesus replied to him: *Let it be so now* (Mt. 3:15)....

For this reason I took on all flesh. For this reason I became one of my own creations. For all these reasons I was made manifest to the world. For these reasons I was seen *in the likeness of a servant* (Phl. 2:6). Take courage, then, and joyfully approach the undertaking.

On hearing those words, John, the baptist and precursor, like a faithful servant, in fear and trembling performed the liturgy ... and baptized the Lord and Savior....

O! how wonderful! The Son was baptized. The Father testified from above. The Holy Spirit joined in bearing testimony. How truly great is the mystery of the Incarnation, great, and extraordinary, and surpassing all understanding! The Trinity was manifested at the river Jordan. The oneness of substance of the divinity was confirmed there, or rather the divinity in three persons was recognized there. In the presence of the Jews, John was struck with terror. The Jordan was sanctified, while Christ, God of all, was baptized by John in the Jordan, sanctifying all nature.

To Him be power and the glory for all ages. Amen.

> The feast of the Epiphany underwent a complex evolution on account of the acceptance of Christmas in the East, on the one hand, and, on the other hand, on account of its own passage and acceptance in the West. Though of definite Eastern origin, as its Greek name indicates, the first indisputable reference to its celebration in the West comes from Gaul about 361. In Jerusalem, at the time of Egeria,

Epiphany and Nativity were the one feast, without any reference to baptism or the miracle of Cana. But in the West, generally at the beginning of the fifth century, Epiphany, or *Apparitio,* meant the three miracula or manifestations, first to the Magi, then at the baptism, and finally at Cana, and they were celebrated separately on the feast and on the first and second Sundays after the feast.

In the Greco-Roman world the word *Epiphaneia* meant the manifestation or appearance of a divinity coming to the help of a human in need: the earliest Latin translations of this Greek word bring out the wealth of its significance, and *manifestatio, apparitio* and *adventus* appear for the first time in the new literature. These new Latin terms can be seen especially in sermons 199 and 204 in St. Augustine's immense collection of sermons devoted to the Epiphany. Here are some samples:

[43]A few days ago we celebrated the day on which the Lord was born of the Jews. Today we are celebrating the day on which He was adored by the Gentiles. For *salvation is of the Jews* (Jn. 4:22) but this salvation is even to the ends of the earth (cf. Acts 13:47). Thus, too, on the previous day the shepherds adored. Today, the Magi. Angels announced Him to the shepherds, a star to the Magi.

[44]Today's feast is known throughout the whole world. What joy it brings to us, or what lesson the feast has for us on its annual return—the season suggests that we also make this the topic of the sermon which we give at this time each year. The Greek *Epiphania*, it is clear, can be translated in Latin by the word *Manifestatio.* It is on this day that the Magi are said to have *adored the Lord (Mt. 2:11).*

The Lord was also *made manifest* (Lk. 2:15), and that on the day of His birth, to the shepherds who were informed by an angel. And on that day news of Him was given by a star also to those men still far off in the East and this is the day on which

---

[43]Text: PL 38.1026 = ACW 15.154
[44]Text: *ibid.* 1033 = ACW 15.169-170

they adored Him. Therefore, the universal Church of the Gentiles adopted this day as a day to be celebrated in a most devout manner; for even these Magi—what were they but the first fruits of the Gentiles?

[45]...It was therefore proper for us, that is, the Church gathered from the Gentiles, to add the celebration of this day, the day on which Christ was made manifest to the first fruits of the Gentiles, to the celebration of that day on which Christ was born of the Jews and to preserve the memory of so great a mystery in a twin festival.

> Despite the early connection of Epiphany in the East with the administraton of baptism, the feast in the West generally concentrated on the visit of the Magi rather than on the baptism in the Jordan. Leo the Great is particularly anxious to sever the connection between Epiphany and baptism. Writing to all the bishops of Sicily he reminds them that he has a divine and apostolic mandate to keep watch over the state of all the churches and, if necessary, to recall men "with speedy care either from the stupidity of ignorance or from forwardness and presumption." In this case the error is that in Sicily baptisms are being done at Epiphany.

[46]Accordingly when it reached my ears on reliable authority (and I already, beloved, felt a brother's affectionate anxiety about your actions) that in what is one of the chief sacraments of the Church, you depart from the practice of the apostles' consitution by administering the sacrament of baptism to greater numbers on the feast of Epiphany than at Easter time, I was surprised that you or your predecessors could have introduced so unreasonable an innovation as to confound the mysteries of the two festivals and believe that there was no difference between the day on which Christ was worshipped by the wise men and that on which He rose from the dead.

---

[45]Text: *ibid.* 1038 = ACW 15.180
[46]Text: PL 54.696 = LNPF ser. 2,12.27

He goes on to insist that Easter and Pentecost are the only two feasts on which baptism is to be administered. His reason for excluding it at Epiphany is clear:

[47]But if anyone thinks that the feast of Epiphany, which in proper degree is certainly to be observed in due honor, claims the privilege because, according to some, the Lord came to John's baptism on the same day, let him know that the grace of that baptism and the reason of it were quite different and is not of equal footing with the power by which they are reborn of the Holy Spirit ... For the Lord ... desired to be baptized just as He desired to be circumcised, and to have a victim offered for the purification ... that He might become under the law.... But the sacrament of baptism He founded in His own person ... and He ratified the power of rebirth ... when from His side there flowed out the blood of ransom and the water of baptism.... Therefore, in accordance with the apostolic rule of purging by exorcisms, sanctifying by fastings and instructing by frequent sermons two seasons only are to be observed for baptism, namely Easter and Whitsuntide.

This prohibition of baptism on the feast of the Epiphany eventually identified the feast in the West with the manifestation to the Magi. Peter Chrysologus (c.460) is a witness to this rapid spread of the new understanding at Ravenna:

[48]Do you think that the Evangelist taught that the Chaldaean watchers of the stars, the Magi journeying with the aid of the stars, studying the affairs of the heavens in the darkness of the nights, attributing the causes of birth and death to the movements of the stars, asserting that good or evil comes to men through the decision of these luminous bodies—do you think that the Evangelist taught that it was by the mere natural guidance of a star that they today discovered the birth of the Christ hidden from the ages?

Let no one have such a thought! That is what the world

[47]Text: *ibid.* 701 = LNPF ser. 2,12.29
[48]Text: PL 54. 612 = FOTC 17.265

thinks, what the pagans understand, what the reading yields at first sight. But the Gospel text speaks matters not human, but divine; matters not ordinary, but new; matters not deceptive through cleverness, but based upon truth...

Thus when the Magus saw that human cares had come to naught, that his own arts had failed, that the labors of worldly wisdom had been exhausted, that the perspiration of all the sects had congealed and the treasures of all philosophy had been emptied out, that the night of paganism had fled and the clouds of opinions dissolved, that the very shadows of the devils had skulked into hiding, that the star was not, like a comet with its surrounding tail, hiding what it was announcing, covering up what was shining—when the Magus saw all this, he spoke: 'It is a divine decree that I see you in Judaea, resplendent with a new ray, a significant light, and a steady splendor, and there—above the law of the universe, above the arrangement of flesh, above the nature of men—there pointing out the King now born.'

With his error thus dispelled, he follows, he runs, he arrives, he finds, he rejoices, he falls prostrate, he adores. For, not through the star, not through his skill, but through the help of God has he found, in astonishment, God in human flesh. Therefore, brethren, the passage read today does not establish the error of magic, it dissolves it. Let these remarks suffice for today, that with God's help the matters which follow may become clear.

3. New Year's Day

Since the middle of the second century B.C. Roman consuls began their tenure on the first day of January: with the reorganization of the Roman calendar in 46 B.C. under Caesar it became the first day of the new year instead of March 1, and, consequently, a feast in honor of Janus, the pagan god who faces in both directions, as Caesarius of Arles explains:

[49]The day of those calends which are called the Calends of January, beloved brethren, derived its name from the dissolute and wicked man, Janus. This Janus formerly was the chief leader of the pagans. Ignorant and rustic men feared him as if he were a king, and they began to worship him as a god; while they were afraid of his kingly power, they conferred unlawful honor upon him. Men at that time, truly foolish and ignorant of God, esteemed as gods those whom they perceived to be more exalted among men. Thus it happened that worship of the one true God was carried over to the many names of deities or rather of demons. For this reason they named the day of today's calends after the name of Janus, as was already said, so that they assigned the end of one year and the beginning of another to the man upon whom they wished to confer divine honors. Now because to them the calends of January were said to complete one year and begin another, they placed this Janus, as it were, both at the beginning and at the end, for he was believed to end one year and begin another. From this stems the fact that ancient worshippers of idols themselves fashioned two faces for Janus, one facing the front and the other the rear: one to look at the past year, and the other to see the coming one. Moreover by thus ascribing two faces to him, foolish men have made him a monster, even while they want to make him a god; what is unnatural even in animals they have willed to be a marked characteristic of their god. And so, in the clearest manifestation of their error and in judgment upon it, while wishing, in their empty devotion to images, that he seem a god, they have openly revealed him a demon.

The festivities of this day were greatly frowned upon by the Fathers of the early fifth century, especially Augustine, two of whose sermons on the feast are extant:

[50]My brethren, seeing that you have gathered together today as for a solemn feast and that you have come in greater numbers than usual, I admonish you in your devotedness to

[49]Text: CCL 104.779 = FOTC 66.26
[50]Text: PL 38.1024 = FOTC 38.55

remember what you have just sung so that your voice may not resound while your heart is silent, but, rather, that what you have uttered for one another's ears may reach the ears of God. For this is what you sang: *Save us, O Lord our God: and gather us from among the nations: that we may give thanks to Thy holy name* (Ps. 106:47). Now, if this feast of the pagans which is celebrated today with such joy of the world and of the flesh, with the singing of meaningless and base songs, with banquets and shameful dances, if these things which the pagans do in the celebration of this false festival do not please you, then you shall be gathered from among the nations. . . . Many will wrestle in their hearts today with the word which they have heard for I said: 'Do not give gifts, but give to the poor.' It is not enough merely to give—you should give generously. Do you not wish to give more? Well, just give. But you object: 'When I give New Year's gifts, I myself give to myself.' What then? Do you receive nothing when you give to the poor? You surely would not believe what the pagans believe; you surely would not hope for what the pagans hope for. But if you say that you get nothing when you have given to the poor, you have become one of the pagans and without justification you have sung: *Save us, O Lord our God: and gather us from among the nations* (Ps. 106:47). Do not be unmindful of that passage which says: *He that giveth to the poor shall not want* (Prov. 28:27). Have you already forgotten what the Lord is going to say to those who have given alms to the poor: *Come, blessed of my Father, take possession of the Kingdom* (Mt. 25:34), and what will He say to those who have not given alms: *Cast them into everlasting fire* (Mt. 25:41)? Here at this moment, those who gladly heard what the Lord said are standing with those who were not so glad to hear it.

Now, I speak to the true Christians. If you believe, hope, and love otherwise (than the pagans do), then live otherwise and gain approval for your distinctive faith, hope, and charity by distinctive actions. . . . *You were once darkness, but now you are light in the Lord. Walk, then, as children of light* (Eph. 5:8-9), so that we, too, who preach the word of the Lord to you, may wish you and because of you rejoice in perpetual light.

Gregory of Nyssa (c.394) was also familiar with the Roman custom of New Year's Day gifts, but was not opposed to the practice: "for thus it happened; on that day as I was going to the metropolis of the Cappodacians, I met a friend who handed me this present, your letter, as a New Year's gift. And I, being overcome by my good luck threw open my treasure to all who were present; all shared in it . . . without any rivalry, and I was none the worse off."[51] This letter also explains the practice to Libanius, presuming the great master of rhetoric and teacher of Chrysostom and the Cappadocians to be unfamiliar with it: "It was a Roman custom to celebrate a feast in wintertime when the days began to lengthen and the sun began to climb. The beginning of every month is holy but the first day of this month contains within it the future of a whole year; thus they devote themselves to forecasting lucky accidents, health and wealth."[52] In time, turning points are many and varied but always sacred, whether the beginning of a year be civil or religious, or the season be that of spring or autumn. Thus again the cosmic experience invites the biblical event, not just by way of opposition, but also by way of instruction or revelation. Naturally the octave of Christmas was celebrated eventually on January 1, and after the Council of Ephesus (431) Marian devotion made this octave the day of circumcision: *When the eighth day arrived for His circumcision, the name Jesus was given the child, the name the angel had given Him before He was conceived* (Lk. 2:22). Circumcision, the name of Jesus, and the Motherhood of Mary, were all biblical themes that became associated in Christian tradition with this sacred day or cosmic experience. Again Caesarius of Arles provides the evidence.

[53]Our Savior, dearest brethren, was born of the Father as true God before all ages, and at the end of ages the same Son of God was Himself born as true man. For the redemption of the

[51]Text: cf. PG 46.1052

[52]Cf. *ibid.* 1053

[53]Text: CCL 104.778 = FOTC 66.25

human race He wished to experience the condition of human weakness, He wanted to fulfill all of the precepts of the Law, and on the eighth day, which we commemorate today, He willed to be circumcised in His body. This was not to cleanse His flesh, but to free us from all wickedness and to extend everything that was accomplished by Him to our profit. But someone will say: Why was Christ circumcised, or even presented in the temple according to the Law? We will reply to him that *He came, not to abolish the law, but to fulfill it* (Mt. 5:17), in order not to be different from the fathers of whose race He was begotten. Thus the Jews may not excuse themselves and say: You are unlike our fathers, and therefore we are unwilling to believe in you.

What is the circumcision of Christ, dearest brethern, except our chastity, whereby God is delighted in us? For it behooves us to be circumcised, not in body, but in spirit; that is, every vice should be cut out of us so that we may be *holy and blameless in his sight* (Eph. 1:4), subduing desires of the flesh, *growing in the knowledge of God and multiplying good works of every sort* (Col. 1:10).

4. Ascension Day

John Chrysostom regarded the Ascension as an ancient and universal feast: according to Augustine it was celebrated throughout the world and, like the feast of Easter and Pentecost, originated with the apostles; for Egeria in Jerusalem around the same time, though possibly earliest in the circumstances, the feast was celebrated on the day of Pentecost, although she also mentions a fortieth day celebration:

[54]On the fortieth day after Easter—this is a Thursday— everyone goes to Bethlehem after the sixth hour of the day before, that is Wednesday, to celebrate the vigil.... On the

---

[54]Text: SC 296.297 = ACW 38.117

following day, Thursday, the feast of the fortieth day, the divine service is celebrated in the prescribed manner—the priests and the bishop delivering sermons appropriate to the day and the place.

> The difficulties of Chrysostom and Augustine remain; but it was not until the last quarter of the fourth century that the Ascension was celebrated as an historical event on the fortieth day, thereby enabling the gift of the Spirit to be celebrated as a separate feast on the fiftieth day. The development of the theology of the Spirit in Cappadocia and the fact of Christ, *appearing to them during forty days* (Acts 1:3), probably prompted a special feast for the Third Person of the Trinity—Pentecost Day, and another historical celebration for the Word made Flesh—namely Ascension Day.
>
> Both feasts are acknowledged by the Fathers of the late fourth century: John Chrysostom, on the one hand, in a Pentecost homily, delivered between 386 and 398, seems to attest a separate Ascension feast, in the East:

[55]Recently we have celebrated the feasts of the crucifixion, passion, and resurrection, and after this the Ascension of our Lord Jesus Christ into Heaven. Today we have come to the end of these blessings, to this metropolis of feasts, we have attained to the fruit of the Lord's promise. *For if I go away*, He said, *I will send you another Paraclete* (Jn. 14:16), and *I will not leave you orphans* (Jn. 14:18).

> On the other hand, Philastrius, bishop of Brescia, in his *Book of Different Heresies*, composed between 385 and 391 gives a list of the principal feasts for the West

[56]Four days of superior festivity have been instituted annually in order for our salvation: first, the Nativity, second, the Epiphany, that is, twelve days later; next, the Pasch, on

[55]Text: PG 50.463
[56]Text: CCL 9.304; cf. Cabié, 188-189, Talley 68

which He suffered, and finally the Ascension Day around Pentecost, which consummated His victory.

> Gregory of Nyssa may, as is thought, have been especially instrumental in the spread of this feast: certainly (preaching in 388), he is its earliest exponent:

[57]Today's celebration, sufficiently important in itself, is magnified by the joy brought to it by the apposite choice of David's psalms. In one of them he orders you to become a sheep being shepherded by God and lacking in no blessings. To you the good shepherd becomes the grass of pasturage, and the water of repose, nourishment, and shelter, and a beaten track, and a guide, and everything else, usefully allocating his favor for every eventuality. Through all of these things He educates His Church, for it is necessary for you first of all to become a sheep of the good shepherd, learning the way to the pasturage and fountains of divine teachings through good instruction so that you be buried with Him in death in baptism, and not be afraid of such a death.... Having gratified us with such thoughts in one of his psalms, David rouses our soul to greater and more perfect joy in the succeeding psalm. Let me explain, if you please, the thought of it to you, synopsizing it briefly. *To the Lord belong the earth and its fullness* (Ps. 24:1). What is strange, O man, if the Lord has appeared on earth, if He has lived with men? The earth is His foundation, He has made it. Therefore, there is nothing strange, nothing unbecoming, in the Lord coming unto His own. For He is not in somebody else's world, but in the one which He established, *He who founded the earth upon the seas* (Ps. 24:2) and provided it with a well-arranged passage of rivers.

What, then, is the reason for His presence among men? In order that He may banish you from the pits of sin and lead you to the mountain, using the chariot of the kingdom, that is, the virtuous way of life, for the ascent. For it is impossible to ascend to that mountain, unless the virtues are your fellow

[57]Text: PG 46.689

travellers, unless your hands are clean and you are unsullied by any wicked deed, pure in heart, directing your soul to no folly, and mounting no wicked stratagems against your neighbor. Benediction is the reward for this ascent (cf. Ps. 24:5). To this the Lord gives His stored up mercy. *This is the generation of those who seek him* (Ps. 24:6), of those who ascend on high through virtue, *of those seeking the face of the God of Jacob* (Ps. 24:6). The rest of this psalm is perhaps more sublime than the teaching of the Gospel itself.˙ For the Gospel tells of the Lord's stay on earth and His ascent to heaven. But this lofty prophet, surpassing himself, as if he were not burdened with the appendage of the body, mingles with the heavenly powers and narrates their words for us, when, in escorting the Lord on His return to heaven, they order the entrances of the earthly angels to be raised, those angels entrusted with the life of mortals, saying: *Raise your gates, principalities, and lift up, you eternal gates, for the king of glory will enter* (Ps. 24:7). . . .

You see how David has made our celebration more congenial, in mingling his gracious words with the heartfelt joy of the Church. Accordingly, let us, insofar as we can, imitate the prophet in charity towards God, in gentleness of life, in magnanimity toward those who hate us, so that the teaching of the prophet may escort us in our way of life to God, in Christ Jesus our Lord, to whom be glory , for ever and ever. Amen.

> In the same year that Gregory of Nyssa preached the Ascension in the East, Chromatius, the new Bishop of Aquileia, preached it in the Latin West:

[58]Today's solemnity has no small festive grace. For on this day, the fortieth after the resurrection, as you heard, dearly beloved, in the present reading, our Lord and Savior, in the presence of His disciples and in their full view ascended bodily into heaven. . . . Our flesh which was unwilling to reign in paradise reigns in heaven. It was the admiration and exaltation of the angels and the joy of the whole world, but the confusion

---

[58]Text: CCL 9A.33

and veritable damnation of the devil. Even David in the psalm shows this admiration of the angels at the Lord's ascension into heaven when he exclaims in such terms of wonder, saying, *Gates, raise your heads, rise, you ancient doors, let the king of glory in* (Ps. 24:7).

> For Augustine, "There are two glorifications of the Lord, according to His human nature: one, because He rose from the dead on the third day; the other, because He ascended into heaven before the eyes of His disciples.... There remains a third, which will also take place in the sight of men, when He will come to judge."[59] This embryonic theology of the Ascension can be seen developing in his five surviving sermons on the feast:

We are celebrating the feast of the Ascension:

[60]The Resurrection of the Lord is our hope; the Ascension of the Lord is our exaltation. Now today, we are celebrating the feast of the Ascension. If, therefore, we celebrate the Ascension of the Lord with due ceremony, with faith, devotion, holiness, and reverence, let us ascend with Him and let us have our hearts lifted up to Him. Moreover, though we ascend, let us not be lifted up.

On the fortieth day after His Resurrection:

[61]Today, therefore, we celebrate the day of His Ascension. In addition, this day marks a local solemnity for this particular Church. On this day the burial of holy Leontius, the founder of this basilica, took place. However, let the star deign to be obscured by the Sun, and therefore, as I had begun, let me choose to speak about the Lord. This good servant rejoices when the master is praised.

On this day, therefore, that is, on the fortieth day after His

[59]Cf. PL 38.1222

[60]Text: *ibid.* 1202 = FOTC 38.379

[61]Text: *ibid* 1208 = FOTC 38.388

Resurrection, the Lord ascended into heaven. We did not witness His Ascension, but let us believe. Those who did witness it proclaimed it and filled the entire world (with their preaching). You know that, concerning those who witnessed it and who told us about it, the Scripture had predicted: *There are no speeches nor languages, where their voices are not heard. Their sound hath gone forth into all the earth: and their words unto the ends of the world* (Ps. 19:4-5). Hence, their voices have reached us and have aroused us from sleep. Behold, this day is being celebrated throughout the whole world.

He ascended in order to protect us from heaven above:

[62]The glorification of our Lord Jesus Christ was completed by His Resurrection and Ascension. We celebrated His Resurrection on Easter Sunday; today we are celebrating His Ascension. Both feasts belong to us, for He rose again to give us a token of our resurrection; He ascended in order to protect us from heaven above. Hence, we have our Lord and Savior Jesus Christ hanging on a cross, now enthroned in heaven. He paid our price when He hung upon the cross; He gathers what He purchased when He sits enthroned in heaven. As a matter of fact, when He has collected all whom He will gather together throughout all time, He will come at the end of the world just as it is written: *God shall come manifestly* (Mt. 25:31), not as He came first, in obscurity, but, as the Scripture says, *manifestly*. For it was fitting that He should come in obscurity so that He might be judged; but He shall come manifestly when He is to pass judgment.

We cherish all this by faith:

[63]Even now, in truth, how great is His glory because He ascended into heaven, because He sits at the right hand of the Father! But we do not see this with our mortal eyes because we

---

[62]Text: *ibid.* 1209 = FOTC 38.391

[63]Text: *ibid.* 1210 = FOTC 38.393

did not see Him hanging on the cross. We cherish all this by faith; we see it with the eyes of our hearts. For on this day, my brethren, as you have heard, our Lord Jesus Christ ascended into heaven; may our hearts, too, ascend with Him. Let us hearken to the Apostle when he says: *If you have risen with Christ, seek the things that are above, where Christ is seated at the right hand of God. Mind the things that are above, not the things that are on the earth* (Col.3:1-2). For, just as He ascended into heaven without departing from us, so we, too, are already there with Him although that which He promised us has not yet been accomplished in our body. He has already been exalted above the heavens. Nor must we despair of reaching that perfect and angelic heavenly dwelling because of the fact that He said: *No one has ascended into heaven except Him who has descended from heaven: the Son of Man who is in heaven* (Jn. 3:13). But this was said on account of the unity by which He is our Head and we are His Body. Although He ascended into heaven, we are not separated from Him. He who descended from heaven does not begrudge it to us; on the contrary, He proclaims it in a certain manner: *Be My members if you wish to ascend into heaven* (Jn. 15:7). By this word let us be strengthened in the meantime.

The grace of Christ has been diffused throughout the world:

[64]In the use of the number forty to designate this period of time, a reference seems to be made to those who are called to grace through Him who came not to destroy the Law but to fulfill it. For, there are ten precepts of the Law. Now, the grace of Christ has been diffused throughout the world and the world is divided into four parts. Furthermore, when ten is multiplied by four, since those *that have been redeemed by the Lord He hath gathered out of the countries, from the rising and from the setting of the sun, from the north and from the south* (Ps. 107:2-4), the result is forty. Hence, He fasted for forty days before the death of His body as if to say: 'Abstain from the desires of the world,' but He ate and drank during the

[64]Text: *ibid.* 1211 = FOTC 38.395

forty days after the resurrection of His body as if to say: *Behold, I am with you . . . even to the consummation of the world* (Mt. 28:20).

Why do you stand looking up to heaven?

[65]He associated with them on earth for forty days, coming in and going out, eating and drinking, not because He needed to do so, but in order to manifest the truth. Therefore, on the fortieth day which we celebrate today, while they looked on and followed Him with their eyes, He ascended into heaven.

Then, therefore, they afterwards marveled at the fact that they saw Him ascending and they rejoiced that He went up to heaven, for the precedence of the Head is the hope of the members. Moreover, they heard the angelic message: *Men of Galilee, why do you stand looking up to heaven? This Jesus . . . shall come in the same way as you have seen Him going up to heaven* (Acts 1:11). what is the significance of *He shall come in the same way?* He shall come in that same form, so that the Scriptures may be fulfilled: *They shall look upon Him whom they have pierced* (Zach. 12:10). *He shall come in the same way.* He shall come to men; He shall come as a Man; but He shall come as the God-Man. He shall come as true God and true Man to make men like unto God. He has ascended as Judge of heaven; He has expressed Himself as Herald of heaven. Let us have a good cause so that we may not fear the judgment that is to come. As a matter of fact, He did ascend; those who announced it to us witnessed it. The people who did not see it believed; some incredulous persons mocked, *for not all men have the faith* (2 Thess. 3:2). Furthermore, because *not all men have the faith* and because *the Lord knows who are his* (2 Tim. 2:19), why do we take exception to the fact that God ascended into heaven? Rather, let us wonder that God decended into hell. Let us wonder at the death of Christ; but let us praise rather than wonder at His resurrection. Ours is the loss; ours is the sin; but the blood of Christ is our redemption.

[65]Text: *ibid.* 1219 = FOTC 38.409

Our ark is in the flood:

[66]Therefore, look upon this whole period of time which is presented to us as forty days, my brethren. As long as we are here on earth, during this entire period, our ark is in the flood. As long as Christians are baptized and cleansed through water, the ark seems to float upon the waves just as Noah's ark rested upon the water for forty days. But the Lord, remaining with His disciples for forty days, deigned to indicate that throughout this period faith in the Incarnation of Christ is necessary for all, since it is necessary for the weak.

> As with the resurrection we have two surviving sermons from Leo the Great on the Ascension. Samples from both will show the same preoccupaton on his part with the theological and pastoral implications of the developing feast.

From the first:

[67]Today, dearly beloved, marks the close of the forty days which followed the blessed and glorious resurrection of our Lord, Jesus Christ, in which by His divine power He restored in three days the true temple of God which had been destroyed by the impiety of the Jews. The number of holy days, ordained by a divine economy, and employed for the benefit of our instruction, is now complete. Its purpose was that the Lord by extending His bodily presence would strengthen with necessary proofs faith in His resurrection.

Therefore, beloved, these days which have elapsed between the resurrection and ascension of the Lord have not gone by aimlessly and leisurely; great mysteries have been confirmed during this period, great truths revealed. During this time the fear of harsh death has been taken away, and the immortality not just of the soul but of the body has been declared. During these days the Holy Spirit has been poured on all the apostles

[66]Text: *ibid.* 1216 = FOTC 38.404
[67]SC 74.135

by the Lord breathing on them (cf. Jn. 20:22), and on the blessed apostle, Peter, above the others, to whose care the Lord's flock is entrusted after he is given the keys of the kingdom. It was during these days that the Lord was joined as a third to the two disciples on the way (cf. Lk. 24:13) and, to remove from our eyes all the mists of doubt, He rebuked them for their slowness to believe as they feared and trembled. Their hearts were illuminated and took flame with faith, and those hearts which had been lukewarm became burning when He opened for them the Scriptures. In the breaking of bread also as they sat at table with Him their eyes were opened. The opening of the eyes of those to whom the glory of their nature has been manifested is a cause for greater joy than the opening of the eyes of the princes of this world on whom their crime brings confusion.

From the second:

[68]This faith, increased by the Lord's ascension and strengthened by the gift of the Holy Spirit, was not intimidated by chains, or prisons, or exile, or hunger, or fire, or wild beasts, or tortures devised by the cruelty of persecutors. On behalf of this faith not just men but women, not just young men but tender virgins, have contended throughout the world even to the shedding of their blood. This faith has cast out demons, banished diseases, raised the dead. Whence also the blessed apostles themselves, though strengthened by so many miracles and educated by so many discourses, has been terrified by the atrocity of the Lord's passion, and had only accepted the truth of the resurrection with misgivings. But they were so fortified by the Lord's ascension that whatever previously caused them fear was turned into joy. They had concentrated the entire contemplation of their souls on the divinity of the one sitting on the right hand of the Father and the sight of His body no longer hindered them from concentrating their mental agility on that which had not been taken away by descending from the Father, and had not departed by ascending from the disciples.

[68]Text: *ibid.* 139

The celebration on the separate days of Ascension and Pentecost, although in keeping with the Trinitarian and Christological developments of the time, fragmented the unity of the original Paschal season. Vigils and fasts were introduced for feasts and octaves, and early in the fifth century John Cassian warned: "The ten days between the Ascension and Pentecost must be celebrated with the same solemnity and joy as the forty days that precede them." The trend continued and in Gaul at the end of the century the rogation days or lesser litanies, days of fast, procession and intercessory prayers, were introduced for three days before the Ascension feast. A greater litany already existed in Rome for April 25th, to correct the abuses of Robigalia— the procession and intercession, made in honor of Robigus, God of Mildew, to protect the young growth from blight as Caesarius of Arles explains:

[69]Now days which are healing for the soul, that is, the Rogation Days, are approaching. On these days the wounds of sins which human frailty is wont to incur the rest of the time, with God's help, should be restored to their former health by means of prayers, vigils, fasting, and almsgivng. That is why I beseech and admonish you, brethren, and at the same time I warn you. On these three days, from the fourth to the sixth day of the week, no one should withdraw himself from the assembly in Church, unless perhaps some bodily infirmity does not permit him to come to Church. It ought to be enough for us, brethren, that throughout the space of the entire year we are busy with some bodily advantage or need; at least on these three days let us reflect more carefully on the salvation of our soul. Let each one arrange for a small meal to be prepared for himself as in Lent, and in order that the very fast may be helpful for his soul, he should give what he intended to eat to strangers or to the poor. The man who willingly listens to me and willingly fulfills what I am humbly suggesting will quickly rejoice over the good condition of his soul. But the man who acts otherwise will be doubly guilty, because he has both

[69]Text: CCL 104.836 = FOTC 66.92

despised his father who was humbly admonishing him and has not sought a remedy for his soul. We trust in God's mercy, however, that He will deign to inspire your hearts in such a way that you will be able to receive a reward because of your humble obedience. Therefore, dearly beloved, let us live in such a way that the days of healing may benefit us as a healing remedy, not as wounds. May He Himself help and assist us, who lives and reigns for ever and ever. Amen

5. Presentation Day

The fortieth day after Epiphany[70] is indeed celebrated here with the greatest solemnity. On that day there is a procession into the Anastasis, and all assemble there for the liturgy; and everything is performed in the prescribed manner with the greatest solemnity, just as on Easter Sunday. All the priests give sermons, and the bishop, too; and all preach on the Gospel text describing how on the fortieth day Joseph and Mary took the Lord to the temple, and how Simeon and Anna the prophetess, the daughter of Phanuel, saw Him, and what words they spoke on seeing the Lord, and of the offering which His parents brought. Afterwards, when all ceremonies have been performed in the prescribed manner, the Eucharist is then celebrated and the dismissal is given. (Egeria)

> This fortieth day celebration in Jerusalem seems to mark the end of an Epiphany quarantine there on February 14, forty-days after January 6, and was in keeping with the forty day seasons that were now surrounding the great feasts, as we shall see in a later chapter on the new seasons. The Church of Jerusalem observed this day as an extension of Epiphany—this Christ-centered feast of Hypapante, or meeting of the Messiah with Simeon the Just, and not as the Marian feast of the Purification. The creation of the feast is another example of the impact of the biblical sites on the making of the liturgical year.

[70]Text: SC 296.255 = ACW 38.96

By the middle of the fifth century the feast appears in
Rome on February 2, once more forty days after December
25, Christmas in the West, and in conjunction with a
candlelight procession. Again it was intended to replace an
ancient pagan procession of expiation, celebrated at the
beginning of February, in the form of a procession around
the boundaries of the city—a further example of biblical
event and cosmic experience.

Sophronius, Bishop of Jerusalem (633) expresses the
spirit of this feast, two centuries later, with its new
significance:

[71]Let us all run to meet Him, we who honor and venerate
the mystery of the Lord with pious devotion. Let us all go to
meet Him with eager minds. Let there be no one who does not
share in this meeting, let no one refuse to carry a light.

We add to this the bright shining of candles. In this way we
show forth the divine splendour of the coming of Him who
makes all things bright, in the abundance of whose eternal light
all things are bathed in light when the evil shadows have been
driven away. In this way we show the brightness of soul with
which we must go to meet Christ.

The most chaste Virgin Mother of God bore in her arms the
true light and came to the help of those who were lying in
darkness. In the same way we must hurry out to meet Him who
is truly light, enlightened by the beams of His brightness and
bearing in our hands the light which shines for all men.

Indeed this is the mystery which we celebrate, that the light
has come into the world and has given it light when it was
shrouded in darkness, and that the day-spring has visited us
from on high and given light to those who were sitting in
darkness. That is why we go in procession with lamps in our
hands and hasten, bearing lights showing both that the light
has shone upon us, and signifying the glory which is to come to
us through Him. Therefore let us all run together to meet God.

That true light, which enlightens every man coming into this
world (Jn. 1:9), has come. Brethren, let us all be enlightened,

[71]Text: PG 87.3291

let us all be filled with light.

Let none of us remain a stranger to this brightness, let no one who is filled with it continue in the darkness, but let us all go forth shining with light, let us all go together bright with that light to welcome with old Simeon that everlasting shining light. Rejoicing with Him in our souls, let us sing a hymn of thanks to the Begetter and Father of the light, who has sent the true light and driven away the darkness and made us all to shine with light.

For we too have seen through Him the salvation of God which He has prepared before the face of all peoples, and has shown forth for the glory of us who are the new Israel; and we have been freed at once from that mysterious and ancient sin just as Simeon was released from the bonds of this present life when he had seen Christ.

We have embraced Christ in faith as He came to us from Bethlehem, and have been made the people of God instead of Gentiles, for He is the salvation given us by our God and Father. We have seen God made flesh with our very eyes and we are called the New Israel now that we have seen the visible presence of God and have cradled Him in our minds. That presence we celebrate with a yearly festival: we shall never forget it.

> In the West the influence of Christmas replaced that of the Epiphany in the East, and eventually the feast of Hypapante became a Marian one, known as the Purification of the Blessed Virgin Mary on account of the Gospel reading of the day and centuries later became the Presentation of our Lord, popularly called Candlemas Day. But the notion of presentation as purification was already preached in Jerusalem in the fifth century by Hesychius (d. 450) in his homily *On Hypapante*—the oldest extant address on this feast which, as has been seen, originated in Jerusalem.

[72]This indeed is called the feast of the Purification nor would

[72]Text: PG 93.1467

anyone be mistaken who called this feast of feasts, or Sabbath of Sabbaths, the holyday of holydays.

Indeed the whole mystery of the Incarnation of Christ, the only-begotten Son of God, is recalled and proclaimed: on this day the child is lifted as Christ and confessed as God; the author of our nature is held high by human hands, presiding, as it were, on a throne.

> Although the spirit of the homily is clearly Christological and in keeping with the feast of Hypapante, nevertheless, the Marian dimension is no less obvious in the exposition of the letter of the Mosaic law governing the rite of purification:

[73]If, moreover, a woman should give birth to a daughter she shall be unclean for twice seven days. Why the doubled number?

Because an Eve is again born from Eve. A fragile vessel, a weak receptacle, a container pierced through, a leader of disobedience, a collaborator of the serpent. But as you have heard the complaint brought against the woman come now and learn what was done right by her. A woman brought virginity to life. She contained in her womb God whom creation cannot contain. She bore in the flesh Him who fashioned our race. A woman was the first to welcome Jesus from the dead (cf. Mk. 16:9), first to begin the proclamation of the resurrection (cf. Mk. 16:10), first to announce the joy to the disciples. *Any woman*, Scripture says, *who received seed* (Lev. 12:2). The Mother of God was indeed a woman. But she did not experience the things of women. Her womb did not know the plow. The virginal vine did not submit to the pruning fork so that the offering was made not for herself but for the whole (human) race. For the sake of us Christ is circumcised. For the sake of us He is also baptized. For us He fulfills the purifications of the law. If He weeps, He washes our nature. If He is scourged, He frees our captivity. If He carries the cross, He relieves us from the yoke of sin. If He is spat upon, He frees Adam from the spit of the curse.

[73]Text: *ibid.* 1470

Chapter Four

NEW WEEKS OF THE LORD

The creation story of Genesis, as has been seen, detached its week from the lunar month, and thereby established a calendar of successive, uninterrupted weeks, linked to the eternal God, and unconnected in origin with the phases of the moon. But by fixing Easter on the first Sunday after the first full moon of spring, the Council of Nicaea (325) restored to biblical time a lunar quality, which brought together into one, so to speak, two weeks that would otherwise have stood side by side. This is the night of which Scripture says, *The night will be as illumined as the day* (Ps. 139:12).[1] So night and day became in fourth-century Jerusalem Holy Week and Easter Week: "Let slaves rest from their work all the great week and let them do likewise throughout the week that follows; let them do the former in memory of the Passion and the latter in memory of the resurrection. There is a great need for instruction and they should know who it is that suffered and died, and who it is that raised them from the dead."[2] So spoke the *Apostolic Constitutions*.

In contrast with the eschatological expectations of earlier Christians, converts of this post-Constantinian age were concerned with the Jesus of history, and consequently with biblical times and places. Ceremonial, too, reflected this

---

[1] *Exultet, Missale Romanum*

[2] Text: PG 1.1133 = ANF 7.495

new trend and developed accordingly by fragmenting the unity of the ancient Paschal triduum into a triduum of Maundy Thursday, Good Friday and Holy Saturday in honor of the death and burial of Christ, and a triduum of Easter Sunday, Monday and Tuesday in honor of His resurrection and risen life. Holy Week and Easter Week belong to this new development of ritual as historical representation or re-enactment: the origin, growth and significance of each week form the main divisions of this chapter.

1. Holy Week

The death and resurrection of Christ took place at a time of fast and festival in Jerusalem. In Rome towards the end of that first century, public fast was a recognized form of worship, especially on Wednesdays and Fridays, which were known as Station days, or days of assembly, when Christians fasted and kept watch. In the *Shepherd of Hermas* we read:

³While fasting and sitting on a certain mountain, and giving thanks to the Lord for all His dealings with me, I see the Shepherd sitting down beside me, and saying, 'Why have you come hither (so) early in the morning?' 'Because, sir,'I answered, 'I have a station.''What is a station?' He asked. 'I am fasting, sir,' I replied. 'What is this fasting,' He continued, 'which you are observing?''As I have been accustomed, sir,' I reply, 'so I fast.''You do not know,' He says, 'how to fast unto the Lord: this useless fasting which you observe to Him is of no value.''Why sir,' I answered, 'do you say this?''I say to you,' He continued, 'that the fasting which you think you observe is not a fasting. But I will teach you what is a full and acceptable fasting to the Lord. 'Listen,' He continued: 'God does not desire such an empty fasting. For fasting to God in this way you will do nothing for a righteous life; but offer to God a fasting of the following kind: do no evil in your life, and serve

³Text: SC 53.225 = ANF 2.33

the Lord with a pure heart: keep His commandments, walking
in His precepts, and let no evil desire arise in your heart; and
believe in God. If you do these things, and fear Him, and
abstain from every evil thing, you will live unto God; and if you
do these things, you will keep a great fast, and one acceptable
before God.'

> In North Africa about a hundred years later a passionate
> controversy arose concerning the increasing number of fast
> days and the stricter forms of their observance. In his
> Montanist period Tertullian (d. 220) defended those
> excesses, and violently attacked those Catholics, "enthralled
> with voluptuousness and bursting with gluttony," who
> counselled moderation and invoked tradition:

⁴Some at all events . . . think that those days were definitely
appointed for fasts in which *the Bridegroom was taken away*
(Lk. 5:35); and that these are now the only legitimate days for
Christian fasts, the legal and prophetical observances of old
having been abolished: for wherever it suits their wishes, they
recognize what is the meaning of *the Law and the prophets
until John* (Mt. 11:13). Accordingly for them . . . fasting was
to be indifferently observed in the New Discipline; it was to be
of choice and not of command, according to the times and
needs of each individual: such in their opinion was the
observance of the apostles who imposed no obligation of
definite fasts . . . nor were the Stations imposed on the fourth
and sixth days binding on all in the same way . . . but
depended upon the judgment of each, especially as regards the
protraction of the fast beyond the last hour of the day.

> But even in this treatise on the nature and history of
> fasting, Tertullian never separates fast and festival:

⁵But if there is a new creation in Christ, our solemnities, too,
will be bound to be new: else, if the apostle has erased *all*

⁴Text: PL 2.956 = ANF 4.103
⁵Text: *ibid.* 977 = ANF 4.112

devotion absolutely *of seasons, and days, and months, and years* (Gal. 4:10), why do we celebrate the Passover by an *annual* rotation in the *first month*? Why in the *fifty* ensuing *days* do we spend our time in all exultation? Why do we devote to Stations the *fourth* and *sixth days of the week, and to fasts the preparation day*? Anyhow, you somtimes continue your Station even over the Sabbath—a day never to be kept as a fast except at the Passover season, according to a reason elsewhere given. With us, at all events, every day likewise is celebrated by an ordinary consecration. And it will not, then, be, in the eyes of the apostle, the differentiating principle—distinguishing (as he is doing) things new and old—which will be ridiculous; but (in this case, too) it will be your own unfairness, while you taunt us with the form of antiquity all the while you are laying against us the charge of novelty. (*On Fasting*)

> The same stress on the unity of fast and festival can be seen also in Irenaeus (c. 180), who, on the one hand, maintained that "this mystery of the Lord's resurrection should be observed only on the Lord's Day," and, on the other hand, accepted the position of the Quartodecimans concerning the different ways of celebrating the Paschal fast: Eusebius provides the reference:

[6]Churches of God, which maintain a more ancient custom, should not be cut off ... for this controversy not only concerns the day of the Pasch, but also concerns the very fast of the Pasch and the manner of the celebration. Some think they should fast for one day, others for two days, while others still think they should fast for more. Furthermore there are even those who reckon their day as consisting of forty hours—day and night. This variety in the observance of the fast for the Paschal feast did not originate in our time, but long before us in the days of our ancestors: indeed it is very likely that they did not hold to strict accuracy but rather went their own simple ways ... a good custom for their posterity for they lived in

[6]Text: SC 41.70

peace and harmony ... and their disagreement about the fast
only confirms their agreement about the faith.

> Fast and festival were integral parts of the original
> Paschal night celebrations, and together they symbolized in
> a single rite that transition from death to life that is the
> Pasch: the Quartodecimans continued this tradition and on
> the night of the Pasch concluded their fast with the festival
> of the eucharistic meal. But the widespread and growing
> practice of celebrating the new Pasch on the Lord's Day
> after the Pasch of Israel loosened the bond of fast and
> festival, and began the triduum of the death, burial and
> resurrection, which naturally involved two days of fast and
> mourning in preparation for the festival day of rejoicing.
> Soon there followed a fast of six days as the triduum was
> transformed by the power of the week, which remained in
> the Church the basic unit of time that it was in Israel. This
> six-day fast is mentioned by Dionysius of Alexandria
> (c.250): for him it was desirable, but, unlike the more
> ancient fast of two days, it was not of obligation. A more
> detailed description of this six-day fast is found in the
> *Didascalia* (c.250):

[7]And so in the night when the fourth day of the week drew
on, (Judas) betrayed our Lord to them. But they made the
payment to Judas on the tenth of the month, on the second day
of the week; wherefore they were accounted by God as though
on the second day of the week they had seized Him....
Therefore you shall fast in the days of the Pasch from the
tenth, which is the second day of the week; and you shall
sustain yourselves with bread and salt and water only, at the
ninth hour, until the fifth day of the week. But on the Friday
and on the Sabbath fast wholly, and taste nothing....
Especially incumbent on you therefore is the fast of the
Friday and of the Sabbath....
Fast on the Friday, because thereon the People killed

---

[7]Cf. Connolly, *Didascalia Apostolorum*, 189

themselves in crucifying our Savior; and on the Sabbath also, because it is the sleep of our Lord; for it is a day which ought especially to be kept with fasting ... for Moses bound them beforehand with mourning perpetually, in that he set apart and appointed the Sabbath for them. For they deserved to mourn, because they denied their Life, and laid hands upon their Savior and delivered Him to death. Wherefore, already from that time there was laid upon them a mourning for their destruction.

But let us observe and see, brethren, that most men in their mourning imitate the Sabbath; and they likewise who keep Sabbath imitate mourning. For he that mourns kindles no light: neither do the People on the Sabbath, because of the commandment of Moses; for so it was commanded them by him. He that mourns takes no bath: nor yet the People on the Sabbath. He that mourns does not prepare a table; neither do the People on the Sabbath, but prepare and lay for themselves the evening before because they have a presentiment of mourning, seeing that they were to lay hands on Jesus. He that mourns does no work, and does not speak, but sits in sorrow: so, too, the People of the Sabbath; for it was said to the People concerning the mourning on the Sabbath thus: *Thou shalt not lift thy foot to do any work* (Ex. 20:10), and *thou shalt speak no word out of thy mouth* (Deut. 5:14).

> In this new fast of six days the notion of the week prevails, even though a new triduum of Maundy Thursday, Good Friday and Holy Saturday preserves a certain unity, identity, and prominence. Here then is also evidence from the third century of the Church's new attitude to history that would follow the Peace of Constantine (313), as each day of this week of fast is linked to an historical episode of the passion. Furthermore the Council of Nicaea (325), by fixing the date of Easter on the first Sunday after the first full moon of spring, confirmed this ritual separation of Christ's death and resurrection; thus fast and ceremonial were now free to present in a week-long ritual the mystery of Christ's redemptive death in preparation for the festival of His resurrection. Epiphanius (c.377), the bishop of Salamis,

gives a clear picture of this developing week with its days of fast, its vigils and different services, which everywhere appeared in the latter half of the fourth century:

[8]Throughout the six days of the Pasch, all the peoples persevere in strict abstinence—I mean they then partake of bread and salt and water towards evening. But the zealous fast completely for two, three or four days together, and some the whole week until cockcrow at dawn on Easter Day. They observe vigils on the six days, and again they hold services the same six days and throughout the whole of Lent, from three in the afternoon until evening. But in some cases they have vigils on Thursday evening until dawn on Friday, and on Saturday evening until dawn on Easter Day. And in some places the Eucharist is celebrated on Thursday at 3 p.m., and so the people are dismissed and continue in the same strict abstinence. But in other places the Eucharist is not celebrated except at dawn on Easter Day.

At this very time there developed in Jerusalem, probably under the influence of Cyril (313-386), the bishop, a liturgy of Holy Week, that reflected the time and place interests of the new age. Egeria in *her Diary* describes in great detail this new drama of redemption, which she experienced there as a pilgrim towards the end of the fourth century:

[9]The following day, Sunday, marks the beginning of Holy Week, which they call here the Great Week. On this Sunday morning, at the completion of those rites which are customarily celebrated at the Anastasis or the Cross from the first cockcrow until dawn, everyone assembles for the liturgy according to custom in the major Church, called the Martyrium. It is called the Martyrium because it is on Golgotha, behind the Cross, where the Lord suffered His Passion, and is therefore a shrine of martyrdom. As soon as

[8]Text: PG 42.364
[9]Text: SC 296.271 = ACW 38.103

everything has been celebrated in the major church as usual, but before the dismissal is given, the archdeacon raises his voice and first says: 'Throughout this whole week, beginning tomorrow at the ninth hour, let us all gather in the Martyrium, in the major Church.' Then he raises his voice a second time, saying: 'Today let us all be ready to assemble at the seventh hour at the Eleona.' When the dismissal has been given in the Martyrium or major Church, the bishop is led to the accompaniment of hymns to the Anastasis, and there all ceremonies are accomplished which customarily take place every Sunday at the Anastasis following the dismissal from the Martyrium. Then everyone retires to his home to eat hastily, so that at the beginning of the seventh hour everyone will be ready to assemble in the church on the Eleona, by which I mean the Mount of Olives, where the grotto in which the Lord taught is located.

At the seventh hour all the people go up to the church on the Mount of Olives, that is, to the Eleona. The bishop sits down, hymns and antiphons appropriate to the day and place are sung, and there are likewise readings from the Scriptures. As the ninth hour approaches, they move up, chanting hymns, to the Imbomon, that is, to the place from which the Lord ascended into heaven; and everyone sits down there. When the bishop is present, the people are always commanded to be seated, so that only the deacons remain standing. And there hymns and antiphons proper to the day and place are sung, interspersed with appropriate readings from the Scriptures and prayers.

As the eleventh hour draws near, that particular passage from Scripture is read in which the children bearing palms and branches came forth to meet the Lord, saying: *Blessed is He who comes in the name of the Lord* (Mt. 21:9; Ps. 118:26). The bishop and all the people rise immediately, and then everyone walks down from the top of the Mount of Olives, with the people preceding the bishop and responding continually with *Blessed is He who comes in the name of the Lord* (Mt. 21:9; Ps. 118:26) to the hymns and antiphons. All the children who are present here, including those who are not yet able to walk because they are too young and therefore are carried on their parents' shoulders, all of them bear branches, some carrying palms; others, olive branches. And the bishop is led in the same manner as the Lord once was led. From the top of the mountain as far as the city, and from there through the entire city as far as the Anastasis, everyone accompanies the bishop the whole way on foot, and this includes distinguished ladies and men of consequence, reciting the responses all the while; and they move very slowly so that the people will not tire. By the time they arrive at the Anastasis, it is already evening. Once they have arrived there, even though it is evening, vespers is celebrated; then a prayer is said at the Cross and the people are dismissed.

> For the most part this Sunday order was continued on the Monday, Tuesday and Wednesday of the Great Week. In Egeria's *Diary* the dynamics of the age and place can be easily felt: hence the inclusion here of her detailed description of the Passion triduum:

[10]On Thursday whatever is customarily done from the first cockcrow until morning and what is done at the third and sixth hours takes place at the Anastasis. At the eighth hour all the people gather as usual at the Martyrium, earlier, however, than on other days, because the dismissal must be given more quickly. When all the people have assembled, the prescribed rites are celebrated. On that day the sacrifice is offered at the Martyrium, and the dismissal from there is given around the tenth hour. Before the dismissal is given, however, the archdeacon raises his voice, saying: 'At the first hour of the night let us assemble at the church which is on the Eleona, for much toil lies ahead of us on this day's night.' Following the dismissal from the Martyrium, everyone proceeds behind the Cross, where, after a hymn is sung and a prayer is said, the bishop offers the sacrifice and everyone receives Communion. Except on this one day, throughout the year the sacrifice is never offered behind the Cross save on this day alone. The dismissal is given there, and everyone goes to the Anastasis,

[10]Text: *ibid.* 278 = ACW 38

where a prayer is said, the catechumens as well as the faithful are blessed, as is customary, and the dismissal is given.

Everyone then hurries home to eat, because, immediately after having eaten, everyone goes to the Eleona, to the church where the grotto in which the Lord gathered with His disciples on that day is located. And there, until around the fifth hour of the night, they continually sing hymns and antiphons and read the scriptural passages proper to the place and to the day. Between these, prayers are said. Moreover, they read those passages from the Gospels in which the Lord spoke to His disciples on that day while sitting in the same grotto which lies within this Church. And from here, around the sixth hour of the night, everyone goes up to the Imbomon, singing hymns. That is the place from which the Lord ascended into heaven. There also they sing hymns and antiphons and read scriptural passages proper to the day; and whatever prayers are said, whatever prayers the bishop recites, they will always be proper to the day and to the place.

As soon as it begins to be the hour of cockcrow, everyone comes down from the Imbomon singing hymns and proceeds toward the very place where the Lord prayed, as it is written in the Gospel: *And He went as far as a stone's throw and He prayed* (Lk. 22:41), and so forth. On that spot stands a tasteful church. The bishop and all the people enter there, where a prayer fitting to the day and the place is said, followed by an appropriate hymn, and a reading of that passage from the Gospel where He said to His disciples: *Watch, that you enter not into temptation* (Mk. 14:38). The whole of this passage is read there, and a second prayer is then said. Next, everyone, including the smallest children, walk down from there to Gethsemani, accompanying the bishop with hymns. Singing hymns, they come to Gethsemani very slowly on account of the great multitude of people, who are fatigued by vigils and exhausted by the daily fasts, and because of the rather high mountain they have to descend. Over two hundred Church candles are ready to provide light for all the people.

On arriving in Gethsemani a suitable prayer is first said, followed by a hymn, and then the passage from the Gospel describing the arrest of the Lord is read. During the reading of this passage there is such moaning and groaning with weeping from all the people that their moaning can be heard practically as far as the city. And from that hour everyone goes back on foot to the city singing hymns, and they arrive at the gate at the hour when men can begin to recognize one another. From there, throughout the center of the city, all without exception are ready at hand, the old and the young, the rich and the poor, everyone; and on this day especially no one withdraws from the vigil before early morning. It is in this fashion that the bishop is led from Gethsemani to the gate, and from there through the whole city to the Cross.

When they finally arrive before the Cross, it is already beginning to be broad daylight. There then is read the passage from the Gospel where the Lord is led before Pilate, and whatsoever words are written that Pilate spoke to the Lord or to the Jews, all this is read. Afterwards, the bishop addresses the people, comforting them, since they have labored the whole night and since they are to labor again on this day, admonishing them not to grow weary, but to have hope in God who will bestow great graces on them for their efforts. And comforting them as he can, he addresses them saying: 'Go, for the time being, each of you, to your homes; sit there awhile, and around the second hour of the day let everyone be on hand here so that from that hour until the sixth hour you may see the holy wood of the cross, and thus believe that it was offered for the salvation of each and every one of us. From the sixth hour on we will have to assemble here, before the Cross, so that we may devote ourselves to prayers and scriptural readings until nightfall.'. . . .

After this, following the dismissal from the Cross, which occurs before sunrise, everyone now stirred up goes immediately to Sion to pray at the pillar where the Lord was whipped. Returning from there then, everyone rests for a short time in his own house, and soon all are ready. A throne is set up for the bishop on Golgotha behind the Cross, which now stands there. The bishop sits on his throne, a table covered with a linen cloth is set before him, and the deacons stand around the table. The gilded silver casket containing the sacred wood of the cross is brought in and opened. Both the wood of the cross and the inscription are taken out and placed on the table. As soon as they have been placed on the table, the bishop, remaining seated, grips the ends of the sacred wood with his hands, while the deacons, who are standing about, keep watch over it. There is a reason why it is guarded in this manner. It is the practice here for all the people to come forth one by one, the faithful as well as the catechumens, to bow down before the table, kiss the holy wood, and then move on. It is said that someone (I do not know when) took a bite and stole a piece of the holy cross. Therefore, it is now guarded by the deacons standing around, lest there be anyone who would dare come and do that again. . . .

All the people pass through one by one; all of them bow down, touching the cross and the inscription, first with their foreheads, then with their eyes; and, after kissing the cross, they move on. No one, however, puts out his hand to touch the cross. As soon as they have kissed the cross and passed on through, a deacon, who is standing, holds out the ring of Solomon and the phial with which the kings were anointed. They kiss the phial and venerate the ring from more or less the second hour; and thus until the sixth hour all the people pass through, entering through one door, exiting through another. All this occurs in the place where the day before, on Thursday, the sacrifice was offered. . . .

When the sixth hour is at hand, everyone goes before the Cross, regardless of whether it is raining or whether it is hot. This place has no roof, for it is a sort of very large and beautiful courtyard lying between the Cross and the Anastasis. The people are so clustered together there that it is impossible for anything to be opened. A chair is placed for the bishop before the Cross, and from the sixth to the ninth hours nothing else is done except the reading of passages from Scripture. . . .

First, whichever psalms speak of the Passion are read. Next, there are readings from the apostles, either from the epistles of the apostles or the Acts, wherever they speak of the Passion of the Lord. Next, the texts of the Passion from the Gospels are read. Then there are readings from the prophets, where they said that the Lord would suffer; and then they read from the Gospels, where He foretells the Passion. And so, from the sixth to the ninth hour, passages from Scripture are continuously read and hymns are sung, to show the people that whatever the prophets had said would come to pass concerning the Passion of the Lord can be shown, both through the Gospel and the writings of the apostles, to have taken place. And so, during those three hours, all the people are taught that nothing happened which was not first prophesied, and that nothing was prophesied which was not completely fulfilled. Prayers are continually interspersed, and the prayers themselves are proper to the day. At each reading and at every prayer, it is astonishing how much emotion and groaning there is from all the people. There is no one, young or old, who on this day does not sob more than can be imagined for the whole three hours, because the Lord suffered all this for us. After this, when the ninth hour is at hand, the passage is read from the Gospel according to Saint John where Christ gave up His spirit. After this reading, a prayer is said and the dismissal is given...

As soon as the dismissal has been given from before the Cross, everyone gathers together in the major church, the Martyrium, and there everything which they have been doing regularly throughout this week from the ninth hour when they came together at the Martyrium, until evening, is then done. After the dismissal from the Martyrium, everyone comes to the Anastasis, and, after they have arrived there, the passage from the Gospel is read where Joseph seeks from Pilate the body of the Lord and places it in a new tomb. After this reading a prayer is said, the catechumens are blessed, and the faithful as well; then the dismissal is given....

On this day no one raises his voice to say the vigil will be continued at the Anastasis, because it is known that the people are tired. However, it is the custom that the vigil be held there. And so, those among the people who wish, or rather those who are able, to keep the vigil, do so until dawn; whereas those who are not able to do so, do not keep watch there. But those of the clergy who are either strong enough or young enough, keep watch there, and hymns and antiphons are sung there all through the night until morning. The greater part of the people keep watch, some from evening on, others from midnight, each one doing what he can. . . .

On the following day, which is Saturday, there is as usual a service at the third hour and again at the sixth hour. There is not service, however, at the ninth hour on Saturday, for preparation is being made for the Easter vigil in the major church, the Martyrium.

> In this century of historical interest, pilgrimages, especially to the biblical sites, became popular, and Gregory of Nyssa (335-395), who visited Jerusalem about the same time as Egeria, wrote a short treatise entitled *Pilgrimages*: the contrast is interesting between the experience of the bishop and that of the nun, if indeed a nun the good lady was:

[11]When the Lord invites the blest to their inheritance in the kingdom of heaven, He does not include among their good deeds a pilgrimage to Jerusalem: . . . indeed the inns, hosteleries and cities of the East are so given to license and vice that it is not possible to pass through such smoke without at least smarting the eyes. . . . What advantage, moreover, is had by him who reaches those celebrated spots themselves? He cannot imagine that our Lord is living, in the body, there at the present time . . . or that the Holy Spirit is everywhere in Jerusalem, but unable to travel as far as us. Whereas, if it is really possible to infer God's presence from visible symbols, one might more justly consider that He dwells in the Cappadocian nation more than in any of the spots outside it. For how many altars are there here on which the name of the Lord is glorified! One could hardly count so many in all the rest of the world. Again, if the divine grace was more abundant in Jerusalem than elsewhere, sin would not be so much the fashion among those that live there; but as it is, there is no form of uncleanness that is not perpetrated amongst them; rascality, adultery, theft, idolatry, poisoning, quarrelling, murder, are rampant and rife; and the last kind of evil is so excessively prevalent, that nowhere in the world are people so ready to kill each other as there; where kinsmen attack each other like wild beasts, and

[11]Text: G. Pasquali, ed. *Gregorii Nysseni Epistulae*, Leiden, 1959, 14-19

spill each other's blood, merely for the sake of lifeless plunder. Well, in a place where such things go on, what proof, I ask, have you of the abundance of divine grace?...

We confess that the Christ who was made manifest is very God, as much before as after our sojourn at Jerusalem; our faith in Him was not increased afterwards any more than it was diminished. Before we saw His grave we believed in His resurrection from the dead; apart from seeing the Mount of Olives, we confessed that His Ascension into heaven was real. We derived only this much of profit from our travelling thither, namely that we came to know by being able to compare them, that our own places are far holier than those abroad. Wherefore, O ye who fear the Lord, praise Him in the places where ye now are. Change of place does not effect any drawing nearer unto God, but wherever you may be, God will come to you, if the chambers of your soul are of such a sort that He can dwell in you and walk in you. But if you keep your inner man full of wicked thoughts, even if you were on Golgotha, or the Mount of Olives, or even on the memorial rock of the resurrection, you will be as far away from receiving Christ into yourself, as one who has not even begun to confess Him. Therefore, my beloved friend, counsel the brethren to be absent from the body to go to our Lord, rather than to be absent from Cappadocia to go to Palestine.

> Nevertheless the pilgrimage to Jerusalem continued and certainly inspired the spread of the historical representation of redemption throughout the Christian world, in the East and the West, in a week of fast and ceremonial, that was known throughout as holy and great. The ceremonial of this week naturally differed from place to place depending on the emphasis: but the spirit of the week was everywhere the same, aroused as it was by the same selection of Scripture, whether in the catechumenate of Cyril in Jerusalem or of Ambrose in Milan. These common Scriptures were preached by the Greek and Latin Fathers within the framework of a ceremonial fast of mourning in preparation for the festival of rejoicing. By looking briefly at the characteristics of the principal days of this new week, as expressed by the Fathers,

we can come to a greater understanding of the week as a whole.

PALM SUNDAY

The distinctive feature of Palm Sunday, according to Egeria, was the procession of palms and the reading of Matthew's Gospel account of Jesus entering Jerusalem. Already in Origen one can see the allegorical approach that will so well suit the preaching of this New Week: "And Jesus sat upon the garments of those who by their preaching instructed both the ass and the colt, that is the Jews and the Gentiles... and along the way the great multitude placed their garments ... so that all might go up to Jerusalem through places that were free of earth and earthly things and unstained by its dust."[12] To a certain Methodius, a distinguished adversary of Origen (d.253), is wrongly attributed a homily placing this biblical event on a definite day:

[13]Let us all receive Him gladly, and hold our feast with all honesty. Instead of our garments, let us strew our hearts before Him, in psalms and hymns, let us raise to Him our shouts of thanksgiving; and, without ceasing, let us exclaim, *Blessed is He that cometh in the name of the Lord* (Mt. 21:9; Ps. 118:26) for blessed are they that bless Him, and cursed are they that curse Him. Again I will say it, nor will I cease exhorting you to good: Come, beloved, let us bless Him who is blessed, that we may be ourselves blessed of Him. Every age and condition does this discourse summon to praise the Lord; kings of the earth, and all people; princes, and all judges of the earth; both young men and maidens—and what is new in this miracle, the tender and innocent age of babes and sucklings hath obtained the first place in raising to God with thankful confession the hymn which was of God taught them in the strains in which Moses sang before to the people when they came forth out of

[12]Cf. PG 13.1458
[13]Text: PG 18.384 = ANF 6.294

Egypt—namely, *Blessed is He that cometh in the name of the Lord* (Mt. 21:9; Ps. 118:26). . . .

Today, holy David rejoices with great joy, being by babes despoiled of his lyre, with whom also, in spirit, leading the dance, and rejoicing together, as of old, before the Ark of God, he mingles musical harmony, and sweetly lisps out in stammering voice, *Blessed is He that cometh in the name of the Lord* (Mt. 21:9; Ps. 118:26). Of whom shall we inquire? Tell us, O prophet, who is this that cometh in the name of the Lord? He will say it is not my part today to teach you, for He hath consecrated the school to infants, who hath out of the mouth of babes and sucklings perfected praise to destroy the enemy and the avenger, in order that by the miracle of these the hearts of the fathers might be turned to the children, and the disobedient unto the wisdom of the just. Tell us, then, O children, whence is this, your beautiful and graceful contest of song?

> The allegorical approach of Origen and the Alexandrians to the Scriptures was well suited to the developing liturgy of Holy Week and can be seen clearly in Ambrose's *Commentary on Palm Sunday:*

[14]And He was in a village, and a colt was tied there and an ass; it could not be loosed save by the command of the Lord. An apostolic hand loosed it. Such was the means, such the life, such the grace. Be you of such a kind: that you also may loose those that are bound. . . . Now let us ponder who they were, who, discovered in sin, were cast out of paradise, and banished to a village. And see how Life recalls those whom death had driven forth. And so we read, according to Matthew, *an ass* and *a colt* (Mt. 21:2-11), so that as in the person of two human beings each sex was driven out, in the two animals either sex is recalled. Consequently in the mother ass we have a figure of Eve who erred; in the colt a figure of the people of the Gentiles. And He is seated on the colt of the ass; and, rightly, *on which no man ever hath ridden* (Lk. 19:30): because no man before

[14]Text: PL 15.1795

Christ had called the people of the Gentiles into the Church. And Mark too has the same: *Upon which no man yet hath ridden* (Mk. 11:2). It was, however, held fast tied by the bonds of unbelief, in bondage to an evil master, enslaved by falsehood: but he had no just claim to dominion whom guilt, not nature, had made master. And because of this when Lord is said, One only is held true Lord: for there are many gods and many lords; but for us there is but One Lord and One God. And though He is not named as Lord, yet is it indicated, not by conjunction of a person, but through community of nature. . . .

Mark introduces the beast as, *bound before the gate without* (Mk. 11:4): for whosoever is outside of Christ is without in the way; but he that is in Christ is not outside in the way. In the meeting of two ways, he adds, where he is the certain possession of no one; and there is no stall, no roof, no manger. Unhappy the servitude with none but uncertain rights: for he that has no master will have many. Strangers will tie him fast, to make him theirs. Another frees him, that he may keep him for himself; so he makes acquaintance with harsher gifts than fetters.

> On the other hand, Chrysostom was more literal, but in a sense no less figurative, for clearly he goes beyond the text to a deeper meaning:

[15]He said: *You shall find an ass* (Mt. 21:2). He foretells that no one will oppose them; and that those who would hear them would say nothing. This was no light condemnation of the Jews, that He persuades men who knew Him not at all, and whom He had not seen, to give up without a word what was theirs, and this through His disciples. Yet this people refused to obey Him when He performed signs and wonders in their presence. . . .

Do not look upon what happened on this occasion as being of slight importance. For who was it persuaded them not to oppose the disciples when their property was taken from them: poor men that they were, and tillers of the soil? What am I

[15]Text: PG 58.627

saying, not to oppose them? Not even to answer, or, at least, having answered them to fall silent and yield? For both facts are alike wonderful; that they said nothing when their beasts were taken away, and that when they heard that the Lord had need of them they yielded and did not oppose them; especially since they did not see the Lord Himself, but only His disciples. From this He teaches us that He could have restrained the Jews, even against their will, when they were getting ready to lay hands on Him; and could have stricken them dumb. But He willed not to. From this He likewise teaches His disciples, that whatsoever He might ask of them they should give. Even should He bid them give up life itself, even that must not be denied.

> "By this ass," said Jerome, "we are to understand the synagogue, which was tamed and broken to the yoke, and had borne the yoke of the Law. The colt of the ass, wanton and unbroken, is the people of the Gentiles, upon whom Christ sat, and His two disciples were sent, one to the circumcision, and the other to the Gentiles."[16]
>
> Although Palm Sunday was observed in Milan in the fourth century, in Spain in the fifth, in Gaul in the seventh, and in England at the beginning of the eighth century, it was not admitted into Rome until the twelfth century. Hence in Rome the emphasis from the time of Pope Leo was on this day as the first day of the Passion, and not as the day of palms:

[17]And when morning was come all the chief priests and elders of the people took counsel against Jesus to put Him to death.... After this condemnation of Christ, brought about more by the cowardice than the power of Pilate,... the license of the people, obedient to the looks of the priests, heaped many insults on the Lord, and the frenzied mob wreaked its rage on Him, who meekly and voluntarily endured it all. But because, dearly-beloved, the whole story is too long to go through

[16]Cf. PL 26.147
[17]Text: PL 54.322

today, let us put off the rest till Wednesday, when the reading
of the Lord's Passion will be repeated.

SPY WEDNESDAY

> Wednesday, the fast day of the *Didache*, and the Station
> day of the *Shepherd of Hermas,* became in the *Didascalia*
> (c.250) the day of the betrayal, popularly translated in
> English as Spy Wednesday:

[18]For while He was yet with us before He suffered, as we
were eating the Passover with Him, He said to us: *Today, in
this night, one of you will betray me* (Mt. 26:21)....

Now this was done on the fourth day of the week. For when
we had eaten the Passover on the third day of the week at even,
we went forth to the Mount of Olives; and in the night they
seized our Lord Jesus. And the next day, which was the fourth
of the week, He remained in the house of Caiaphas the high
priest....

Fast, therefore, not after the custom of the former people,
but according to the New Testament which I have appointed
you: that you may be fasting for them on the fourth day of the
week, because on the fourth of the week they began to destroy
their souls, and apprehended Me. For the night after the third
of the week belongs to the fourth of the week, as it is written:
There was evening and there was morning, one day (Gen.
1:5).... And so in the night when the fourth day of the week
drew on, Judas betrayed our Lord to them.

> In Jerusalem at the end of the fourth century the
> ceremonial of Monday and Tuesday was repeated on the
> Wednesday, according to Egeria, with the additional
> reading of Judas bargaining with the Jews on the price of
> betrayal. In Rome, on the other hand, there is less
> ceremonial, and Monday and Tuesday were not days of
> assembly: hence Pope Leo (c.440) had to await the

[18]Cf. Connolly, *op. cit.* 181

Wednesday Station, or assembly, to complete the exposition of the Passion begun on the previous Sunday:

[19]In speaking but lately of the Lord's Passion, we reached the point in the Gospel story, where Pilate is said to have yielded to the Jews' wicked shouts that Jesus should be crucified. And so when all things had been accomplished, which the Godhead, veiled in frail flesh, permitted, Jesus Christ the Son of God was fixed to the cross which He had also been carrying, two robbers being similarly crucified, one on His right hand, and the other on the left: so that even in the incidents of the cross might be displayed that difference which in His judgment must be made in the case of all men; for the believing robber's faith was a type of those who are to be saved, and the blasphemer's wickedness prefigured those who are to be damned. Christ's Passion, therefore, contains the mystery of our salvation, and of the instrument which the iniquity of the Jews prepared for His punishment, the Redeemer's power has made for us the stepping-stone to glory.

All Leo's Passion sermons end abruptly on the Sunday with the promise of resuming on the Wednesday following: for example, on Sunday he concludes: "From this point, dearly-beloved, our sermon must pass to the consideration of the details of the Lord's Passion, and lest we should burden you with prolixity, we will divide our common task, and put off the rest till the fourth day of the week."[20] On the following Wednesday he resumes: "Having discoursed, dearly beloved, in our last sermon, on the events which preceded the Lord's arrest, it now remains, by the help of God's grace, to discuss, as we promised, the details of the Passion itself."[21]

[19]Text: PL 54.323
[20]Cf. *ibid.* 337
[21]Cf. *ibid.* 337

HOLY THURDSAY

The practice of antiquity in reckoning the beginning of a day from the previous evening naturally brought Holy Thursday into the triduum of the death, burial and resurrection. But the ceremonial embellishment of this day that took place in the fourth century contributed greatly to the new triduum of Maundy Thursday, Good Friday and Holy Saturday. Maundy, from the Mandatum or new commandment of Christ concerning the washing of the feet, describes the Thursday of this ritual: but the rite probably originated in the West, with the exception of Rome, as part of the rite of baptism and consequently was performed on the Saturday. Ambrose is our witness:

[22]We are not unaware of the fact that the Church in Rome does not have this custom, whose character and form we follow in all things. Yet it does not have the custom of washing the feet. So note: perhaps on account of the multitude this practice declined. Yet there are some who say, and try to allege in excuse, that this is not to be done in the mystery, nor in baptism, nor in regeneration, but the feet are to be washed as for a guest. But one belongs to humility, the other to sanctification. Finally, be aware that the mystery is also sanctification: *If I wash not thy feet, thou shalt have no part with me* (Jn. 13:8). So I say this, not that I may rebuke others, but that I may commend my own ceremonies. In all things I desire to follow the Church in Rome, yet we, too, have human feeling; what is preserved more rightly elsewhere we, too, preserve more rightly.

In Jerusalem the *Mandatum* on Holy Thursday appeared in the fifth century. In the West the spread of the Roman liturgy caused the Saturday rite of Ambrose to disappear gradually, but it came into use again in monasteries, as a service to the brethren and to the poor, and was ordered by the Council of Toledo (694) for the Churches of Spain and

[22]Text: PL 16.433 = FOTC 44.291

Gaul for Holy Thursday. On this custom Augustine comments:

²³Concerning the washing of feet, although the Lord commended it as a form of the humility which He had come to teach, the question is raised about the time when such a great practice should best be taught by example, and it coincided with that time at which His teaching made a deeper religious appeal. Many have been unwilling to accept it as a custom, lest it should seem to be a part of the sacrament of baptism. Some have not even shrunk from abolishing it as a custom. But others, in order to promote it at a less conspicuous time, and to separate it from the sacrament of baptism, have chosen to do it either on the third day of the octave—because the number three has such pre-eminence in many sacraments—or on the octave day itself. . . .

I wonder why you wanted me to write you some comments on customs which vary in different places, since there is no obligation about them, and there is one completely safe rule to be followed in such things, namely, when they are not contrary to faith or morals, and they have some effect in encouraging us to a better life, wherever we see them in use, or know that they are used, we do not censure them, but support them by our approval and imitation—all this, of course, unless they might cause harm to others whose faith is weak.

But the dominant feature of this day from the fourth century was the celebration of the Eucharist, which was not celebrated on any other day of this week. According to Egeria, as has been seen, it was celebrated twice on this day in Jerusalem and this custom is also found in Africa in the time of Augustine (c. 400), and occasioned his comments on liturgical custom and diversity of practice:

²⁴What ought to be done on the Thursday of the last week of Lent? Is the Sacrifice to be offered in the morning and again

²³Text: PL 33.220 = FOTC 12.289
²⁴Text: *ibid.* 202-203 = FOTC 12.257

after supper, because it is said, *In like manner after He had supped* (1 Cor. 11:25), or is one to remain fasting and offer it only after supper, or is one to fast and then to sup after the offering as we are used to doing? To this, therefore, I make the answer that, if the authority of the divine Scripture prescribes which of these is to be done, there is no doubt that we should do as we read, and that our discussion should turn not on how it is to be administered, but on how the sacrament is to be understood; likewise, if any of these customs is common to the whole Church throughout the world, it is the most unheard of madness to doubt that such custom is to be followed. But, what you ask belongs to neither of these suppositions. It follows, then, that it is of that third sort which varies according to locality and country. Let each one, then, do what he finds in that church which he attends.

GOOD FRIDAY

The Friday of Preparation, now called Good, in English, was honored in the second century with a fast according to Irenaeus. Early in the third century Origen (d.253) observed certain days—"the Lord's Day, the Preparation, the Passover, Pentecost":

[25]He also, who is without ceasing preparing himself for the true life, by abstaining from the pleasures of this life, which lead so many astray, and by chastising his body and bringing it into subjection, is truly and without doubt keeping the day of preparation every day ... yet ... we are required by the law of God to keep its festival by eating the bread of affliction or unleavened with bitter herbs by humbling our souls because it is impossible for a man of spirit and flesh to keep the feast with his whole nature: either he does so with his spirit and afflicts his body, or else he does so with his body and his spirit is unable to share in it.

[25]Text: SC 150.222

This Preparation day of Origen, already on a par with the Lord's Day, Passover, and Pentecost, was, nevertheless, the fast day of the *Didascalia* (c.250), which became the festival day, though indeed a mournful one, of Egeria. The veneration of the cross, supposedly discovered by the Empress Helena in the year 320, was the most striking feature of this new liturgy in Jerusalem. The dissemination of relics of this true cross spread this new liturgy of veneration throughout the West, but Rome did not adopt it until the eighth century, when the Pope, barefoot, carried the relic of the cross in procession from the Lateran Basilica to the Church of the Holy Cross, which the Empress Helena had built nearby.

The second feature of the Jerusalem liturgy was the vigil. Egeria was particularly impressed by the rigors of the vigil from Thursday to Friday: "At the first hour of the night let us assemble at the church which is on the Eleona, for much toil lies ahead of us on this day's night."[26] The vigil from Friday to Saturday was less demanding and not of obligation; yet "the greater part of the people kept watch, some from evening on, others from midnight, each one doing what he can."[27]

Cyril of Jerusalem (315-386) was the guiding genius of this liturgy that developed there and centered so much around the cross:

[28]About the third hour a gigantic cross formed of light appeared in the sky above holy Golgotha stretching out as far as the holy Mount of Olives. It was not seen by just one or two, but was most clearly displayed before the whole population of the city. Nor did it, as one might have supposed, pass away quickly like something imagined, but was visible to sight above the earth for some hours, while it sparkled with a light above the sun's rays. Of a surety, it would have been overcome and

[26]Cf. SC 296.278 = ACW 38.107
[27]Cf. *ibid.* 290 = ACW 38.113
[28]Text: PG 33.1170

hidden by them, had it not exhibited to those who saw it a brilliance more powerful than the sun, so that the whole population of the city made a sudden concerted rush into the Martyrium, seized by a fear that mingled with joy at the heavenly vision. They poured in, young and old, men and women of every age ... not only Christians but pagans from elsewhere sojourning in Jerusalem, all of them as with one mouth raised a hymn of praise to Christ Jesus our Lord, the only-begotten Son of God, the worker of wonders.

> In this letter to the Emperor Constantius he makes a passing reference to the discovery of the True Cross, "fraught with salvation" in the days of Constantine. In the *Catechesis* this fact is also mentioned: "The whole world has now been filled with pieces of the wood of the cross":

[29]His witness is the holy wood of the cross, seen among us even to this day, and by those who have taken portions of it, from hence filling almost the whole world. His witness is the palm tree in the valley which supplied branches to the children who shouted His praises. Gethsemane is His witness, all but showing Judas still, to those who understand. This holy mount of Golgotha, conspicuous in its elevation, bears witness to Him. The holy sepulcher bears witness, and the stone which lies there even to this day....

[30]Jesus truly suffered for all men, for the cross was no illusion ... His death was not imaginary ... He was crucified and we do not deny it ... if I should now deny it, Golgotha here beside us, close to which we are now gathered, refutes me: the wood of the cross, now distributed piecemeal from Jerusalem over all the world, refutes me. I confess the cross.... Since the cross was followed by the resurrection, I am not ashamed to vow it.

> At Antioch in the fourth century the liturgy of Good Friday took place in the Martyrium, or Church of the Great

[29]Text: *ibid.* 685
[30]Text: *ibid.* 776

Cemetery, which was outside the city, for as Chrysostom explained in his literal way, "Christ was crucified outside Jerusalem."[31] This ceremony lasted for the whole day and for the greater part of the night, and Chrysostom preached on the Holy Cross and on the death of the Savior. In his *Catechesis*, particularly, he develops in his literal, but nonetheless figurative way, his understanding of the power of Christ's blood:

[32]If you desire further proof of the power of this blood remember where it came from, how it ran down from the cross, flowing from the Master's side. The Gospel records that when Christ was dead, but still hung on the cross, a soldier came and pierced His side with a lance and immediately there poured out water and blood. Now the water was a symbol of baptism and the blood, of the holy Eucharist. The soldier pierced the Lord's side, he breached the wall of the sacred temple, and I have found the treasure and made it my own.... *There flowed from His side water and blood* (Jn. 19:34). Beloved, do not pass over this mystery without thought; it has yet another hidden meaning, which I will explain to you. I said that water and blood symbolized baptism and the holy Eucharist. From these two sacraments the Church is born. Since the symbols of baptism and the Eucharist flowed from His side, it was from His side that Christ fashioned the Church, as He had fashioned Eve from the side of Adam. Moses gives a hint of this when he tells the story of the first man and makes him exclaim: *Bone from my bones and flesh from my flesh* (Gen. 2:23)! As God then took a rib from Adam's side to fashion a woman, so Christ has given us blood and water from His side to fashion the Church. God took the rib when Adam was in a deep sleep, and in the same way Christ gave us the blood and the water after His own death.

In North Africa, as can be inferred from Augustine, there was on Good Friday a Liturgy of the Word, but no

---

[31]Cf. PG 49.393
[32]Text: SC 50.160

ceremony of veneration. At Rome it was similar, and Pope Leo's (c.450) sermon on the cross was preached at the ordinary Friday Station:

[33]How marvelous the power of the cross; how great beyond all telling the glory of the Passion: here is the judgment seat of the Lord, the condemnation of the world, the supremacy of Christ crucified. . . .

Lord, you drew all things to yourself so that the devotion of all peoples everywhere might celebrate in a sacrament made perfect and visible, what was carried out in the one temple of Judaea under obscure foreshadowings. . . .

Now there is a more sacred anointing for the priesthood, because your cross is the fount of all blessings, and the cause of all graces. Through the cross the faithful receive strength from weakness, glory from dishonor, life from death.

HOLY SATURDAY

The most primitive feature of Holy Saturday, as is clear from the *Didascalia*, is the total fast that was kept on that day. But the *Diary of Egeria* describes the Friday-Saturday vigil and ceremonial, as "some of the clergy and the greater part of the people kept watch." This watching by the tomb was the feature that develped into the forty-hour watch and fast, calculated from the hour of evening and death to the hour of dawn and resurrection, and became in time the devotion of the forty hours of eucharistic watch. But the tomb and its silence is the theme that emerges in the preaching of the Fathers for this day and in this ancient homily, attributed perhaps wrongly to Epiphanius:

[34]Something strange is happening—there is a great silence on earth today, a great silence and stillness. The whole earth keeps silence because the King is asleep. The earth trembled

[33]Text: PL 54.341
[34]Text: PG 43.461

and is still because God has fallen asleep in the flesh and He has raised up all who have slept ever since the world began. God has died in the flesh and hell trembles with fear. . . .

He has gone to search for our first parent. Greatly desiring to visit those who live in darkness and in the shadow of death, He has gone to free from sorrow the captives Adam and Eve, He who is both God and the son of Eve. The Lord approached him bearing the cross, the weapon that had won Him the victory. At the sight of Him, Adam, the first man He had created, struck his breast in terror and cried out to everyone: 'My Lord be with you all.' Christ answered him: 'And with your spirit.' He took him by the hand and raised him up, saying, 'Awake, O sleeper, and rise from the dead, and Christ will give you light.' I am your God, who for your sake have become your life. Out of love for you and for your descendants I now by my own authority command all who are held bondage to come forth, all who are in darkness to be enlightened, all who are sleeping to arise. I order you, O sleeper, to awake. I did not create you to be held a prisoner in hell. Rise from the dead, for I am the life of the dead. Rise up, work of my hands, you who were created in my image. Rise, let us leave this place, for you are in me and I am in you; together we form only one person and we cannot be separated.

> Amphilochius of Iconium (c. 340-400), cousin of Nazianzus and friend of the great Basil, in his Cappodacian way expresses the mood of this day:

[35]Today we celebrate the sepulchral feast of our Savior. He has dissolved the bonds of death among the dead, and filled Hades with His light. He has aroused the dead from sleep. Let us rejoice and dance upon the earth as we contemplate the resurrection and no longer dread corruption or fear that it might prevail over incorruption: Scripture says, *You will not let your holy one see corruption* (Ps. 16:10). And perhaps the Jews and the Greeks laugh at our philosophy, for the Jews expect another Messiah, and the Greeks shut up their hopes in

---

[35]Text: PG 39.89

the tomb, concerning whom the prophet has aptly said: *Their sepulchres are their homes forever* (Ps. 49:12). But those who now laugh will one day weep (they will weep, I say, *looking at the one they have transfixed* and injured)(Zach. 12:10), but we who are now in tears will temper this suffering with joy. . . .

Death snatched away Christ, our Lord. But it will not retain life by itself. Death devoured Him without recognizing Him, but has vomited forth many with Him. He is now willingly in detention. But tomorrow, having laid waste Hades, He will rise. Yesterday, the sun was darkened at His crucifixion and night descended at midday: today, death lost its power when it received one more dead. Yesterday creation suffered and donned darkness as a mourning garb: *today the people who sat in darkness have seen a great light* (Isa. 9:1)

> Holy Saturday, for the most part, had no distinctive and proper liturgy in the early Church and this very vacuity in itself symbolized the repose of the tomb. Gregory of Nyssa wrote a work entitled, *On the Three Days Between the Death and Resurrection of Our Lord Jesus Christ*; Sabbath and repose dominate this work:

[36]This is the blessed Sabbath of our first creation. Recognize through this Sabbath that other Sabbath, the day of repose which God blessed above all other days. On this day the only begotten Son of God truly rested from all His works, having procured the repose for His flesh through the economy of His death. And returning through His resurrection to His former state He has raised up with Himself everything reposing (in death), having become life, resurrection, dawn, daybreak for all those in darkness and in the shadow of death.

> The death and resurrection of Jesus Christ made the Wednesdays and Fridays of the pagan week the axes of a new Christian week of fasting in preparation for Sunday, the Lord's Day of rejoicing. But the annual celebration of this same event, called by Augustine the *Sacratissimum*

[36]Text: PG 46.601

> *Triduum Crucifixi, Sepulti, Suscitati,* also brought into a
> renewed prominence the Sabbath rest of the Saturday now
> called holy, "good and great":[37]

[38]Let us now see ... why that calculation is made to ensure
that a Sabbath occurs when we celebrate Easter, for that is
peculiar to the Christian religion—the Jews only figured the
month of new corn and the moon from the fourteenth to the
twenty-first day. Because their Pasch, on which the Lord
suffered, so fell that there was a Sabbath between His death
and resurrection, our fathers have seen fit to make the
additional requirement that our feast should be distinguished
from the Jewish feast. As we must believe that His action was
not without meaning, who is before time, and by whom time
was created, and who came in the fullness of time, and who
had power to lay down His life and to take it up again;
therefore, He awaited His hour, not a chance one, but one
appropriate to the mystery which He ordered to be observed
when He said: *My hour is not yet come* (Jn. 2:4), so that the
memory of His Passion might be kept by posterity in a yearly
observance.

> This emphasis on the Sabbath rest of Holy Saturday
> grew out of Augustine's figurative approach to the Old
> Testament in general and to the third commandment of the
> decalogue in particular: certainly the connection between
> Sabbath rest and sepulchral silence was easily made by the
> figurative or symbolic mind, and so Saturday became an
> integral part of Augustine's triduum and therefore holy and
> great:

[39]Note, therefore, the three sacred days of His crucifixion,
burial and resurrection. Of these three, the cross signifies what
we do in this present life, but the burial and resurrection, what
we perform by faith and hope. In this present time it is said to

[37]Cf. PG 39.440
[38]Cf. PL 33.211 = FOTC 12.273
[39]Text: PL 33.215

man: *Take up thy cross and follow me* (Mt. 16:24). . . .

We walk, therefore, in the act of laboring, but in the hope of rest, in the oldness of the flesh, but in the newness of faith. For he says: *The body indeed is dead because of sin, but the spirit is life because of justice; and if the Spirit of Him that raised up Jesus Christ from the dead dwells in you, He that raised up Christ from the dead shall quicken also your mortal bodies, because of His Spirit that dwelleth in you* (Rom. 8:10-11). These are the truths which by the authority of the divine Scriptures and the consent of the universal Church, which is spread throughout the world, are commemorated by the yearly celebration of Easter, truly a great sacramental observance, as you now understand. In the Old Testament, no other time is prescribed for keeping the Pasch, except the month of new corn and the days between the fourteenth and the twenty-first of the moon. Since it is clear from the Gospel on what days the Lord was crucified and rested in the tomb and rose again, there is added, through the Councils of the Fathers, the requirement of retaining those same days, and the whole Christian world is convinced that the Pasch should be celebrated in that way.

> In contrast with the eschatological expectations of earlier Christians, converts of this new age, pre-eminently Constantine himself, were concerned with the Jesus of history and consequently with biblical times and places, and most especially with the cross and tomb of death and resurrection:

[40]One act, however, I must by no means omit to record, which this admirable prince performed in my own presence. On one occasion, emboldened by the confident assurance I entertained of his piety, I had begged permission to pronounce a discourse on the subject of our Savior's sepulcher in his hearing. With this request he most readily complied, and in the midst of a large number of auditors, in the interior of the palace itself, he stood and listened with the rest. I entreated him, but in vain, to seat himself on the imperial throne which

[40]Text: PG 20.1181 = LNPF series 2,1.548

stood near: he continued with fixed attention to weigh the topics of my discourse, and gave his own testimony to the truth of the theological doctrines it contained. After some time had passed, the oration being of considerable length, I was myself desirous of concluding; but this he would not permit, and exhorted me to proceed to the very end. On my again entreating him to sit, he in his turn was displeased and said that it was not right to listen in a careless manner to the discussion of doctrines relating to God; and again, that this posture was good and profitable to himself, since it was reverent to stand while listening to sacred truths. Having, therefore, concluded my discourse, I returned home, and resumed my usual occupations (Eusebius).

2. Easter Week

> The festival of Redemption was celebrated by the ancients on a single night: later it developed into the triduum of the death, burial and resurrection; later still it became the triduum of Maundy Thursday, Good Friday and Holy Saturday in honor of the death and burial, and the triduum of Easter Sunday, Monday and Tuesday in honor of the resurrection and life. But just as the triduum of death and burial became the Holy Week of fast and ceremonial, so, too, the triduum of resurrection and life became the Easter Week of celebration and catechesis according to Egeria:

[41]The eight days of Easter are observed just as at home with us. The liturgy is celebrated in the prescribed manner throughout the eight days of Easter just as it is celebrated everywhere from Easter Sunday to its octave. There is the same decoration, and the same arrangement for these eight days of Easter, as for the Epiphany, both in the major church and in the Anastasis, in the Cross as well as the Eleona, in Bethlehem, and in the Lazarium, too, and indeed everywhere, for this is Easter time.

[41]Text: SC 296.292 = ACW 38.114

On that first Sunday, Easter Day, everyone assembles for the liturgy in the major church, in the Martyrium, and on Monday and Tuesday also. But it always happens that, once the dismissal has been given from the Martyrium, everyone comes to the Anastasis singing hymns. On Wednesday everyone assembles for the liturgy in the Eleona; on Thursday, in the Anastasis; on Friday, at Sion; and on Saturday, before the Cross. On Sunday, however, on the octave, that is, they go once again to the major church, to the Martyrium. During the eight days of Easter, everyday after lunch, in the company of all the clergy and the neophytes—I mean those who have just been baptized—and of all the *aputactitae*, both men and women, and of as many of the people as wish to come, the bishop goes up to the Eleona. Hymns are sung and prayers are said, both in the church which is on the Eleona and where the grotto in which Jesus taught His disciples is located, and at the Imbomon, the place, that is, from which the Lord ascended into heaven. After psalms have been sung and a prayer has been said, everyone comes down from there, singing hymns, and goes to the Anastasis at the hour for vespers. This is done throughout the eight days.

On Easter Sunday, after the dismissal from vespers at the Anastasis, all the people, singing hymns conduct the bishop to Sion. When they have arrived there, hymns proper to the day and the place are sung, and a prayer is said. Then is read the passage from the Gospel describing how on this day and in this very place where there is now this same Church of Sion, the Lord came to His disciples, although the doors were closed, at the time when one of the disciples, namely, Thomas, was not there. When he returned, he said to the other apostles, who had told him that they had seen the Lord: *I will not believe, unless I see* (Jn. 20:25). After this passage has been read, a prayer is again said, the catechumens and then the faithful are blessed, and everyone returns to his home late, around the second hour of the night.

Then on Sunday, on the octave of Easter, immediately after the sixth hour all the people go up to the Eleona with the bishop. First of all everyone sits down for a time in the church which is there; hymns are sung as well as antiphons proper to the day and to the place. Then, everyone, singing hymns, goes from there up to the Imbomon above; and what was done in the Eleona is done in like manner again here. When it is time, all the people and all the *aputactitae*, singing hymns, lead the bishop to the Anastasis. They arrive at the Anastasis at the hour when vespers is customarily celebrated, and the vespers service is held both at the Anastasis and at the Cross.

From there, all the people without exception, singing hymns, lead the bishop as far as Sion. When they have arrived there, hymns proper to the place and to the day are sung as usual. Then they read the passage from the Gospel where, on the octave of Easter, the Lord came into where the disciples were, and He reproved Thomas because he had not believed. The whole passage from Scripture is then read. After a prayer has been said and the catechumens and the faithful have been blessed according to custom, then everyone returns to his home at the second hour of the night, just as on Easter Sunday.

When it is Easter week, during the eight days from Easter Sunday to its octave, as soon as the dismissal has been given from the church, everyone, singing hymns, goes to the Anastasis. Soon a prayer is said, the faithful are blessed, and the bishop stands up. Leaning on the inner railing, which is in the grotto of the Anastasis, he explains everything which is accomplished in baptism. At this hour no catechumen goes into the Anastasis; only the neophytes and the faithful who wish to hear the mysteries enter the Anastasis. Indeed, the doors are closed, lest any catechumen come that way. While the bishop is discussing and explaining each point, so loud are the voices of praise that they can be heard outside the church. And he explains all these mysteries in such a manner that there is no one who would not be drawn to them, when he heard them thus explained.

A portion of the population in this province knows both Greek and Syriac; another segment knows only Greek; and still another, only Syriac. Even though the bishop may know Syriac, he always speaks Greek and never Syriac; and, therefore, there is always present a priest who, while the bishop speaks in Greek, translates into Syriac so that all may understand what is being explained. Since whatever scriptural texts are read must be read in Greek, there is always someone present who can translate the readings into Syriac for the people, so that they will always understand. So that those here who are Latins, those consequently knowing neither Greek nor Syriac, will not be bored, everything is explained to them, for there are other brothers and sisters who are bilingual in Greek and Latin and who explain everything to them in Latin. But this above all is very pleasing and very admirable here, that whatever hymns and antiphons are sung, whatever readings and prayers are recited by the bishop, they are said in such a manner as to be proper and fitting to the feast which is being observed and to the place where the service is being held.

> Proclus (d. 446), patriarch of Constantinople, places the same emphasis on the Paschal week: "Glorious is our paschal festival; and truly splendid the comings and goings of the Christian people . . . for the celebration of this week, or rather the joy of this week is such that not alone does man rejoice on earth throughout it, but the very powers of heaven are one with us in our celebration of Christ's resurrection."[42]
>
> But the great makers of this whole week of Paschal celebration and catechesis were Cyril in Jerusalem for the Greek East, and Ambrose in Milan for the Latin West:

[43]After Easter's holy day of salvation, you will come every day, starting Monday, immediately after the assembly into the holy place of the resurrection, where, God willing, you will hear other lectures. In these you will be instructed again in the reasons for everything that has been done, reasons warranted by proofs from the Old and the New Testaments; first concerning what is done immediately before baptism; then how you were cleansed by the Lord *in the bath of water by means of the word* (Eph. 5:26); how like priests you have become partakers of the name of Christ; and how the seal of the fellowship of the Holy Spirit has been given to you. You

42Cf. PG 57.795

43Text: PG 33.1056 = FOTC 64.138

will be instructed concerning the mysteries at the altar of the New Testament, those mysteries first instituted here in Jerusalem. You will hear what the Sacred Scriptures have delivered to us, and of the efficacy of these mysteries; how you must approach them, when and how to receive them; and, last of all, how you must behave in word and deed worthily of the grace received, that all of you may be able to enjoy life everlasting. These points will, God willing, be the burden of our talks.

Cyril's catecheses for Easter Week are called Mystagogical for they are discourses on the mysteries of salvation:

[44]It has long been my wish, true-born and long-desired children of the Church, to discourse to you upon these spiritual, heavenly mysteries. On the principle, however, that seeing is believing, I delayed until the present occasion, calculating that after what you saw on that night I should find you a readier audience now when I am to be your guide to the brighter and more fragrant meadows of this second Eden. In particular, you are now capable of understanding the diviner mysteries of divine, life-giving baptism. The time being now come to spread for you the board of more perfect instruction, let me explain the significance of what was done for you on that evening of your baptism.

The same emphasis on mystery is found in the preaching of Ambrose during this Easter week of instruction: in fact one collection of these homilies is simply called *The Mysteries*, and the other is known as *The Sacraments*.

[45]We have given a daily sermon on morals, when the deeds of the patriarchs or the precepts of the Proverbs were read, in order that, being informed and instructed by them, you might become accustomed to enter upon the ways of our forefathers and to pursue their road, and to obey the divine commands,

[44]Text: *ibid.* 1065 = FOTC 64.153
[45]Text: PL 16.389 = FOTC 44.5

whereby, renewed by baptism, you might hold to that manner of life which befits those who are washed.

Now time warns us to speak of the mysteries and to set forth the very purpose of the sacraments. If we had thought that this should have been taught those not yet intitiated before baptism, we would be considered to have betrayed rather than to have portrayed the mysteries; then there is the consideration that the light of the mysteries will infuse itself better in the unsuspecting than if some sermon had preceded them.

> On the other hand, many of the Fathers throughout this week of instruction were less mystagogical and more exegetical. Their word-for-word exposition of the Gospel texts of the resurrection and post-resurrection appearances were linked together by St. Thomas Aquinas (d. 1250) in a sort of continuous commentary known as the *Catena Aurea*, or golden chain, where the preface explains the method: "In quoting the testimony of the Fathers, it was necessary many times to cut away some parts, so as to avoid undue length, and for greater clarity ... to change about the actual sequence of the parts quoted ... and to seek not alone the literal meaning but also the mystical."[46] In the following abbreviated excerpt from the *Catena Aurea,* the message of the Fathers on Mark's account of the resurrection, read on Easter morning, can be heard:

[47]*And when the sabbath was over* (Mk. 16:1)...

JEROME: After the sadness of the sabbath a day of happiness now shines forth, which holds the primacy among all days, the First Light shining upon it; and upon it the Lord rises triumphant from the dead.

And very early in the morning, the first day (Mk. 16:2)...

JEROME: Very early, therefore, he says, where another Evangelist says, very early in the morning; the time between

---

[46]A. Gaurienti, *Catena Aurea*, Marietti, 1953, 4
[47]Cf. *ibid.* 560-566

the darkness of the night and the brightness of the day. In which time the salvation of the human race appeared as the sun: His blessed nearness must be announced in the Church, which, as it rises, sends before it a roseate aurora, that the eye prepard by the grace of this shining glow may see, when the hour of the Lord's resurrection has shone out; that the whole Church, after the example of the holy women, might then sing the praises of Christ, when by the proof of His resurrection He has awakened mankind from sleep, when He has given them life, and poured into them the light of belief.

And they said one to another: Who shall roll us back (Mk. 16:3). . .

SEVERIANUS: Your heart was sealed, your eyes were shut, and so you saw not before you the splendor of the wide open tomb. For there follows:

And looking, they saw the stone rolled back from the door. (Mk. 16:4)

BEDE: How the stone was rolled back Matthew sufficiently explains (cf. Mt. 28). This rolling back of the stone mystically suggests the unlocking of the Mysteries of Christ, which were concealed by the covering of the Law: for the Law was written on stone. There follows: For it was very great. Severianus: Great in size, yet greater in significance than in size, which sufficed to shut in and cover the Body of the Creator of the world.

And entering into the sepulcher, they saw (Mk. 16:5). . .

SEVERIANUS: The holy women, therefore, enter into the sepulcher, that, buried with Christ, they may rise with Christ from the tomb. They see a young man, that they may see the age of our resurrection: for resurrection knows no old age; and where man is neither born nor dies, there age allows of no loss, nor does it need to gain: whence is it they see a young man, not an old one, not an infant, but one in the joyous time of life.

Who saith to them: Be not affrighted (Mk. 16:6). . .

GREGORY: But let us hear what the Angel goes on to say. You

seek Jesus of Nazareth. Jesus in the Latin language is interpreted to mean Savior. But then there could have been many called Jesus, in name, but not in the reality. Accordingly, the place also is added, so that it may be clear of what Jesus he is speaking, namely: of Nazareth. And he immediately adds their motive: Who was crucified.

But go, tell His disciples and Peter that He goeth (Mk. 16:7)...

JEROME: A saying brief in its words, but a promise immense in its significance. There is the fountain of our joy, and the source that was prepared of our eternal salvation. There are gathered the multitudes that were dispersed; and the contrite of heart are healed. There, he says, you shall see Him; but not as you have seen Him.

> Augustine distinguishes between "Easter ... a feast with the strongest scriptural authority, and the eighth day of the neophytes, which rest on a decree of the Church." Easter was, therefore, no mere week of instructions, mystagogical or moral, but a sacramental experience or gesture which could not be contained within the space of a day: first, it ran its course for three days, "because the number three has such pre-eminence in many sacraments," and then for eight, "so that the eighth harmonizes with the first."[48] Hence the following divisions of this section: a) the day, b) the triduum and c) the week of Easter:

[49]Therefore, this renewal of our life is in a sense a passing from death to life, which begins by faith, that we may rejoice in hope and be patient in tribulation, while still *our outward man is corrupted, yet the inward man is renewed day by day* (2 Cor. 4:16). Because of this very beginning of new life, because of the new man which we are ordered to put on, and to put off the old, *purging out the old leaven, that we may be a new dough,*

[48]Cf. PL 33.220
[49]Text: *ibid.* 206

for Christ our Pasch is sacrificed (1 Cor. 5:7), because of this newness of life, the first month among the months of the year is selected for this celebration. It is called the month of the new corn, because, truly, in the whole time of the world, the third period has now come, and therefore, we celebrate the resurrection of the Lord for three days. For, the first period was before the Law, the second under the Law, the third under grace, where we have now the revealing of a mystery previously hidden in prophetic obscurity. This is also signified in the lunar number: because the number seven in Scripture commonly has a mystic connection with some sort of perfection, the Pasch is celebrated in the third week of the moon, that is, a day which falls between the fourteenth and the twenty-first.

EASTER SUNDAY

The controversy of the Lord's Day and the Pasch, as distinct from the Quartodeciman question, concerns the priority of Sunday over Easter or *vice versa,* as the more ancient Christian festivals. In Asia Minor, as has been already discussed (chapter 2), the Pasch was certainly celebrated in the mid-second century on the fourteenth Nisan and in keeping with the practice of the Jews; but in Rome there was neither a Paschal fast nor festival until the time of Pope Soter (c. 166-174). Certainly for Justin (*Apol.* 1:67; *Dial. Trypho*, 138), Sunday seems to have been the only commemoration of the resurrection, and thus the first Christian festival or day of worship. Indeed the Scriptures seem to suggest this conclusion for *on the evening of that day, the first day of the week ... Jesus came and stood among them* (Jn. 20:19), *as they sat at table,* (Mk. 16:14). *Eight days later, His disciples were again in the house ... but Jesus came and stood among them* (Jn. 20:26). On the other hand, there is clear evidence of a Paschal awareness in Paul's letter to the Corinthians: *Christ our passover has been sacrificed. Let us celebrate the feast not with the old yeast, that of corruption and wickedness, but with the unleavened bread of sincerity and truth* (1 Cor. 5:7-9).

The second century saw the development of the Sunday Easter and its Vigil: the possible priority of Sunday as the most ancient day of Christian worship could easily explain the early emergence of the Vigil by way of preparation for the feast, but the priority of the Vigil could scarcely necessitate the celebration of the Sunday by way of completing what was already begun on the evening before. At any rate in the East as in the West there was in the fourth century a widespread practice of preaching on the resurrection on Easter Sunday: "the day of the resurrection! What an auspicious beginning! Radiantly let us celebrate this day, giving one another the kiss of peace. Let us pardon one another in honor of the resurrection." So spoke Gregory (d.390) on his first sermon preached on Easter Sunday at the age of thirty-two in his home town of Nazianzus:

[50]Yesterday I was crucified with Christ; today I will be glorified with Him. Yesterday I died with Christ; today I will return to life with Him. Yesterday I was buried with Christ; today I will rise with Him from the tomb.

Let us then carry our first fruits to Him who has suffered and risen for us. Do you think perhaps that I am talking of gold, silver, garments, or precious stones? Insubstantial earthly goods, transitory, tied to earth, owned for the most part by the wicked, the slaves of materialism and the prince of this world? No, let us offer ourselves: it is the most precious and dearest gift in the eyes of God. Give to His image what resembles it most. Recognizing our greatness, honor our model, understanding the force of this mystery and the reasons for Christ's death....

Give all, offer all, to Him who has given Himself for us as a prize and ransom. We will give nothing as great as ourselves if we have grown by the power of this mystery and have become for Him all which He has become for us....

[50]Text: PG 35.396

Gregory of Nyssa (d.394), is no less rhetorical on the text:
*This is the day the Lord has made; let us be glad and rejoice
in it* (Ps. 118:24):

[51]Today . . . there are no travellers on the strees: today the
sea is free of sailors and seamen. The laborer has left hoe and
plough aside, and dressed up in his Sunday best to celebrate:
The stores are closed. Riots have disappeared, like winter
when summer appears. Disturbances, crowds, and the
agitations of life have subsided in the peace of the feast. The
poor man is decked out like the rich man; the rich man appears
in greater splendor than usual. The elder runs like a youngster
to share in the joyous occasion. The man who is ill is
strengthened in his weakness; the child by a change of clothes
celebrates the feast in external appearance since he cannot yet
understand what it is all about. The virgin rejoices exceedingly
in spirit, for she sees the remembrance of her own hope so
splendidly honored; the married woman rejoices as she keeps
festival with her entire household. For now she herself, her
husband, children, servants and all join in the festivities. And
just as a swarm of bees, new and recently born, emerging fresh
from the hive or the shelter, fly into the air and daylight and
attach themselves in a body to a branch of a tree, so on this
feast whole families swarm to the family hearth. And truly by
imitation, today is rightly compared to the last day; for both
are rallying points for men, the last day for the whole world,
today for individuals. To speak more truly, in respect to what
pertains to joy and happiness, today is more pleasant than the
last day, since it will be necessary on the last day to see some
weeping because their sins are uncovered. But today's joy
admits of no sad faces. For the just man is joyful, and the man
whose conscience is not clear hopes for forgiveness from his
contrition and all grief sleeps today. For there is no one so
overwhelmed with pain that he does not get relief from the
splendor of the feast.

[51]Text: PG 46.456

Ambrose in Milan (339-396) is a clear witness in the West to an Easter day liturgy with the resurrection account of Mark to replace the pericope of Matthew in the Vigil. His sermon, entitled the *Sunday of the Resurrection*, is truly a Paschal commentary on the scripture text:

[52]Now since you are celebrating the holy Pasch, you should know, brethren, what the Pasch is. Pasch means the crossing-over; and so the festival is called by this name. For it was on this day that the children of Israel crossed over out of Egypt, and the Son of God crossed over from this world to His Father. What gain is it to celebrate the Pasch unless you imitate Him whom you worship; that is, unless you cross over from Egypt, that is, from the darkness of evil-doing to the light of virtue, and from the love of this world to the love of your heavenly home?

For there are many who celebrate this holy festival, and honor this solemnity, and yet do so unworthily and because of their own wickedness: because they will not cross over from this world to their Father; that is, they will not cross over from the desires of this world, and from bodily delights, to the love of heaven. O unhappy Christians, who still remain in Egypt, that is, under the power of the devil, and taking delight in this evil!

Because of these things I warn you, brethren, that you must celebrate the Pasch worthily, that is, that you cross over.

In a homily for Easter Sunday, Jerome says: "I say a new thing, and one that is borne out by the words of the Scriptures: this day is at once one of seven and is outside seven. It is this day which is called the eighth day (octave); whence also certain psalms have the title 'for the octave.' This is the day on which the synagogue ended and the Church was born. It is this day whose number was the number of souls saved in the Ark."[53] But, Augustine his contemporary, is without doubt, the most prolific preacher

[52]Text: PL 17.672
[53]Cf. CCL 78.545

in the West of the Easter mystery with sermons for the vigil, the day, the Scriptures, and the liturgical texts. In a sermon on the theme: Death of Death, he says:

[54]Where is death? Seek it in Jesus Christ, for it exists no longer. It was in Him but it exists no longer. O life, the death of death! Take courage and it will die also in you. What has begun in our Head will continue in His members. Death will die also in us. When? At the end of the world. At the resurrection of the dead in which we believe without the slightest doubt. *He who believes and is baptized will be saved* (Mk. 16:16)

Read what follows—it is formidable: *He who does not believe shall be condemned* (Mk. 16:16). Death will die in us but it will be victorious in those who are condemned. There will be everlasting death where death itself does not die because the torments will be everlasting. In us, however, death will die and will exist no more.

I am going to cite some words of those who have vanquished death. Reflect on them, sing them in your heart, and they will provide an objective for your hope and a meaning to your faith and good works. Hear the victorious words to be repeated when death will be no more, when death will perish in us as it has already perished in Christ our head. *This corruptible body*, says St. Paul, *must put on incorruption and this mortal body must put on immortality. Then shall be fulfilled the Scripture saying, Death is swallowed up in victory* (1 Cor. 15:53). As I have said already, death will die in us. Death is swallowed up in victory. That is the death of death.

Around the same time Maximus, Bishop of Turin (d.420), poet and mystic, develops the symbolism of the Christ as the Light of Day:

[55]This is called 'today' because, like a living, unfailing splendor, it does not cease to inflame the world in perpetual

[54]Text: PL 38.1114

[55]Text: PL 57.606

light and because this unceasing flame seems to be one uninterrupted day. *A thousand years are in your sight as one day* (Ps. 4), writes the prophet. Yes, Christ is clearly this one day, because the eternity of divinity in Him is one.

It is our 'today': the past, by reason of antiquity, does not escape Him; and the future, which is unknown, has no secrets for Him. But like a sovereign light, He contains all things, He knows all things, He is ever present and possesses all things. Before Him the past cannot escape, and the future cannot hide. And when God said to his Son, *Today I have begotten you* (Heb. 1:5; Ps. 2:7), understand that this 'today' is not the time in His humanity when He was born of the Virgin Mary, nor in His divinity when He proceeded from the mouth of God, His Father, but the time when He rose from the dead. *He has raised up the Lord Jesus Christ* (1 Cor. 6:14), says the apostle Paul, as also it is written in the second Psalm, *you are my son, this day have I begotten you* (Acts 13:33; Ps. 2:7). Truly, then, this is our 'today' when He rises from the dense night of hell to illumine men like a bright light. That is rightly called day which the black deed of the Jews could not obscure. And nothing could be better than for us today to accept the light; He has restored day and salvation to all the dead; by the presence of life today He has raised up men long dissolved in death.

> In Rome the sacramental nature of Easter was realistically expressed by Pope Leo, who preached the mystery of the cross on Easter Sunday, presumably because Good Friday, as has been seen, was not a ceremonial day in Rome. Two of Leo's Paschal homilies survive, both characterized by Leo's twin concerns of theological exposition and pastoral exhortation. Here are selections from both:

[56]In my last sermon, dearly beloved, we called on you, not unreasonably, if I may say so, to share the cross of Christ in such a way that the very life of the faithful might incorporate the Paschal mystery and that what is honored in the feast might be celebrated in your mortal lives. You yourselves testify

[56]Text: SC 74.123

to the utility of this approach, and from your devotion you have learned how profitable to soul and body are extended fasts, more frequent prayers, and more generous almsgiving. Practically everybody has profited from this exercise and has stored in the depths of his conscience some genuine cause for rejoicing. These gains, however, must be jealously guarded. Any relaxation of our efforts may afford the devil in his envy a chance to rob us of God's grace.

Since, then, our objective in the observance of Lent was to experience something of the cross of Christ at the time of His Passion, we should strive likewise to be found sharers in His resurrection and to pass from death to life, even in our present mortal state. For everyone who changes by any conversion from one state to another, the last word is not to be what he was, and the first, to be what he was not. But it makes a difference for what one lives or dies. Because it is death which is the cause of life, and life, the cause of death. Nowhere except in this transitory life are both objectives pursued, and the differences of our eternal retributions depend on the quality of our passing actions. We must die, then, to the devil, and live to God.

Again:

[57]This feast which we name the Pasch is called . . . Passover, by the Hebrews as the Gospel testifies, saying, before the feast of the Pasch, Jesus knowing that His hour had come that *He should pass over from this world to the Father* (Jn. 13:1). But to which of the two natures is this passing over reserved except to ours since the Father is inseparably united with the Son and the Son to the Father? But because the Word and the Flesh constitute but one person the nature assumed is not separated from the nature assuming it, and the honor given to Him who is going to be elevated is called an increase for Him who is elevated according to the word of the apostle already quoted: *For this reason God elevated Him and gave Him a name which is above every other name* (Phil. 2:9). In this, of course, it is the

[57]Text: *ibid.* 133

elevation of man assumed by the Word which is taught, so that just as the divinity remains inseparable from Him in his sufferings, so the humanity remains coeternal with the divinity in glory. For this sharing in His ineffable gift the Lord Himself was preparing a blessed passing over for His faithful when, with His Passion imminent, He prayed not only for His apostles and disciples, but also for the whole Church, saying, *I pray not only for these, but for those also who through their words will believe in me, so that they all may be one, as you Father are one in me and I in you, they also may be one in us* (Jn. 17:20-21)...

You, however, rightly rejoice, on this festival, and your joy is wholesome because you admit no falsehood in the truth, either concerning Christ's nativity according to the flesh, or His Passion and death. Or have you any doubts about His bodily resurrection, since you recognize without any separation from His divine nature, Christ truly born from the Virgin's womb, true wood of the cross, true in the burial of His flesh, true in the glory of resurrection, true on the right hand of the majesty of His Father.

> Towards the end of the patristic age Gregory the Great (c.600) followed the exegetical manner of preaching, and in his Easter homilies explained the gospel text phrase by phrase and ended with his usual exhortation:

[58]Let us, beloved, love with all our hearts this glorious resurrection, which was first made known to us by a Figure, and then made known in deed; and for love of it let us be prepared to die. See how in the resurrection of our Author we have come to know His ministering angels as our own fellow citizens. Let us hasten on to that great assembly of these fellow citizens. Let us, since we cannot see them face to face, join ourselves to them in heart and desire. Let us cross over from evil-doing to virtue, that we may merit to see our Redeemer in Galilee.

[58]Text: PL 76.1173

THE EASTER TRIDUUM

The major Church of the Martyrium was the place of congregation for everyone in Jerusalem on Sunday, Monday and Tuesday of Easter week: on the remaining days of this week the assemblies were held each day in one or other of the minor Churches. (Egeria 39). At Constantinople Chrysostom "celebrated the resurrection of the Lord for three days;" [59]and Augustine spoke of... "celebrating the days of Easter, in which Christ, our Pasch, is sacrificed, while the Jews continue in their expectation, although the time has already come." [60]Little is known about the actual ceremonial of these days other than their "decorative observance everywhere ... for this is Easter time" (Egeria 39). But Monday and Tuesday were probably a repetition of Easter day with, as Augustine tells us, a different gospel reading: "It is our custom during these days to read from all books of the Gospel an account of the resurrection of Our Lord Jesus Christ."[61]

The reading of Matthew's account of the resurrection at the Easter Vigil, Mark's on Easter morning, Luke's on Monday, and probably on Tuesday also, and John's for the rest of the week was the norm in Rome at the time of Pope Innocent I (401-417), who desired liturgical uniformity everywhere, but with Rome as center. Augustine's practice was for the most part similar as he also read the evangelists in their proper sequence on the first days of the Paschal celebrations. But this practice already represents the transformation of the first days, or triduum, into the more biblical notion of the week, which suited the needs of the neophytes. Hence a week of ceremonial and catechesis replaced the triduum of scriptural celebration.

[59]Cf. PG 46.600
[60]Cf. PLS 2.723
[61]Cf. SC 116.244

[62]Listen to me, especially you who are now reborn to a new life and for that reason are called infants, while I explain, as I promised, what it is that you see before you here on the altar. Pay attention also you, the faithful, who are long accustomed to view this sacred rite, because it is for your benefit, too, that we recall these things, otherwise you might forget them. The food you see here on the Lord's table, you are accustomed to see on your own tables at home, as far as outward appearances go. It has the same appearance, but not the same worth.

The Apostle has shown us briefly what this bread is. Now consider the matter more carefully and see how it comes about. How is bread made? Wheat is threshed, ground, moistened, and baked. By moistening, the wheat is purified, and by baking it is made firm. In what does your threshing consist? You also underwent a form of threshing, by fasting, by the Lenten observances, by night watches, by exorcisms. You were ground when you were delivered from the devil by exorcism. But moistening cannot be done without water; as a consequence, you were immersed. Baking is troublesome yet necessary. What, then, is the baking process? The fire of temptations of which no life is free. And how is this beneficial? *The furnace trieth the potter's vessels, and the trial of affliction just men* (Isa. 48:10). As one loaf results from combining the individual kernels and mixing the same together with water, so also the one body of Christ is represented in the grains of wheat, so also is the blood represented in the grapes. For wine pours forth from the wine press out of what were formerly many individual grapes, now flowing together as one liquid to become wine. Hence both in the bread and in the chalice the sacrament of unity is present.

At the table of the Lord you hear the words, *Dominus vobiscum*, the Lord be with you. We are wont to say these words when we greet you from our place in the apse and also when we begin our prayers, because our well-being demands that the Lord be with us, since without Him we are nothing. Recall, moreover, the words that resounded in your ears, the ones you say when you are gathered at the altar of God. For we

[62]Text: PLS 2.554

summon you, as it were, and admonish you, declaring, *Sursum cor*, lift up your heart. Do not let it sink to the earth, for the heart would decay on the earth, but lift it heavenward. But whereto lift the heart? What do you respond? Whereto lift the heart? *Habemus ad dominum*, we have lifted it up to the Lord. To keep one's heart aloft is sometimes a good thing and sometimes a bad thing. In what way can it be bad? It is bad for those of whom it is said, *When they were lifted up thou hast cast them down* (Ps. 73:18). To lift up the heart, but not to the Lord, is not virtue but arrogance. Therefore, when we say, 'Lift up your heart,' you reply, since in itself this could be nothing but arrogance, 'We have lifted it up to the Lord.' And thus it becomes a worthy deed and not a mark of pride. But because it is praiseworthy to elevate the heart to God, is that a matter of our own doing? Do we accomplish this by our own powers? Do we who were but dust raise it up toward heaven? By no means! He did so Himself, He deigned to do so, He stretched forth His hand, He lavished His grace, He lifted up what was fallen. Thus when we say, 'Lift up your heart,' and you make the response, 'We have lifted it up to the Lord,' lest you arrogate to yourselves the elevation of your heart, I added the words, *Gratias agamus Domino Deo nostro*, let us give thanks to the Lord our God. These mystery-laden words are short in measure but great in their content. What we proclaim is very tersely put, yet it issues from the depths of our being. You utter these sentiments quickly, without the aid of a book, without reading them, without use of many words. Yet always remember what you are and in whom you must place your confidence, so that you may finally attain the joys which God has promised.

The exegetical approach of the earlier triduum, nonetheless, remained, and can be seen especially in the homilies for the first days of this week. Luke's account of the resurrection was read on the Monday of the Easter triduum, for only Luke reports the reproval of the disciples for their unbelief: "In the Gospel for today we see how the Lord Jesus reproved his disciples, His first members, the ones who were always at His side, because they who had just mourned His death now refused to believe that He was alive. Although they were the fathers of the faith, they themselves were lacking in faith."[63]

The Lucan account of the resurrection may also have been read by Augustine on the Tuesday, as it was in the Rome of Innocent I, on account of the Emmaus pericope which reports what happened on "that same day": the following truncated excerpt from the *Catena Aurea* shows how widely Luke's Gospel was preached during those early centuries, Greek and Latin, especially the pericope *On the Road to Emmaus:*

[64]*And behold, two of them went that same day to a village called Emmaus* (Lk. 24:13).

THEOPHYLACTUS: These two disciples talked to one another of the things that had happened, not as believing, but rather as astounded at events so strange.

BEDE: And as they speak of Him, the Lord draws near and joins them, to the intent that He may kindle in their hearts faith in His resurrection, and also that He may fulfill His promise, Where two or three are gathered together in My name, there am I in the midst of them.

THEOPHYLACTUS: For having now obtained a spiritual body, no difference of place hindered His being present with those with whom He willed to be; and He ruled His body no longer after the laws of nature, but spiritually, in a manner that transcended nature. Wherefore Mark says, *He appeared unto them in another form* (Mk. 16:12), in which it was not granted them to know Him. And this was so that they might open to Him the entire pattern of their doubt, and by showing their wounds might receive their cure. It was to teach them also that, although the very body that had suffered has arisen, it was no longer such as to be seen by all, but only by those by whom He willed it to be seen.

---

[63]Cf. SC 116.244
[64]Cf. *Catena Aurea* v.2. 313-315

GREGORY: The two disciples in their inmost hearts both loved and doubted. So when they spoke of Him, He showed His presence; but, because they doubted, He concealed from them the form they knew.

And one of them ... said, Art Thou only a stranger? (Lk. 24:18)

GREGORY: They thought Him a stranger to Jerusalem, whose face they did not know. But He was in truth a stranger to them; for now that He had gotten the glory of the resurrection He was far removed from the weakness of their nature, and was moreover an outsider to their faith, while as yet they did not know Him risen.

THEOPHYLACTUS: Yet these men seem to have been not altogether unbelieving; for, after relating the Passion they say, *and besides all this, today is the third day since these things were done* (Lk. 24:21), which seems to show that they remembered that the Lord had said that He would rise again on the third day.

O fools and slow of heart to believe all that the prophets have spoken! (Lk. 24:25).

THEOPHYLACTUS: O fools, He says, rebuking their excess of doubt, for they had used almost the same words as those who stood by the cross, *He saved others; Himself He cannot save* (Lk. 23:35). And it becomes us in all things to give credence to the prophets, both in the inglorious things foretold of Christ and in the glorious; for He entered on the glory through enduring the ills.

Ought not the Christ to have suffered these things, and to enter into His glory? (Lk. 24:26).

ISIDORE: Yet though it behooved the Christ to suffer, nevertheless those who crucified Him were guilty; for they were not concerned with the fulfillment of God's plan. So their carrying out of it was wicked, but the providence of God, in turning their wickedness to the profit of mankind, like using viper's flesh as a health-giving antidote, was very wise.

And they drew nigh unto the village whither they went, and He made as though He would have gone further (Lk. 24:28).

GREGORY: Because He was a stranger to faith in their hearts, He made as though He would go on. The simple Truth did nothing of deceit in this; He only behaved outwardly according to their inward thought of Him. But because these men with whom Love was walking could not be themselves strangers to love, they ask Him as a stranger, to come and be their guest, saying, *Abide with us* (Lk. 24:29). And, lo, when Christ is received through His members, He seeks His receivers also through Himself, for it goes on, *And He went in with them* (Lk. 24:29). They set the table, they bring food; and God, whom they had not known in the expounding of the sacred Scriptures, they knew in the breaking of bread.

Their eyes were opened, and they knew Him (Lk. 24:31).

AUGUSTINE: They were not walking with their eyes shut earlier, but there was something in them that would not suffer them to know that which they saw.

THEOPHYLACTUS: Here also He implies another thing, that the eyes of those who take the holy bread are opened, so that they may know Him; for the flesh of the Lord has a great and unspeakable power.

AUGUSTINE: Or else the Lord means that men may come to know Him by exercising hospitality, so that when He had departed far from men above all heavens He would be nonetheless with those who did thus to His servants.

EASTER WEEK

The triduum of Easter was easily expanded in the late fourth century to meet the needs of the neophytes. This was their week and the Gospel of John became their text. The apparitions of the Risen Lord were expressions of the presence and power of the sacraments which initiated them into the mysteries of salvation. *The Catena Aurea* summarizes the message of the Fathers on the apparitions to

Mary Magdalen, and to the apostles on the eighth day, which were read from John's Gospel during the remainder of Easter week:

[65]*But Mary stood without at the sepulcher, weeping* (Jn. 20:11).

AUGUSTINE: The eyes that sought the Lord and found Him not gave place to tears, grieving the more that He Who had been slain upon the tree had now been taken from the sepulcher, since of so great a Master, after His life was taken, not even a memorial remained.

CHRYSOSTOM: For a tomb that can be seen is a great consolation. See, therefore, what she does; for her greater comfort she stoops and looks into the sepulcher, wanting to see the place where the body had lain.

AUGUSTINE: For her grief was beyond measure; she could not easily believe either her own eyes nor those of the apostles. Or was it rather by a divine impulse within her soul that she looked in?

GREGORY: She sought the body, and could nowhere find it; so she went on looking. And it so happened that she found out that longings disappointed grew the greater and, growing, became great enough to find. For holy longings grow by disappointment; and if fulfillment is not thus deferred, then they are not longings. She, therefore, who so loves, and has already looked into the tomb, stoops to do so again—with what result?

She sees two angels in white sitting, one at the head, and the other at the feet, where the body of Jesus had lain (Jn. 20:12).

CHRYSOSTOM: The woman's mind was not so exalted as that she should perceive the resurrection from the linen clothes; so she beholds angels in glad apparel, that her own sorrow may be soothed thereby.

[65]Cf. *ibid.* 579-581

GREGORY: One angel sits at the head, because the apostle declares that *in the beginning was the Word.* The other sits at the feet, because it is said, *the Word was made flesh.*

They say unto her, Why weepest thou? (Jn. 20:13).

AUGUSTINE: She tells them the reason of her tears. *They have taken away my Lord* (Jn. 20:13), she says, describing as *the Lord* His lifeless body, just as we all confess that Jesus Christ the Son of God was buried, though it was His flesh only that suffered burial.

CHRYSOSTOM: But why, when speaking to the angels and not yet hearing His voice, did she turn herself back? It seems to me that Christ appeared behind her, and the angels, beholding their Ruler, forthwith declared by their aspect and movement that they saw the Lord; that was what made the woman look behind her.

GREGORY: Mary turned backwards to see Jesus, because by not believing in His resurrection, she had already, as it were, turned her back on the face of the Lord. But because she loved and doubted, she saw Him, but she did not know Him.

Jesus saith unto her, Woman, why weepest thou? (Jn. 20:15)

GREGORY: He asks the reason of her sorrow to increase her longing, so that in naming Him for whom she sought, a yet more ardent love for Him might kindle her.

She, supposing Him to be the gardener (Jn. 20:15)...

GREGORY: Maybe this woman was not wrong in mistaking Jesus for the gardener. For was He not the gardener of her spirit, who by the power of His love implanted living seeds of virtues in her heart?

He saith unto her, Mary! (Jn. 20:16)

GREGORY: She had not recognized Him when He called her 'Woman,' now He says her name, which is as though He said, 'Know Him who knows you.' So Mary, called by name, recognizes Him who speaks her name; for it was He whom she was seeking outwardly, and it was also He who inwardly was teaching her to seek. Wherefore it follows, *She turned herself and saith unto Him, Rabboni, which is to say, Master!* (Jn. 20:16)

Touch me not, for I am not yet ascended to My Father (Jn. 20:17).

AUGUSTINE: Touch, as it were, sets bounds to cognizance, and He did not want the heart thus set on Him to think that He was only what He seemed.

CHRYSOSTOM: This woman wanted to be with Christ, just as she had been before the Passion. So He says, *Touch Me not,* that she may have great awe in speaking to Him. In saying *I am not yet ascended,* He shows how He is hastening and speeding thither. And it was not fitting that He who was to depart thither and walk no more with men should be regarded with the same mind as He had been before. And this He shows by adding, *Go to My brethren, and say unto them, I ascend to My Father and your Father, to My God and your God* (Jn. 20:17). He does not say *our Father,* but *My Father and your Father.* Mine in one sense, yours in another; Mine by nature, yours by grace. Nor does He say *our God,* but My God, in that I am Man, and your God, between whom and you I am the Mediator.

Mary Magdalen came and told the disciples that she had seen the Lord (Jn. 20:18).

GREGORY: Behold, the guilt of mankind is put away by the same means whereby it came about. For in paradise the woman gave the man death to eat, and from the tomb a woman brought news of life to men, and she who had repeated the death-dealing serpent's words repeats the sayings of her Quickener.

> Again the *Catena Aurea* on the *Second Appearance to the apostles*:

[66]*After eight days again His disciples were within, and Thomas with them; then came Jesus again* (Jn. 20:26).

[66]*Ibid.* 583-585

CHRYSOSTOM: Consider the Lord's clemency, how even for one soul He shows Himself as bearing wounds, and comes to save one man. He sought Thomas alone. Yet did He not appear to him forthwith, but *after eight days*, so that he might be kindled to a greater longing by the encouragement of the disciples? So Jesus stands, and does not wait for Thomas to address a question to Him, but to show that He was present when he spoke with his fellow disciples He uses the same words.

And be not faithless, but believing (Jn. 20:27).

AUGUSTINE: Had the Lord so willed, He could have removed all marks of any scar whatever from His risen and glorified body; but He knew why He must keep His scars. For as He showed His wounds to Thomas, who was not going to believe unless he touched and saw, so also will He show them to His enemies.

Because thou hast seen, thou hast believed (Jn. 20:29).

AUGUSTINE: But He will not say to them, as He said to Thomas, *Because thou hast seen, thou hast believed;* to them the Truth will say for their conviction, 'Behold the Man you crucified! You see the wounds you made, and you perceive the side you pierced; for it was opened both by you and for you, and you would not enter in.'

GREGORY: The Lord offered to be touched the flesh that He had brought in through closed doors; and herein are two marvellous things that seem to human reason to contradict each other, for after the resurrection He showed His body to be incorruptible, and yet it could be touched. For that which can be touched is of necessity corruptible, and that which is not subject to corruption is impalpable. So He showed Himself to be at once incorruptible and touchable; so that directly He was risen His body might be shown to have at once the same nature as before, and another glory. Our body also in that glory of the resurrection will have a certain subtlety from the effect of spiritual power; yet from the truth of its nature it will be touchable.

AUGUSTINE: Thomas saw and touched the Man, and he confessed the God whom he neither saw nor touched. Through what he saw and touched, he now believed, all doubt removed.

My Lord and my God (Jn. 20:28).

THEOPHYLACTUS: He who before he touched the Savior's side was unbelieving, after that touch showed himself an excellent theologian, for he declared the two natures in Christ's single Person, confessing His humanity by calling Him Lord, and His divinity by calling Him God, and both the One and Selfsame God and Lord.

These eight days of Easter were for the celebration and the instruction of the neophytes. Asterios Sophistes (c.340), a Cappadocian, reveals a Paschal celebration that lasted for a week: this week began with baptism at the vigil, and was devoted to mystagogical catechesis until its close on the following Sunday.[67] Cyril of Jerusalem (d. 386) has left us the mystagogical catechesis for this week, that are sometimes attributed to John his successor and which Egeria experienced. Ambrose in Milan (d. 397) during this week explained baptism, confirmation and eucharist to his neophytes, first as mysteries and later as sacraments. Augustine in Hippo said: "I must speak to you, the newborn infants, little children in Christ, new offspring of the Church, the gift of the Father, the fruitfulness of the Mother. God-fearing offshoots, the new colony, flower of our parenthood, fruit of our labor, my joy and my crown, all who stand fast in the Lord ... may you be clothed with the Life put on by you in the sacrament."[68]

But Chrysostom has left us a sermon on the feast of Easter that is a model of its kind. In it we find the traditional catechesis: the parallelism of the two Adams and the tree of Eden and the tree of the cross. The presence of the neophytes smells of spring and suggests images of trees and fields in full bloom, which prefigure the new creation.

[67]Cf. Talley, *op. cit.*, 56
[68]Cf. ML 1.35

⁶⁹Today we must all exclaim with blessed David: *Who can utter the mighty doings of the Lord or show forth all his praises?* (Ps. 106:2). Today we have come to a longed-for and salutary festival: it is the day of the resurrection of our Lord Jesus Christ, a day which has seen the end of the war and the conclusion of peace, a day when our reconciliation has been sealed, a day when death has been destroyed and the devil vanquished. Today is the day when men are united to angels, and mortals join in chanting hymns with the angelic powers. Today is the day that the devil's tyranny is abolished, the bonds of death are broken, and the triumph of hell is annihilated. Today is the day that the word of the prophet can be repeated: *O death, where is thy sting? O death, where is thy victory?* (1 Cor. 15:55).

Today Jesus Christ our Lord has broken the gates of brass and has caused the very person of death to disappear. Did I say 'the very person of death?' He has even changed its name. Death is no longer called 'death' but 'repose' and 'sleep.' Before the coming of Jesus Christ and the economy of the cross, the name death had a fearful ring. The first man, Adam, heard his condemnation in the sentence: *On whatever day you eat of the fruit of this tree you will die the death* (Gen. 2:17). And blessed Job called it by this name, saying, *Death is rest for man* (Job 3:23). The prophet David also said, *The death of sinners is worst* (Ps. 34:22). Not only is this separation of the soul from the body called death, but even hell. Listen to the words of the patriarch Jacob, *You will lead with sorrow my white head to hell* (Gen. 42:38). And again, hear another prophet: hell has opened its abyss (Isa. 5:14). And another prophet: *he will deliver me from the depths of hell* (Ps. 86:13). And you will find many other passages of the Old Testament calling departure from this life *death* and *hell.* But since Jesus Christ our God was offered for us in sacrifice and rose from the dead, our loving Lord has removed these names and introduced a new and extraordinary convention into human life. For departure from this life is no longer called death but repose and sleep.

⁶⁹Text: PG 52.765

What is the proof of this? Jesus Christ himself says, *Lazarus, our friend, sleeps. But I go that I may wake him from sleep* (Jn. 11:11). Just as it is easy for us to awaken and rouse a sleeping man, so it was easy for the Lord of us all to raise a man from the dead. And since His remark appeared novel and strange, and the apostles failed to comprehend it, He put it in clearer terms in deference to their weakness.

And the blessed Paul, the teacher of the world, writing to the Thessalonians said: *But we would not, brethren, have you ignorant concerning those who are asleep, lest you should grieve, even as the others who have no hope* (1 Thess. 4:13). Elsewhere he says, *Hence they also who have fallen asleep in Christ have they perished?* (1 Cor. 15:18). And again, *we who live, who survive until the coming of the Lord shall not precede those who have fallen asleep* (1 Thess. 4:15). And further, *For if we believe that Jesus died and rose again, so we ought also believe that with him God will bring those who have fallen asleep through Jesus* (1 Thess. 4:14).

You see death everywhere called 'repose' and 'sleep,' and what was dreaded before Jesus Christ is become easy to accept since His resurrection. You see the illustrious triumph of this resurrection? By it we have received a host of blessings. By it the wiles of the devil have lost their effectiveness. By it we laugh at death. By it we overlook the present life. By it we hasten to the prospect of future blessings. By it, though still clothed in a mortal body, we can, if we wish, enjoy the same privileges as the incorporeal angels.

Today we celebrate a great triumphal victory. Today our Lord has erected a trophy over vanquished death, destroyed the tyranny of the devil, and opened to us through His resurrection the way to salvation. Let us all then rejoice, exult and be glad. For though our Lord alone was victor and erected the trophy, we should share in His joy and happiness. It is for our salvation that He has accomplished all these things. And He has triumphed over the devil by the devil's own devices. He has taken the devil's own weapons and waged the contest with them. Listen to how He did this.

A virgin, a tree, and death had been the instruments of our defeat. For Eve was a virgin; she had not yet known Adam when she was seduced by the devil. The tree was the tree of knowledge, and death was the penalty it imposed on Adam. You see how a virgin, a tree and death became the instruments of our fall? Now see how they next became the instruments of our victory. Mary takes the place of Eve. The tree of the cross replaces the tree of knowledge of good and evil. The Lord's death replaces the death of Adam. Do you see how the devil is defeated by the very weapons of his prior victory? The devil had vanquished Adam by means of a tree. Christ vanquished the devil by means of the tree of the cross. The tree sent Adam to hell. The tree of the cross has recalled men from there. The tree had shown Adam laid prostrate, naked and low. The tree of the cross manifested to all the victorious Christ, naked and nailed on high. Adam's death sentence passed on to his successors. Christ's death gave life even to His predecessors. *Who can utter the mighty doings of the Lord or show forth all his praises?* (Ps. 106:2). Through death we men have become immortal. Through a fall we have risen. Through a defeat we have emerged as victors.

Do not, then, dishonor this feast, I beg you, but assume sentiments worthy of the favors bestowed on us by the grace of Jesus Christ. Let us not give ourselves up to excesses of drinking and eating, but, considering the liberality of our common Mother who gives equal honor to rich and poor, slaves and freemen, who confers her gifts equally upon all, let us strive to recognize the blessings of God who bears us testimony of so much love. We cannot recognize them better than by a life which is agreeable to Him, by increased carefulness. There is no need, then, on this feast which we solemnize, of riches and great expense, but only of a right will and a pure heart. Today there are no physical advantages: all is spiritual—the preaching of the word, the hallowed prayers, the priests' blessings, participation in the divine mysteries, peace and concord, and, finally, all the spiritual gifts worthy of the generosity of God. Joyfully, then, let us celebrate the day on which the Lord has risen. Yes, He has risen and with Himself He has raised up the whole earth. He has risen after breaking the bonds of death; He has raised us after having broken the bonds of our crimes.

Chapter Five

NEW SEASONS
OF THE LORD

The lunar calendar of the Pasch, unlike the solar calendar of all other feasts, united in a single night, not only the two weeks called Holy and Easter, but also two seasons, one of fast and the other of festival, respectively known as the forty days of Lent and the fifty days of Pentecost. Lent is derived from 'Lecten,' the old English word for spring, when the days are lengthened; Pentecost, on the other hand, is the Greek of the Septuagint for the Jewish feast of seven weeks (Tob. 2:1), or forty-nine days plus one from the Feast of Unleavened Bread to the Feast of First Fruits.

Pentecost, or the fifty days of Christian Pasch, is, as we shall see, the oldest season of the Church's year, dating back, if not to apostolic times, at least to the first century period of Jewish influence. Lent, on the other hand, made haste more slowly, and the observance varied from place to place and age to age; but by the time of Augustine (c.400) these seasons were the final evolution of the "Sacratissimum triduum crucifixi, sepulti, suscitati," mentioned in his letter to Januarius,[1] and thus, a sacrament, in the Augustinian sense, seasons of grace and glory:

[2]In this present life the subject of our meditation should be the praise of God, because divine praise is another name for

[1]Text: PL 33.215
[2]Text: CCL 40.2165

eternity: but we cannot or will not praise God in eternity if we do not prepare ourselves in time by the discipline of prayer: praise in eternity, prayer in time. Then our praise will be marked by joy; now our prayer is marked by groans ... for this reason there are two seasons, even here on earth, two sacraments ... one of temptation and tribulation, the other ... of rest and exultation: in other words there is the season before Easter and the season after Easter. The season before Easter signifies the tribulations in which we now are; the season after Easter signifies the bliss in which we shall then be. The fast we keep before Easter is a sacrament of the present life: the festival we keep after Easter is a sacrament of the life to come. Thus we spend Lent in fast and prayer, but we spend Pentecost in festival and praise: the one is before the Lord's resurrection; the other is after the resurrection. The baptism of the Lord invites us to accept this present life of trial, in which we must work and suffer and die; but the resurrection of the Lord invites us to hope for the life that is to come, when He shall come who shall make every recompense, evil for evil and good for good.

The making of these seasons of 1. Lent, and 2. Pentecost—their origin, development and significance, constitute the two main divisions of this chapter. However, a third section of lesser importance on 3. Advent and Quartertense is added, simply because as a season it is more fitting here than elsewhere.

1. Lent

As a season Lent did not exist in the third century. Holy Saturday was the only day in the year, "when the religious duty of fasting was universal and official" (Tertullian, *Prayer*. 18). Irenaeus (d. 202) knew of forty hours of fast in honor of the forty hours of Christ's death, which could be reckoned as one day or two. (Eus. *E.H.* 5.24). For Hippolytus (d. 235) those two days were the norm *(Apost. Trad.* 20.7), whereas the *Didascalia* (c. 250), as has been seen, recommended six full days of fast at least for the pious.

Even Dionysius (d. 268), whose function it was as bishop of Alexandria to announce each year to the Churches of Egypt the exact date of the Pascha, confined himself to the festival. (Eus. *E.H.* 7.20).

In the fourth century Lent made its appearance as a season first of fast and later of preparation for Easter. Athanasius (295-373) as Bishop of Alexandria, continued the festival letter of his predecessors, announcing to his suffragan sees the duration of the fast and the date of the festival:

[3]We begin the holy fast on the fifth day of Pharmuthi (March 31), and adding to it according to the number of those six holy and great days, which are the symbol of the creation of this world, let us rest and cease (from fasting) on the tenth day of the same Pharmuthi (April 5), on the holy Sabbath of the week. And when the first day of the holy week dawns and rises upon us, on the eleventh day of the same month (April 6), from which again we count all the seven weeks one by one, let us keep feast on the holy day of Pentecost—on that which was at one time to the Jews, typically, the feast of weeks, in which they granted forgiveness and settlement of debts; and indeed that day was one of deliverance in every respect. Let us keep the feast on the first day of the great week, as a symbol of the world to come, in which we here receive a pledge that we shall have everlasting life hereafter. Then, having passed hence, we shall keep a perfect feast with Christ, while we cry out and say, like the saints, 'I will pass to the place of the wondrous tabernacle, to the house of God; with the voice of gladness and thanksgiving, the shouting of those who rejoice' whence pain and sorrow and sighing have fled, and upon our heads gladness and joy shall have come to us! May we be judged worthy to be partakers in these things.

Let us remember the poor, and not forget kindness to strangers; above all, let us love God with all our soul, and might, and strength, and our neighbor as ourselves. So may we receive those things which the eye hath not seen, nor the ear

[3]Text: PG 26.1366 = LNPF, ser. 2,4.509

heard, and which have not entered into the heart of man, which God hath prepared for those that love Him, through His only Son, our Lord and Saviour, Jesus Christ; through whom, to the Father alone by the Holy Spirit be glory and dominion for ever and ever. Amen.

In this *First Festal Letter* for the year 329 Athanasius announced as normative the fast of six days; but from the following year onwards he emphasized again and again the fast of forty days:

[4]We begin the fast of forty days on the thirteenth of the month Phamenoth (March 9). After we have given ourselves to fasting in continued succession, let us begin the holy Paschal week on the eighteenth of the month Pharmuthi (April 13). Then resting on the twenty-third of the same mounth Pharmuthi (April 18), and keeping the feast afterwards on the first of the week, on the twenty-fourth (April 19), let us add to these the seven weeks of the great Pentecost, wholly rejoicing and exulting in Christ Jesus our Lord, through whom to the Father be glory and dominion in the Holy Spirit for ever and ever. Amen.

The brethren which are with me salute you. Salute one another with a holy kiss.

Here endeth the second Festal Letter of the holy lord Athanasius, Bishop of Alexandria.

The fast of forty days, recognized by the fifth Canon of the Council of Nicaea (325) quickly spread to all parts of the Church in the fourth century, but was not observed in the same manner in each place. Again in the *Diary of Egeria* there is a clear description of Lent in Jerusalem at the end of the fourth century and after the time of Cyril, the bishop:

[5]When the season of Lent is at hand, it is observed in the following manner. Now whereas with us the forty days

[4]*ibid.* 1371 = LNPF ser. 2,4.512
[5]Text: SC 296.256 = ACW 38.97

preceding Easter are observed, here they observe the eight weeks before Easter. This is the reason why they observe eight weeks: On Sundays and Saturdays they do not fast, except on the one Saturday which is the vigil of Easter, when it is necessary to fast. Except on that day, there is absolutely no fasting here on Saturdays at any time during the year. And so, when eight Sundays and seven Saturdays have been deducted from the eight weeks—for it is necessary, as I have just said, to fast on one Saturday—there remain forty-one days which are spent in fasting, which are called here *eortae*, that is to say, Lent.

On each day of each week this is what is done. On Sunday, at the first cockcrow, the bishop inside the Anastasis reads from the Gospel the passage of the resurrection of the Lord, as is done on every Sunday throughout the year; and all the same ceremonies are performed until daybreak at the Anastasis and at the Cross as are preformed on every other Sunday during the year. Afterwards, in the morning, as always happens on Sunday, everyone assembles for the liturgy in the major church called the Martyrium, on Golgotha behind the Cross, where the rites customarily performed on Sunday are accomplished. When the dismissal has been given from the church, everyone chanting hymns goes to the Anastasis, as is always done on Sundays. By the time these ceremonies are completed, the fifth hour is at hand. The usual vespers service takes place at its regular hour at the Anastasis and the Cross, just as it does in all holy places. On Sundays there is no service at the ninth hour.

On Monday one also goes to the Anastasis at cockcrow, where everything is done just as it always is until morning. Once again at the third hour everyone returns to the Anastasis, where the ritual customarily observed at the sixth hour throughout the year is now celebrated, for during Lent a service has been added, so that they go at the third hour as well. At the sixth hour and at the ninth hour and at vespers those services take place which customarily are celebrated throughout the year in these holy places. The same ritual is celebrated in exactly the same manner on Tuesday as on Monday.

On Wednesday, while it is still night, they go to the

Anastasis, where the usual ritual is observed until morning; and the third and sixth hours are observed as usual. But as it is always the custom at the ninth hour throughout the year on Wednesdays and Fridays to assemble for the liturgy in the church of Sion at this hour—for in these parts on Wednesdays and Fridays they always fast, even the catechumens, unless the day happens to be the feast of a martyr—they consequently assemble for the liturgy at Sion at the ninth hour. If by chance during Lent the feast day of a martyr occurs on a Wednesday or a Friday, they do not assemble for the liturgy at Sion at the ninth hour. During Lent, as I have already said, on Wednesday everyone assembles for the liturgy at Sion at the ninth hour as is customary throughout the year, and whatever ritual is customarily observed at that time takes place, except for the offering of the sacrifice. So that the people will know the law, the bishop and a priest preach assiduously. When the dismissal has been given, the people, chanting hymns, lead the bishop from there to the Anastasis. They come from there in such a way that it is already the hour of vespers when they enter the Anastasis. Hymns and antiphons are sung, prayers are said, and the vespers service takes place at the Anastasis and the Cross. The vespers service during Lent is always held later than it is on other days throughout the year.

On Thursday everything is done just as on Monday and Tuesday. On Friday everything is done as on Wednesday; and so everyone goes to Sion at the ninth hour, and the bishop is likewise led back from there to the Anastasis to the accompaniment of hymns. But on Friday they celebrate the vigil in the Anastasis from the hour when they have returned from Sion singing hymns until morning, that is, from the hour of vespers until the beginning of morning on the following day, which is Saturday. The sacrifice is offered early in the Anastasis that the dismissal may be given before sunrise. All during the night psalms with responses and antiphons are sung alternately; there are readings from Scripture; and all this continues until morning. The divine service which takes place on Saturdays at the Anastasis—I mean, of course, the offering of the sacrifice—is celebrated before sunrise, so that at the hour when the sun begins to rise, the divine service has taken place at the Anastasis. This is how the ritual is celebrated every week during Lent.

> The historian, Socrates (c.450), who continued the work of Eusebius, and covered the period of the Church from the beginning of the fourth century to the middle of the fifth, describes the practices of other churches that were known to him:

[6]The fasts before Easter will be found to be differently observed among different people. Those at Rome fast three successive weeks before Easter, excepting Saturdays and Sundays. Those in Illyrica and all over Greece and Alexandria observe a fast of six weeks, which they term 'the forty days' fast.' Others commencing their fast from the seventh week before Easter, and fasting three to five days only, and that at intervals, yet call that time 'the forty days' fast.' It is indeed surprising to me that thus differing in the number of days, they should both give it one common appelation; but some assign one reason for it, and others another, according to their several fancies. One can see also a disagreement about the manner of abstinence from food, as well as about the number of days. Some wholly abstain from things that have life: others feed on fish only of all living creatures: many, together with fish, eat fowl also, saying that according to Moses, these were likewise made out of the waters. Some abstain from eggs, and all kinds of fruits: others partake of dry bread alone; still others eat not even this: while others, having fasted till the ninth hour, afterwards take any sort of food without distinction. And among various nations there are other usages, for which inumerable reasons are assigned. Since however no one can produce a written command as an authority, it is evident that the apostles left each one to his own free will in the matter, to the end that each might perform what is good not by constraint or necessity. Such is the difference in the churches on the subject of fasts.

[6]Text: PG 67.633

This reference of Socrates to a fast of three successive weeks in Rome is confusing on account of the biblical association and the widespread practice of the forty days: thus some have understood the weeks in an alternating manner, thereby preserving the fast of six weeks or forty days. Certainly Jerome, writing in Rome in 384, was aware of the forty days: "all year round. Asella observed a continual fast remaining without food for two or three days at a time, but when the forty days arrived she hoisted her every sail, if I may speak in this manner, and fasted well nigh from week's end to week's end with a cheerful and happy countenance."[7]

In the beginning the forty days of Lent were everywhere reckoned according to local custom. In the East generally, seven weeks made forty fast days by excluding the Sundays, but in Jerusalem eight weeks were necessary since there was no fast on Saturdays and Sundays (Egeria 27). In the West, on the other hand, six weeks sufficed at first, when they observed the fast on Saturdays and Sundays: later when the Sunday fast was abandoned, Gregory the Great (c.600) added Ash Wednesday, and the days following, to make the required forty. Ultimately, however, all computation depended exactly on the festival being celebrated—the one Paschal night of the ancients, or "the *Sacratissimum triduum curcifixi, sepulti, suscitati*" of Augustine, or the "*dies Resurrectionis*" of Gregory the Great.

The institution of Lent at the beginning of the fourth century met the needs of the Church at that time by becoming forty days of liturgical and catechetical preparation for faithful and catechumen alike: thus, on the one hand, the high standards of "the little flock" of more ancient times, "the remnant of Israel," so to speak, were preached to the great numbers that trooped into the Church after the Peace of Constantine (313) and, on the other hand, the divine mysteries were explained to the crowds that were still coming. In East and West, Lent became a season of *metanoia* and catechesis, and spring was the simile that ran

---

[7]Text: CSEL 54.216

like a leitmotif through the sermons and instructions of so many preachers and teachers. Asterius, the Sophist (d. 345), is an early example from the Greek East:

[8]The resurrection of Christ has caused a double Spring to rise on the world. How 'double'? Because along with the Spring visible to our senses has arisen the intelligible Spring. The intelligible Sun, Christ, the lamp of souls, illuminator of the darkness, traversing the Passion like Winter, traversing Hades, death, and the tomb like sombre clouds, has shown us in the resurrection a brilliant light and a radiant rising. Since the spring of the resurrection has arisen and since Christ, like the sun, has caused souls to rise by the wood of the cross, the vernal shower of baptism has come and has caused the newly-illuminated to be as resplendent as the flowers of Spring.

Eusebius of Caesarea (d. 339), a contemporary of Asterius, also contributed important developments to the Spring motif: the description is standard. Spring is the most suitable time for salvation: the sun is at the beginning of its course, the moon at its side in full brilliance, transforming the whole course of the night into luminous day. Ended are the furies of the winter storms, ended the long nights, ended the floods. Henceforth in the newness of a shining atmosphere sailors find the sea calm. The fields are filled with ears of grain, the trees laden with fruit. But spring is suitable not just because of its beauty, but because it is the anniversary of the first days of creation. The spring is preferable to the extremes of winter and summer, and preferable to the autumn when the fields are barren and despoiled of their fruits. Spring is to the year what the head is to the body.

Gregory of Nyssa (d. 394) somewhat later examines various earthly phenomena—human birth, the production of pottery, the growth of a blade of grass—to show that re-creation and resurrection of the body are logical and feasible:

[8]Text: SC 187.74

⁹From the grain ... let us pass to an examination of trees, noting how winter brings death to them each year. When their fruits are gathered the leaves fall and the trees remain bare and devoid of beauty. But when the moment of spring comes they are covered in beautiful blossoms and are clothed again with shady leaves. It is a sight to delight the eyes of man, a concert hall full of tuneful birds sitting among the branches.

> From trees he passes to reptiles awakening from their hibernation:

¹⁰The life of reptiles leads me to the same conclusion, for their dynamic spark is dead in winter when they lie completely motionless in their holes for six months. But when the appointed time comes, and thunder reverberates through the world, they hear its sound like some signal of life, and quickly leap up and return to their customary ways after this long interval. What does this mean? Let the one who criticizes and judges the works of God tell me why he admits that thunder restores the serpents from virtual death and yet denies that men are revived at the sound of God's trumpet as the Scripture says: *for the trumpet shall sound and the dead shall rise* (1 Cor. 15:52).

> In a letter sent as an Easter present to Eusebius, bishop of Chalcis in Coele-Syria, he sheds light on the double coincidence that it is in wintertime that we celebrate Christ's birth, but 'it is when the days are as long as the nights that he restores man to life.' Elsewhere he writes:

¹¹It is not the natural custom of spring to shine forth all at once but there come as preludes of spring the sunbeam gently warming earth's frozen surface, and the bud half hidden beneath the clod, and breezes blowing over the earth so that the fertilizing and generative power of the air penetrates deeply

⁹Text: PG 46.669
¹⁰Text: *ibid.* 672
¹¹Text: PG 46.1044

into it. One may see the fresh and tender grass, the return of birds which winter had banished and many such tokens which are rather signs of spring than spring itself.

He goes on to say that the local people are spiteful and malicious layers of mischief congeal like ice forming in their cottages when the rain leaks in. We have 'need of many prayers that the grace of the Spirit may thaw the bitterness of their hatred and melt the frost that is hardening upon them from their malice.'

Thanking a friend for consoling him in trouble he asks:

[12]What flower in spring is so bright, what voices of singing birds so sweet, what breezes that soothe the calm sea so light and mild, what glebe so fragrant to the husbandmen, whether it be teeming with green blades or waving with fruitful ears, as is the spring of the soul lit up with peaceful beams from the radiance which shone in your letter which raised our life from despondency to gladness.

Cyril of Alexandria, (d.444) continued the custom of his predecessors in this ancient see of sending each year to all the Churches of Egypt, in the form of a pastoral letter, an announcement on the date of Easter and the preceding fast. These letters, written between 414 and 442 and wrongly called *Paschal Homilies*, exhort to fast and abstinence, vigilance and prayer, almsgiving and works of mercy, and make frequent use of the Spring simile:

[13]Gone is the hateful threat of winter, the bad weather and darkness have vanished, the rains and sharp winds have subsided. Spring days are here again, summoning the farmer from his torpor and inactivity to work. The meadows are bedecked with flowers. Trees on mountainside and in gardens

[12]Text: PG 46.1040
[13]Text: PG 77.429

begin to sprout new buds, as from nature's womb. Fields are clothed with green. All this is a monument of God's providence.

Allegorical interpretation follows:

Man's nature should contend with mother earth in fecundity, blossoming forth in piety.

In an exegesis of *Song of Songs* 2:10-12, he says:

Spring is especially suitable for the Pasch. It is the time when the earth is warmed by the pure, placid rays of the sun. Trees bud. Grass comes to greenness. Among the flowers laughing in the meadows is the lily. The bee emerges from the hive and pursues its gathering of honey unimpeded by rain. Beasts leave their places of hibernation, lambs frisk. The knife for pruning the vines is sharpened.

All this is allegorically explained:

The many-headed dragon, the devil, is winter's darkness. Christ is the Sun emerging with light to scatter his reign of darkness.

The theme of Spring continued in the East as a simile and a symbol of the annual renewal and increase of the Church, and in the sixth century Leontius of Constantinople (c.540) continues to exhort in the traditional manner:

[14]Let us really rejoice and be glad in it, because we have seen what we desired, because we have grasped what we sought, because we have contemplated what we awaited, because the Christian spring has dawned, because the flowers of the saints have blossomed, because the lilies of the newly-illuminated have matured, because the children of the (baptismal) bath have been resplendent. Truly, *this is the day which the Lord has made. Let us rejoice and be glad in it* (Ps. 118:24).

[14]Text: PG 77.429

The same spirit of Spring also is found in the catechesis of Cyril which permeated the sermons of his brother bishops for the faithful at large: "Already the savor of bliss is upon you, who have come to be enlightened: you have begun to pluck spiritual flowers with which to weave your heavenly crowns. Already are you redolent with the fragrance of the Holy Spirit.... Lo, now the trees are in blossom; grant that the fruit be duly gathered":[15]

[16]At what season does the Savior rise? Is it in summer or at another time? *The winter is past, the rains are over and gone. The flowers appear on the earth, the time of pruning has come* (Cant. 2:12). Is not the land now full of flowers, and are not the vines being pruned? You see how he said also that the winter was past. For in this month (Xanthicus), spring is already come. This is the time, the first month among the Hebrews in which is celebrated the feast of the Pasch, formerly the figurative Pasch, but now the true. This is the season of the creation of the world; for God then said: *Let the earth bring forth vegetation, yielding seed according to its kind and according to its likeness* (Gen. 1:11). Now, as you see, every herb is in seed. At that time God made the sun and the moon and gave them courses of equal day and night; just a few days ago we had the equinox. Then God said: *Let us make man in our image and likeness* (Gen. 1:26). Man received the image but obscured the likeness by his disobedience. His loss of grace and his restoration took place in the same season. At this season created man, by his disobedience, was cast out of Paradise; then, he, who believed by his obedience, was brought in. Salvation came about in the same season as the Fall, when the flowers appeared, and the time of pruning was come (cf. Cant. 2:12).

Just consider the spring, and the various kinds of flowers, so alike and yet so diverse, the deep red of the rose and the pure white of the lily.

[15]Text: PG 33.332
[16]Text: PG 33.836 = FOTC 64.37

Among the Latin Fathers of the West in the fourth century the simile of spring was also common in the preaching and catechesis of Lent for the renewal of the faithful and the initiation of the catechumens. Indeed Spring was a favorite theme in Latin literature: there are the three Spring Odes of Horace (1:4; 4:7; and 4:12), with the familiar images—flocks leaving their hibernation, ploughman quitting his fireside, and dry beached ships being hauled to the water; for Virgil it was springtime, great spring, when the world first began, a temperate spell between the extremes of heat and cold, when heaven held Mother Earth in his arms and comforted her (*Georgics* 2.336-345). Ambrose of Milan belonged to this tradition:

[17] ... the year, has the stamp of a world coming to birth, as the splendor of the springtime shines forth all the more clearly because of the winter's ice and darkness now past. The shape of the circles of years to come has been given form by the first dawn of the world. Based on that precedent, the succession of years would tend to arise, and at the commencement of each year new seedlings would be produced, as the Lord God has said: *Let the earth bring forth the green herb and such as may seed, and the fruit tree, yielding fruit after its kind. And immediately the earth produced the green herb and the fruit-bearing tree* (Gen. 1:11). By this very fact both the constant mildness of divine Providence and the speed in which the earth germinates favor for us the hypothesis of a vernal period. For, although it was in the power of God to ordain creation at any time whatsoever and for earthly nature to obey, so that amid winter's ice and frost earth might bear and produce fruits under the fostering hand of His celestial power, He refrained. It was not in His eternal plan that the land held fast in the rigid bonds of frost should suddenly be released to bear fruits and that blooming plants should mingle with frosts unsightly.

Wherefore, in order to show that the creation of the world took place in the spring, Scripture says: *This month shall be to you the beginning of months, it is for you the first in the*

[17]Text: PL 14.128 = FOTC 42.12

months of the year (Ex. 12:2), calling the first month the springtime. It was fitting that the beginning of the year be the beginning of generation and that generation itself be fostered by the gentler breezes. The tender germs of matter would be unable to endure exposure to the bitter cold of winter or to the torrid heat of summer.

At the same time, one may note, since it belongs here by right, that the entrance into this generation and into this way of life seems to have occurred at the time when the regular transition from this generation to regeneration takes place.

The sons of Israel left Egypt in the season of spring and passed through the sea, *being baptized in the cloud and in the sea* (1 Cor. 10:1), as the Apostle said. At that time each year the Pasch of Jesus Christ is celebrated, that is to say, the passing over from vices to virtues, from the desires of the flesh to grace and sobriety of mind, *from the unleavened bread of malice and wickedness to truth and sincerity* (1 Cor. 5:8). Accordingly, the regenerated are thus addressed: *This month shall be to you the beginning of months; it is for you the first in the months of the year* (Ex. 12:2).

> Gaudentius of Brescia (c.400) sees spring as particularly suitable for the celebration of the fast and the festival "after the fog of autumn and the sadness of winter, but before the heat of summer; for Christ, the Sun of Justice, was to scatter the darkness of Judaism and the ice of paganism before the heat of the future judgment by the peaceful light of the resurrection ... this is why the Son of God raised up the fallen world by His own resurrection at the very season in which He created it out of nothing, so that all things might be refashioned in Him."[18]
>
> Chromatius of Aquileia, a contemporary of Gaudentius and a disciple of Jerome, felt that January, when all things are dead is not the first month of the year: "the Gentiles are greatly mistaken in thinking that it is the first month: Moses was right in saying that the Pasch was the first month, for now the herbs in the meadow rise, as it were, from death;

[18]Text: PL 20.844

likewise the trees that begin to bloom, and the first buds on the vines ... the very air is joyful with this newness of time ... a season when the very elements of the earth are renewed ... indeed the human race itself is renewed, as the newly baptized throughout the world rise in newness of life."[19] To illustrate the reasonableness of fasting at this time, another contemporary, Maximus of Turin (c.410), points to nature as our summons and guide:

[20]For the prescribed forty days coincide in time with that season of the year when nature experiences a thaw; it is the business of fasting to produce a thaw in our soul. This is not a coincidence. God is sketching His will for us through the living motions of nature. The earth during the appointed forty days rids itself of winter's harshness and is cut through by the plough that it might become suitable for earthly crops. We, during the forty days, give up the harshness of sin; fasting digs up our earth to render it receptive to heavenly seeds. And just as this is the season for the young twig of a tree to become fruitful and for new branches to produce buds so also at this time man's lifeless hope revives and lost faith is restored for glory. Nature adorns herself with blossoms and seems to honor the great feast day with her splendor. We, likewise, should now produce roses from our thorns, that is, justice instead of sin, compassion in place of sternness, and instead of avarice, liberality. Only by fasting can we be free of the thorns of our sins. For fasting produces chastity, humility and moderation—the blossoms of our life which blossoms Christ finds fragrant.

In Rome towards the middle of the fifth century there arose during Lent the new practice of the '*Statio*,' when faithful penitents and catechumens processed and assembled at "a fixed place," or Station, for prayer and the Eucharist. At this time Leo the Great (c. 450) was to Rome what Cyril was to Jerusalem the century before, and under his

[19]Text: CCL 9A.77
[20]Text: CCL 23.276

influence the fast of forty days became a feast of spiritual exercises—"*quadraginta dierum exercitatio.*" For these stational celebrations, processional hymns were composed, scripture readings were made to harmonize with each other and with the significance of the particular Church, and indeed with the particular needs of penitents and catechumens. Themes of fasting and conversion, of penance and reconciliation, of almsgiving and mercy, thus made their appearance in the Lenten sermons of Leo, which are the great expressions of the stational season:

[21]*Behold, now is the acceptable time, behold now is the day of salvation* (2 Cor. 6:2). For though there are no seasons which are not full of divine blessings, and though access is ever open to us to God's mercy through His grace, yet now all men's minds should be moved with greater zeal to spiritual progress, and animated by larger confidence, when the return of the day, on which we were redeemed, invites us to all the duties of godliness: that we may keep the super-excellent mystery of the Lord's Passion with bodies and hearts purified. These great mysteries do indeed require from us such unflagging devotion and unwearied reverence that we should remain in God's sight always the same, as we ought to be found on the Easter feast itself. But because few have this constancy, and, because so long as the stricter observance is relaxed in consideration of the frailty of the flesh, and so long as one's interests extend over all the various actions of this life, even pious hearts must get some soil from the dust of the world, the Divine Providence has with great beneficence taken care that the discipline of the forty days should heal us and restore the purity of our minds, during which the faults of other times might be redeemed by pious acts and removed by chaste fasting.

For Leo the forty days are *mystic days*, dedicated to the benefits of fasting, and filled with spiritual delights:

[21]Text: PL 54.275 = LNPF, ser. 2.12.155

²²Let works of piety, therefore, be our delight, and let us be filled with those kinds of food which feed us for eternity. Let us rejoice in the replenishment of the poor, whom our bounty has satisfied. Let us delight in the clothing of those whose nakedness we have covered with needful raiment. Let our humaneness be felt by the sick in their illnesses, by the weakly in their infirmities, by the exiles in their hardships, by the orphans in their destitution, and by solitary widows in their sadness: in the helping of whom there is no one that cannot carry out some amount of benevolence. For no one's income is small, whose heart is big: and the measure of one's mercy and goodness does not depend on the size of one's means. Wealth of good will is never rightly lacking, even in a slender purse. Doubtless the expenditure of the rich is greater, and that of the poor smaller, but there is no difference in the fruit of their works, where the purpose of the workers is the same.

These delights must be increased throughout Lent "that all might be reborn in Christ" and "rescued from the grasp of the Evil One":

²³*Stand, therefore, dearly-beloved*, as the Apostle says, *having the loins of your mind girt in truth, and your feet shod in the preparation of the gospel of peace* (Eph. 6:14). Relying, therefore, dearly-beloved, on these arms, let us enter actively and fearlessly on the contest set before us: so that in this fasting struggle we may not rest sastisfied with only this end, that we should think abstinence from food alone desirable. For it is not enough that the substance of our flesh should be reduced, if the strength of the soul be not also developed. When the outer man is somewhat subdued, let the inner man be somewhat refreshed; and when bodily excess is denied to our flesh, let our mind be invigorated by spiritual delights. Let every Christian scrutinize himself, and search severely into his inmost heart: let him see that no discord cling there, no wrong desire be harbored. Let chasteness drive incontinence far away; let the

²²Text: *ibid.* 270 = LNPF ser. 2,12.155
²³Text: *ibid.* 267 = LNPF ser. 2,12.153

light of truth dispel the shades of deception; let the swellings of pride subside; let wrath yield to reason; let the darts of ill-treatment be shattered, and the chidings of the tongue be bridled; let thoughts of revenge fall through, and injuries be given over to oblivion. In fine, let *every plant which the heavenly Father hath not planted be removed by the roots* (Mt. 15:13). For then only are the seeds of virtue well nourished in us, when every foreign germ is uprooted from the field of wheat.

> For Leo, Lent is the time "when the devil waxes furiously throughout the whole world and the Christian army must do combat ... those that have grown lukewarm and slothful ... through worldly cares ... must be furnished with spiritual armor."[24] Hence the importance of the season for everyone:

[25]On all days and seasons, indeed, dearly beloved, some marks of the divine goodness are set, and no part of the year is destitute of sacred mysteries .... For as the Easter festival approaches, the greatest and most binding of fasts is kept, and its observance is imposed on all the faithful without exception; because no one is so holy that he ought not to be holier, nor so devout that he might not be more devout.

> This positive approach to Lent as a season of spiritual exercises more than external fasts, which Leo emphasized, was continued everywhere afterwards, and is the common theme of Western or Latin Fathers like Caesarius of Arles (d.542). For him Lent was a time of intense Christian living when the faithful were renewed in faith and hope, and charity was seen as the very life of the Church:

[26]For this reason I exhort you, dearest brethren, to rise rather early for the vigils, and above all to come to terce, sext

[24]Text: *ibid.* 303
[25]Text: *ibid.* 302
[26]Text: CCL 104.792 = FOTC 66.42

and none. Let no one withdraw himself from the holy office unless either infirmity or public service or at least great necessity keeps him occupied. Let it not be enough for you that you hear the divine lessons in church, but read them yourselves at home or look for someone else to read them and willingly listen to them when they do. Remember the thought of our Lord, brethren, when He says: *If he were to gain the whole world and destroy himself in the process, what can a man offer in exchange for his very self* (Mt. 16:26)? Above all keep in mind and always fear greatly what is common knowledge: *The burdens of the world have made them miserable.* Therefore busy yourself in your home in such a way that you do not neglect your soul. Finally, if you cannot do more, at least labor as much on behalf of your soul as you desire to labor for the sake of your body ... for ... by fasting, reading, and prayer in these forty days we ought to store up for our souls provisions, as it were, for the whole year. Although through the mercy of God you frequently and devoutly hear the divine lessons throughout the entire year, still during these days we ought to rest from the winds and the sea of this world by taking refuge, as it were, in the haven of Lent, and in the quiet of silence to receive the divine lessons in the receptacle of our heart. Devoting ourselves to God out of love for eternal life, during these days let us with all solicitude strive to repair and compose in the little ship of our soul whatever throughout the year has been broken, or destroyed, or damaged, or ruined by many storms, that is, by the waves of sins. And since it is necessary for us to endure the storms and tempests of this world while we are still in this frail body, as often as the enemy wills to lead us astray by means of the roughest storms or to deceive us by the most voluptuous pleasures, with God's help may he always find us prepared against him....

Therefore, I beseech you again and again. During these holy days of Lent if you cannot cut off the occupations of this world, at least strive to curtail them in part. By fleeing from this world, through an expedient loss and a most glorious gain you may take away from earthly occupations a few hours in which you can devote yourselves to God. For this world either laughs at us or is laughed at by us; either we yield to it and are despised, or we despise it in order to obtain eternal rewards. Thus you either reject and despise the world, or you yield to it and are pursued or even trampled upon by it. But it is better for you to despise the world and by trampling upon it to make a step for yourself whereby you may ascend on high. If, in accord with your usual practice, you both willingly heed and strive faithfully to fulfill, dearest brethren, the truths which we are suggesting for the salvation of all by presuming upon your obedience, you will celebrate Easter with joy and will happily come to eternal life.

For Caesarius the days of Lent are always "holy and spiritual," as they were "mystic" for Leo, when we should bow down in worship and return to the Lord with all our heart:

[27]*Come let us bow down in worship; let us kneel before the Lord who made us* (Ps. 95:6); and again: *Return to me with your whole heart, with fasting, and weeping, and mourning* (Joel 2:12). If we notice carefully, dearest brethren, the holy days of Lent signify the life of the present world, just as Easter prefigures eternal bliss. Now just as we have a kind of sadness in Lent in order that we may rightly rejoice at Easter, so as long as we live in this world we ought to do penance in order that we may be able to receive pardon for our sins in the future and arrive at eternal joy. Each one ought to sigh over his own sins, shed tears, and give alms in such a way that with God's help he may always try to avoid the same faults as long as he lives. Just as there never has been, is not now, and never will be a soul without slight sins, so with the help and assistance of God we ought to be altogether without serious sins.

Now in order that we may obtain this, if burdens of the world keep us occupied at other times, at least during the holy days of Lent *let us reflect on the law of the Lord*, as it is written, *by day and by night* (Ps. 1:2). Let us so fill our hearts with the sweetness of the divine law that we leave no place within us devoid of virtues so that vices could occupy it. Just as at the

[27]Text: *ibid.* 799 = FOTC 66.49

time of the harvest or vintage, brethren, enough is gathered so that the body may be fed, so during the days of Lent as at a time of spiritual harvest or vintage we ought to gather the means whereby our soul may live for ever.

> In all his homilies Caesarius stresses the importance of the spiritual exercises and especially the Word of God: "The soul which is not fed on the food of God's Word is found to be parched and useless, and fit for no good work":[28]

[29]Willingly listen to the divine lessons in church, as you usually do, and read them over again in your own homes. If anyone is so busy that he cannot take time for holy Scripture before lunch, he should not be ashamed to read over something of it at his own little meal. In this way just as the body is fed with food, so the soul is refreshed by the word of God; then the whole man, that is, both the exterior and the interior, may rise up satisfied from the holy and salutary feast. For if only the body is refreshed, but the soul is not fed on the word of God, the handmaid is satisfied but the mistress is tormented by hunger, and your holy selves know how wrong this is. For this reason, as I have already said, you ought to read and listen to the sacred lessons with such eagerness that you may be able to speak about them and teach them to others both in your own homes and elsewhere, wherever you are. As you, like clean animals, masticate the word of God by continuous reflection, you may be able both to procure useful flavor for yourselves, that is, their spiritual meaning, and with God's help give it to others.

> Almsgiving is seen throughout as the fruit of the fast and the charity of the Church:

[30]It is good to fast, brethren, but it is better to give alms. If anyone can do both, those are two good acts; but if he cannot,

[28]*Ibid.* 800
[29]Text: *ibid.* 801 = FOTC 66.51-52
[30]Text: *ibid.* 804 = FOTC 66.54

the almsgiving is better. If there is no possibility of fasting, almsgiving without fasting is enough for a man, but fasting without almsgiving does not suffice at all. Therefore if a man cannot fast, almsgiving without fasting is good; but if he can do so, fasting along with almsgiving is no good unless it happens that a man is so poor that he possesses nothing at all that he can give. For such a man good will is sufficient, if he has nothing to give, according to what is written: *Glory to God in high heaven, peace on earth to men of good will* (Lk. 2:14).

Who will there be who can excuse himself, when our Lord promises that He would give a reward even for a cup of cold water? Now why did He say cold water? Perhaps so no poor man could excuse himself because of lack of wood or say in truth that he had no vessel in which to heat the water. Finally through the blessed prophet, dearest brethren, the Lord exhorts and admonishes us to almsgiving in such a way that almost no one is so poor that he can excuse himself. For thus he speaks: *This is the fasting that I wish, says the Lord: sharing your bread with the hungry* (Isa. 58:6). He did not say that he should give it all, because perhaps that poor man had nothing else, but sharing it, he says. This means that even if your poverty is so great that you have nothing but one loaf, nevertheless break off some of it and give it to the poor. *Sheltering the oppressed and the homeless* (Isa. 58:7), he also says. If anyone is so poor that he has no food to give to the poor, at least he should prepare a little bed for the stranger in some corner of his house. What are we going to say to this, brethren? What excuse will we be able to offer if we have roomy, spacious homes but scarcely ever condescend to receive a stranger? We do not know, or rather do not believe, that Christ is received in all strangers, as He Himself said: *I was a stranger, and you welcomed me* (Mt. 25:35), and *As often as you did it for one of my least brothers, you did it for me* (Mt. 25:40). . . .

Therefore, as we suggested above, dearest brethren, let an abundance of almsgiving make our fasts acceptable, for fasting without almsgiving is like a lamp without oil. Just as a lamp which is lit without oil can smoke but cannot give light, so fasting without almsgiving pains the body, to be sure, but does not illuminate the soul with the light of charity. As for our present course of action, brethren, let us in the meantime fast in such a way that we lavish our lunches upon the poor, so that we may not store up in our purses what we intended to eat, but rather in the stomachs of the poor. Truly the hand of the poor is the treasury of Christ.

> Finally, the practice of chastity among the married was seen as a desirable, if not integral, part of the spiritual exercises of Lent according to Caesarius.

[31]Now I believe that through the inspiration of God as the special feasts approach, you, dear people, always observe chastity even with your own wives several days before that. Nevertheless, although it is unnecessary, at the sight of your dear selves I even remind you of what I believe you are doing. If with God's help you observe chastity throughout Lent and even to the end of Eastertide, then at that sacred Paschal feast when you are clothed with the brightness of charity, purified by almsgiving, adorned by prayer, vigils, and fasts as with heavenly, spiritual pearls, at harmony not only with your friends but also with your enemies, when you approach the altar of the Lord with a secure and easy conscience, you will be able to receive His Body and Blood, not to your judgment, but as a remedy.

> Such was the season of Lent that originated in the East as a fast and grew in the West as a renewal, and which was always seen in the East and West as a preparation for the festival:

[32]The beginning of the fast of forty days is on the fifth of Phamenoth (March 1); and when, as I have said, we have first been purified and prepared by those days, we begin the holy week of the great Easter on the tenth of Pharmuthi (April 1), in which, my beloved brethren, we should use more prolonged

[31]Text: *ibid.* 806 = FOTC 66.57
[32]Text: PG 26.1376 = LNPF ser. 2,4.515

prayers, and fastings, and watchings, that we may be enabled to anoint our lintels with precious blood, and to escape the destroyer. Let us rest, then, on the fifteenth of the month of Pharmuthi (April 10), for on the evening of that Saturday we hear the angels' message, *Why seek ye the Living One among the dead? He is risen* (Lk. 24:5). Immediately afterwards that great Sunday receives us, I mean on the sixteenth of the same month Pharmuthi (April 11), on which our Lord, having risen, gave us peace towards our neighbors. (Cyril of Alexandria)

2. Pentecost

The unity of Lent and Pentecost, fast and festival, as seasonal expressions of the one Paschal night, had been well established by the time of Augustine (c. 400), and imaginatively expressed by him in his *Letter to Januarius*:

[33]The forty-day fast of Lent draws its authority from the Old Testament, from the fasts of Moses and Elias, and from the Gospel, because the Lord fasted that many days, showing that the Gospel is not at variance with the Law and the Prophets. The Law is personified by Moses, the prophets by Elias, between whom the Lord appeared transfigured on the mountain, making manifest what the Apostle said of Him: *being witnessed by the law and the prophets* (Rom. 3:21). In what part of the year, then, could the observance of Lent be more appropriately instituted than that adjoining, so to speak, and touching on the Lord's Passion? In it is portrayed this toilsome life, with its need of self-conquest, to be achieved by withdrawing from the friendship of the world, a deceitful and flattering friendship, always displaying and strewing about its counterfeit enticements. And I think that life itself is represented by the number forty, because the number ten, in which is the perfection of our happiness . . . is made known in time to the world, because the world is divided by four winds, made up of four elements, and goes through the changes of

[33]Text: PL 33.217 = FOTC 12.283

four seasons annually; but four times ten makes forty, and forty, composed of its parts, is added to ten and becomes fifty, which is the reward of labor and self-restraint. Not without reason did the Lord Himself remain on this earth forty days after his resurrection, when He conversed with His disciples in this life, and when He had ascended into heaven, after a space of ten days, He sent the promised Holy Spirit on the perfected day of Pentecost. There is another mystery connected with the fiftieth day, in the fact that seven times seven makes forty-nine, and when there is a return to the beginning, which is the octave, identical with the first, fifty is complete; and these days after the Lord's resurrection form a period, not of labor, but of peace and joy. That is why there is no fasting and we pray standing, which is a sign of resurrection. This practice is observed at the altar on all Sundays, and the Alleluia is sung, to indicate that our future occupation is to be no other than the praise of God, as it is written: *Blessed are they that dwell in thy house: they shall praise thee for ever and ever* (Ps. 84:5).

But, the fifty-day period is also praised in Scripture, not only in the Gospel, because the Holy Spirit came on the fiftieth day, but even in the Old Testament. Therein, fifty days are numbered from the celebration of the Pasch by the killing of a lamb, to the day on which the Law was given on Mount Sinai to the servant of God, Moses. This Law was *written with the finger of God* (Ex. 31:18), and this finger of God the New Testament explicitly identifies with the Holy Spirit. . . .

A lamb is slain, the Pasch is celebrated, and after fifty days the Law, written with the finger of God, is given in fear: Christ is slain, *who was led as a sheep to the slaughter* (Isa. 53:7), as the Prophet Isaiah testifies, the true Pasch is celebrated, and after fifty days the Holy Spirit, who is the finger of God, is given in love. He is opposed to men who seek their own, who therefore bear a hard yoke and a heavy burden, who do not find rest to their souls, because *charity is not self-seeking* (1 Cor. 13:5). . . .

Read Exodus, and see how many days after the celebration of the Pasch the Law was given. God spoke to Moses in the desert of Sinai on the third day of the third month. Notice, therefore, one day after the beginning of that same third month, and see what He says, among other things: *Go down, testify to the people and sanctify them today and tomorrow and the third day, and let them wash their garments, and let them be ready against the third day, for on the third day the Lord will come down in the sight of all the people upon Mount Sinai* (Ex. 19:10). The Law, then, was obviously given on the third day of the third month. Now count the days from the fourteenth of the first month, when the Pasch was kept, to the third day of the third month: you will have seventeen of the first month, thirty of the second, three of the third, which makes fifty. The Law in the Ark is sanctification in the body of the Lord, through whose resurrection future rest is promised to us, to be attained by the charity breathed into us by the Holy Spirit. But, *as yet the Spirit was not given, because Jesus was not yet glorified* (Jn. 7:39). Hence, that prophecy was sung: *Arise, O Lord, into thy resting place, thou and the ark which thou hast sanctified* (Ps. 132:8). Where there is rest, there is also sanctification. So, we have now received a pledge that we may love and desire it. To the repose of the other life, to which we pass over from this life—according to the meaning of Pasch—all are called *in the name of the Father and of the Son and of the Holy Spirit* (Mt. 28:19).

In this text is found Augustine's explanation of the origin and growth of that season and day known in Scripture and tradition as *Pentecoste*, or fiftieth day. This singular adjectival use of the term, in preference to *Pentekonta*, or fifty days, is taken from the Septuagint (Tob. 2:1; 2 Mc. 12:32), to indicate the season of seven weeks that separated the agricultural feasts of *Unleavened Bread* and *First Fruits*. The experience of Exodus and Sinai gave to these primitive feasts the significance of Passover and Covenant, and to the weeks between the flavor of Lamb and Law, prefigurations of Christ and the Spirit. Thus, in a sense, *Night Came and Day Followed . . . the Fiftieth Day, Pentecoste*. Here, season and day, fifty and fiftieth, are aspects of the night as can be seen in Acts 2:1, where the Greek text uses the *Pentecoste* of the Septuagint for the day, and the Latin text—*cum complerentur dies pentecostes*—emphasises the

fulness or completion of the fifty days. But fifty and fiftieth
were for Augustine within the season as were one and eight
within the week: here he is repeating what Asterios, the
Sophist, much earlier called "The Second Eighth Day."

Tradition continued this use of fifty and fiftieth. Irenaeus
mentions Pentecost, during which we do not genuflect, and
"Pentecost, after the Ascension of the Lord, when the Spirit
came down on the disciples ... and offered to the Father
the first fruits of all the nations."[34] Likewise in Tertullian
Pentecost, or the fiftieth day, means the fifty day season:

[35]We, as has been handed down to us, ought to abstain from
genuflecting not merely on Resurrection Day ... but for the
duration of Pentecost, whose celebration is marked by the
same character of joy.

Again:

[36]Why during the fifty ensuing days do we spend our time in
total exultation?

Hippolytus (c. 235), in a fragment of a lost work,
preserved in the *Eranistes* of Theodoret of Cyrus, speaks of
three seasons of the year, but names only two:

[37]That is why three seasons of the year have been prefigured
as a model for the Savior himself, so that the mysteries
announced about Him beforehand might be accomplished: on
the Pasch, to show that He himself was the true lamb who
would be immolated and would be shown as the true Pasch
... and at Pentecost to signify beforehand the kingdom of the
heavens, He himself having first ascended into the heavens and
offering man as a present to God.

[34]Text: SC 211.330
[35]Text: CCL 1.271
[36]Text: CCL 2.1273
[37]Text: PG 83.173

Around the same time Origen, on the other hand, speaks of four days: the Lord's Day, the Preparation, the Passover and Pentecost:

[38]We who are risen with Christ ... are always living in the season of Pentecost, especially, when going up to the upper chamber like the apostles in Jerusalem ... If you recall, the Law orders an offering of first fruits to be made on the day of Pentecost. On this day the shadow was clearly given to the Jews, but the reality was reserved for us. On the day of Pentecost after the sacrifice of prayer was offered, the Church of the Apostles received the first fruits of the coming of the Holy Spirit. This was truly an innovation ... that is why they were said to be full of new wine.

Throughout the fourth century the fifty days remained a most felicitous time, or Tertullian's *laetissimum spatium*.[39] Athanasius called this time or season *the Great Sunday*,[40] for as Sunday was the first and the eighth day so this season began with the day of the resurrection and continued through eight successive Sundays. Thus for Hilary of Poitiers it was an octave of Sundays and a *week of weeks*.[41] This emphasis on the octave of Sundays expressed the eschatological character of those fifty days: for Basil the Great:

[42]... all of Pentecost reminds us of the resurrection which we await in the world to come. ... For that one and first day, if seven times multiplied by seven, completes the seven weeks of the Holy Pentecost; for beginning at the first, Pentecost ends with the same, making fifty revolutions through the same intervening days. And so it is a symbol of eternity, beginning as it does and ending, as in a circling course, at the same point. On

[38]Text: GCS 6.291-292
[39]Cf. CCL 1.293
[40]Cf. PG 26.1366
[41]Cf. CSEL 22.11
[42]Text: SC 17.486

this day the rulers of the Church have trained us to pray in the upright position and by this exercise to lift up our minds to the future and to rise above the present. Moreover, whenever we fall on our knees and rise again we show by that very act the weight of our sins that brings us down to the earth and the kindness of the Creator that lifts us up to Heaven.

Nevertheless, this was also the century when the fiftieth day was celebrated on its own in keeping with the instructions of the Council of Elvira (c. 300). Some years later Eusebius of Caesarea (c. 332) linked the commemoration of the Ascension with this fiftieth day, which now concludes the fifty days:

[43]Each one of these events took place during a most important festival, I mean the august and holy solemnity of Pentecost, which is distinguished by a period of seven weeks, and sealed with that one day on which the holy Scriptures attest the ascension of our common Savior into heaven, and the descent of the Holy Spirit among men. In the course of this feast the emperor received the privileges I have described; and on the last day of all, which one might justly call the feast of feasts, he was removed about midday to the presence of his God, leaving his mortal remains to his fellow mortals, and carrying into fellowship with God that part of his being which was capable of understanding and loving him. Such was the close of Constantine's mortal life. Let us now attend to the circumstances which followed this event.

This emphasis on the fiftieth day as the feast day of the Ascension and the Descent of the Spirit was in keeping with the new trends of this century, mentioned earlier, of separating and solemnizing the different aspects of the one mystery, and can be seen especially in the catechesis of Cyril of Jerusalem (c. 350):

[43]Text: PG 20.1220

[44]The Gospel relates that after His resurrection He breathed on them. But though He bestowed His grace then, He was to lavish it yet more generously; and He says to them, I am ready to give it even now, but the vessel cannot yet hold it: for a while therefore receive you as much grace as you can bear; and look forward for yet more; *but remain in the city of Jerusalem, until you be clothed with power from on high* (Lk. 24:49). Receive it in part now; then, you shall wear it in its fullness. For he who receives, often possesses the gift but in part; but he who is clothed, is completely enfolded by his robe. Fear not, He says, the weapons and darts of the devil; for you shall bear with you the power of the Holy Spirit. But remember what was lately said, that the Holy Spirit is not divided, but only the grace which is given by Him.

Jesus, therefore, went up into heaven, and fulfilled the promise. For He said to them, *I will pray the Father, and He shall give you another comforter* (Jn. 14:16). So they were sitting, looking for the coming of the Holy Spirit; *and when the day of Pentecost was fully come* (Acts 2:1), here, in this city of Jerusalem . . . on the day of Pentecost, I say, they were sitting, and the Comforter came down from heaven, the Guardian and Sanctifier of the Church, the ruler of souls, the pilot of the tempest-tossed, who leads the wanderers to the light, and presides over the combatants, and crowns the victors.

Egeria in Jerusalem describes the celebration there of the Ascension on the fiftieth day, or Pentecost:

[45]On the feast of Pentecost, which falls on Sunday, the day on which there is the greatest strain on the people, everything is done exactly according to custom from the first cockcrow. The vigil is held in the Anastasis, so that the bishop may read the passage from the Gospel which is always read on Sundays, that of the resurrection of the Lord. Afterwards, the customary ritual is carried out in the Anastasis, just as it is throughout the year. As soon as it is morning, all the people assemble for the

[44]Text: PG 33.984
[45]Text: SC 296.298 = ACW 38.118

liturgy in the major Church, in the Martyrium, where everything customarily done is accomplished. The priests preach and afterwards the bishop. All the prescribed rites are accomplished, that is, the sacrifice is offered in the manner in which it is customarily done on Sundays. On this one day, however, the dismissal is moved up in the Martyrium, so that it is given before the third hour.

As soon as the dismissal has been given in the Martyrium, all the people without exception, singing hymns, lead the bishop to Sion, but in such a manner that they are in Sion at precisely the third hour. When they arrive, there is read from the Acts of the Apostles that passage in which the Holy Spirit came down so that all tongues might be heard and all might understand what was being said. Afterwards the divine service is celebrated in the prescribed manner. Now the priests read there from the Acts of the Apostles that passage which is read because this is the place on Sion—the church now is something else—where at an earlier time, after the Passion of the Lord, the multitude was gathered with the apostles, and where that which we mentioned above was done. Afterwards, the divine service is celebrated in the prescribed manner, and the sacrifice is offered. Then, just before the people are dismissed, the archdeacon raises his voice to say: 'Today, immediately after the sixth hour, let us all be ready at the Imbomum on the Eleona.' All the people then return home, each one to rest in his own house.

Immediately after lunch, everyone, insofar as is possible, goes up to the Mount of Olives, that is, to the Eleona, with the result that not a single Christian remains in the city for they have all gone. As soon as they have climbed the Mount of Olives, the Eleona, that is, they go first of all to the Imbomum, that is, to the place from which the Lord ascended into heaven. The bishop sits down there, and the priests and all the people, too. Passages from Scripture are read, hymns are interspersed and sung, and also antiphons proper to the day itself and the place are sung. The prayers which are interspersed are said in such a manner that they fit both the day and the place. Then the passage from the Gospel is read which speaks of the Ascension of the Lord; then there is the reading from the Acts of the Apostles which speaks of the Ascension of the Lord into heaven after the resurrection. When this has been done, the catechumens are blessed and then the faithful. Then at the ninth hour everyone comes down from there and goes, singing hymns, to the church which is also on the Eleona, that is to say in that grotto where the Lord sat teaching the apostles. By the time they arrive there it is already past the tenth hour. Vespers is held there, a prayer is said, the catechumens and then the faithful are blessed.

Then all the people without exception come down from there singing hymns, everyone together with the bishop singing hymns and antiphons proper to the day itself. And in this fashion they make their way slowly and easily to the Martyrium. When they reach the city gate, it is already night, and around two hundred church candles are brought out for the people. Since it is quite far from the city gate to the major church or Martyrium, it is definitely around the second hour of the night when they arrive, because they move slowly and easily all the way so that the people will not be tired out from walking. And when the great doors which are on the market street side are opened, then all the people, singing hymns, enter the Martyrium with the bishop.

After they have entered the church, hymns are sung, a prayer is said, and the catechumens and then the faithful are blessed. From there, everyone, singing hymns, then goes to the Anastasis. When they have arrived at the Anastasis, in like manner hymns and antiphons are sung, a prayer is said, and the catechumens and then the faithful are blessed. And the same thing is done at the Cross.

Then all the Christian people without exception, singing hymns, lead the bishop to Sion. When they get there, appropriate passages from Scripture are read, psalms and antiphons as well are sung, and a prayer is said. The catechumens are blessed and then all the faithful, and the dismissal is given. Once the dismissal has been given, everyone comes forth to kiss the bishop's hand. Everyone then returns to his own home around midnight. And so a great deal of toil is borne on this day, for the vigil at the Anastasis starts with the first cockcrow, and from then on throughout the whole day there is no stopping. Everything that is celebrated is drawn out to the point that only at midnight, after the dismissal has been given at Sion, does everyone return to his home.

> Gregory Nazianzus, around the very time that Egeria was in Jerusalem, preached his *On Pentecost* sermon and followed, as was his custom, the classical structure of Exordium, Encomium and Conclusion.

Exordium:

[46]Let us reason a little about the festival ... spiritually.... Seven was a sacred number among the Jews ... the Sabbath of Israel. The veneration given to this sacred number gave rise to the feast of Pentecost, for seven multiplied by seven is fifty less one day, and this one day was borrowed from the world to come, at once eight and first, one and indestructible. This is the Sabbath of weeks as distinct from the Sabbath of days and that Sabbath of years, called *Jubilees*, and among the Hebrews it gave rise to Pentecost ... a day called holy among them....

And if you read for yourself you may take note of many numbers which contain a meaning deeper than appears on the surface. But let us come to an instance which is most useful to us on the present occasion; the Hebrews honor the day of Pentecost, and we also honor it; just as there are other rites of the Hebrews which we observe ... they were by way of type observed by them, and by us they are celebrated by way of sacrament. And now having said so much by way of preface about the day, let us proceed to what we have to say further.

Encomium:

We are keeping the feast of Pentecost and of the coming of the Spirit, and the appointed time of the Promise, and the fulfillment of our hope. And how great, how august, is the Mystery. The dispensations of the Body of Christ are ended; that of the Spirit is beginning. And what were the things

[46]Text: PG 36.428

pertaining to the Christ? The Virgin, the Birth, the Manger, the Swaddling, the Angels glorifying Him, the Shepherds running to Him, the course of the Star, the Magi worshipping Him and bringing Gifts, Herod's murder of the children, the Flight of Jesus into Egypt, the Return from Egypt, the Circumcision, the Baptism, the Witness from Heaven, the Temptation, the Stoning for our sake, the Betrayal, the Nailing, the Burial, the Resurrection, the Ascension .... Such are the mysteries of Christ....

As regards the Spirit ... may the Spirit be with me, and grant me the gift of speech that I may do justice to this season. He will be with me as my Lord ... for He blows where He wills and on whom He wills and to what extent that He wills. Thus we are inspired both to think and to speak of the Spirit.... Now that I have to some extent prepared you let us return to the subject of the Spirit and hope that you will follow me.

The Holy Spirit always did exist; exists now; and always will exist ... sanctifying, not being sanctified; deifying, not being deified.... Life and Lifegiver; Light and Lightgiver; absolute Good, and Spring of Goodness; the Right, the Princely Spirit; the Lord, the Sender, the Separator; Builder of His own Temple; leading, working as He wills; distributing His own Gifts; the Spirit of Adoption, of Truth, of Wisdom, of Understanding, of Knowledge, of Godliness, of Counsel, of Fear (which are ascribed to Him) by whom the Father is known and the Son is glorified; and by whom *alone* He is known; one class, one service, worship, power, perfection, sanctification. Why make a long discourse of it? All that the Father hath the Son hath also, except the being unbegotten; and all that the Son hath the Spirit hath also, except the Generation. And these two matters do not divide the Substance, as I understand it, but rather are divisions within the Substance.

Are you laboring to bring forth objections? Well, so am I to get on with my discourse. Honor the day of the Spirit; restrain your tongue if you can a little. It is the time to speak of other tongues—reverence them or fear them, when you see that they are of fire. Today let us teach dogmatically; tomorrow we may discuss. Today let us keep the feast; tomorrow will be time enough to behave ourselves unseemly—the first mystically, the second theatrically; the one in the Churches, the other in the marketplace;

> The coming of the Spirit on this day of Pentecost differs from the other manifestations of the Spirit to the disciples which took place before the Passion and after the resurrection:

[47]Now the first of these manifests Him—the healing of the sick and casting out of evil spirits, which could not be apart from the Spirit; and so does that breathing upon them after the resurrection, which was clearly a divine inspiration; and so too the present distribution of the fiery tongues, which we are now commemorating. But the first manifested Him indistinctly, the second more expressly, this present one more perfectly, since He is no longer present only in energy, but as we may say, substantially, associating with us, and dwelling in us. For it was fitting that as the Son had lived with us in bodily form—so the Spirit, too, should appear in bodily form; and that after Christ had returned to His own place, He should have come down to us—*Coming* because He is the Lord; *Sent,* because He is not a rival God. For such words no less manifest the unanimity than they mark the separate individuality.

And therefore He came after Christ, that a Comforter should not be lacking unto us; but *another* Comforter, that you might acknowledge His co-equality. For this word *another* marks an *Alter Ego,* a name of equal lordship, not of inequality. For *another* is not said, I know, of different kinds, but of things consubstantial. And He came in the form of tongues because of His close relation to the Word. And they were of fire, perhaps because of His purifying Power.

[47]Text: *ibid.* 436

Again:

[48]This Spirit shares with the Son in working both the creation and the resurrection, as may be shown by this Scripture; *By the Word of the Lord were the heavens made, and all the power of them by the breath of His mouth* (Ps. 33:6). . . . *You shall send forth your spirit and they shall be created, and you shall renew the face of the earth* (Ps. 104:30).

This Spirit is the author of our spiritual rebirth or regeneration, and here is the proof.

No one can see or *enter into the kingdom, except he be born again of the Spirit* (Jn. 3:3), and be cleansed from the first birth, which is a mystery of the night, by a remolding of the day and of the Light, by which everyone singly is created anew. This Spirit, *for He is most wise and most loving* (Wis. 1:6), if He takes possession of a shepherd makes him a Psalmist, *subduing evil spirits by his song* (1 Sam. 16:23), and proclaims him King; if he possess a gathered and scraper of sycamore fruit, He makes him a prophet. Call to mind David and Amos. If He possess a goodly youth, He makes him a judge of elders, even beyond his years, as Daniel testifies, who conquered the lions in their den (cf. Dan. 6:22). If He takes possession of fishermen, He makes them catch the whole world in the nets of Christ, taking them up in the meshes of the Word. Look at Peter and Andrew and the sons of Thunder, thundering the things of the Spirit. If of publicans, He makes gain of them for discipleship, and makes them merchants of souls; witness Matthew, yesterday a publican, today an evangelist. If of zealous persecutors, He changes the current of their zeal, and makes them Pauls instead of Sauls, and as full of piety as He found them of wickedness. And He is the Spirit of meekness, and yet is provoked by those who sin. Let us therefore make proof of Him as gentle, not as wrathful, by confessing His dignity; and let us not desire to see Him implacably wrathful. He too it is who has made me today a bold herald to you;—if without rest to myself, God be thanked; but if with risk, thanks to Him nevertheless; in the one case, that He may spare those

---

[48]Text: *ibid.* 444

that hate us; in the other, that He may consecrate us, in receiving this reward of our preaching of the Gospel, to be made perfect by blood.

Furthermore:

[49]   *They spoke with strange tongues, and not those of their native land;* and the wonder was great, a language spoken by those *who had not learnt it.* And the sign is to them that believe not, and not to them that believe, that it may be an accusation of the unbeliever as it is written, *With other tongues and other lips will I speak unto this people, and not even so will they listen to Me, saith the Lord* (Isa. 28:11). *But they heard.* (Acts 2:11) Here stop a little and raise a question, how you are to divide the words. For the expression has an ambiguity, which is to be determined by the punctuation. Did they each hear in their own dialect so that, if I may say, one sound was uttered, but many were heard; the air being thus beaten and, so to speak, sounds being produced more clear than the original sound; or are we to put the stop after 'they heard,' and then to add *them speaking in their own languages* (Acts 2:11) to what follows, so that it would be speaking in languages their own to the hearers, which would be foreign to the speakers? I prefer to put it this latter way; for on the other plan the miracle would be rather of the hearers than of the speakers; whereas in this it would be on the speakers' side; and it was they who were reproached for drunkenness, evidently because they by the Spirit wrought a miracle in the matter of the tongues.

But the old confusion of tongues was laudable, when men who were of one language in wickedness and impiety, were building the tower; by the confusion of their language the unity of their intention was broken up, and their undertaking destroyed; so much more worthy of praise is the present miraculous one. For being poured from One Spirit upon many men, it brings them again into harmony.

---

[49]Text: *ibid.* 448

Conclusion:

[50]But let us end this festival now ... enough has been said ... about the earthly festival: later on we shall keep this festival spiritually and forever and understand it more purely and more clearly ... in the Word Himself, God, our Lord Jesus Christ, the true festival and rejoicing of the saved.

> In a homily, *On Pentecost*, Gregory of Nyssa elaborates on a favorite Pentecostal theme, that of new wine in new skins (cf. Lk. 5:37; Acts 2:13):

[51]The enemies of the glory of the Spirit fail to see the tongues of fire the divine Scriptures (cf. Acts 2:12-15) which enlightens what is hidden in darkness and mock those who speak with tongues, accusing them of being filled with sweet new wine. But, in spite of their charges against us, I would advise you, brethren, not to fear their rebuke and not to be intimidated by their deprecatory remarks. Would that they could share in this sweet wine, this newly pressed wine which issues from the winepress which the Lord has trodden in the Gospel so that He might give you to drink of the blood of His own grape. Would that they might be filled also with this sweet wine, called *nouveau* which the innkeepers have not debased by diluting it with the waters of heresy. They could be completely filled with the Spirit, by which those filled with the spirit throw off by foaming the density and slime of lack of faith. But people of that sort cannot receive in themselves the sweet new wine in that they still carry around old wineskins which are unable to contain this new wine but break out in heresy. But now, brethren, as the Prophet says, come, let us rejoice with the Lord, drinking the sweet drink of piety as Esdras recommends (III Esdr. 9:52) and illuminated in the choirs of the apostles and prophets let us rejoice with the gift of the Spirit and exult on that day which the Lord has made, in Christ.

[50]Text: *ibid.* 452
[51]Text: PG 46.700. See R. Cabié, La Pentecôte (Paris, 1969) 224

Here Gregory of Nyssa was, in his own words, "plucking the strings of wisdom on the plectrum of the Spirit":[52] on the same theme John Chrysostom (d. 407) was no less lyrical:

[53]Today we have come to the culmination of blessings, to that very heaven of feasts—the first fruits of the Lord's promise.

What, then, I ask, of those feasts of salvation ... and the power of the Spirit to dispense through them.

Through the Spirit we are liberated from slavery; we are called to liberty; we are led to adoption; we are fashioned anew; we lay aside the grave and fetid burden of sin.

And through the same Spirit we see the choirs of priests and the orders of teachers.

From this new Spirit—the source of all that decorates the Church of God—flows forth the glory of revelation and the grace of healing.

The Latin Fathers of the fourth century also began to focus on the different aspects of the "*laetissimum spatium*" of Tertullian, which they also isolated, so to speak, and began to celebrate separately. St. Ambrose, in Book X of his *Treatise on the Gospel of Luke*, has seasonal reflections on the text, *Pray that your flight be not in winter or on the Sabbath* (cf. Mt. 24:20):

[54]Since the Lord is going to come on the day of judgment before the fire burns (cf. Ps. 50:3), and fire has always the same intensity, or even burns with greater intensity in the summer, why does He say, pray that your flight be not in winter unless perhaps that he who flees to the mountains should not fear the cold and ice, the storms and the hail of sin, but should rather hope for the serenity of the light summer lest our faltering footsteps should totter on the slippery surface of the body.

Whence also the soul, with sureness of foot, rooted firmly

---

[52]Cf. PG 46.496
[53]Text: PG 50.463
[54]Text: SC 52.67

on the ground joyfully says: *Winter is past, the time for pruning has come* (Cant. 2:11). Because in winter the winds strip the trees of their foliage and the rigors of the cold brings the affliction of death to the tender leaves. In spring, however, the seeds rise and the renewal of summer causes nature to green and sprout. The Pasch occurs in spring when I am saved. In summer there is Pentecost when we celebrate the glory of the resurrection as an image of the future.

Jerome (c. 386), too, thought of Pasch and Pentecost as separate seasons:

[55]The Pasch happened at the beginning of Spring ... and Pentecost at the beginning of Summer ... hence the living waters of Spring and the living waters of Summer: many see a reference to baptism of water and baptism of the Spirit in the living waters of Spring and the living waters of Summer; that is to say, at Pasch and Pentecost these waters should be distributed to those who thirst when the Scripture will be fulfilled: *Wash and be clean* (Isaiah 1:16).

Elsewhere, for Jerome, Pentecost clearly means the fiftieth day: "We do not count the seven weeks of Pentecost in the same way as the Jews do; we venerate the descent of the Holy Spirit":[56] Elsewhere Jerome continues:

[57]When the marriage feast has ended and the time of the Passion and Resurrection has passed, then at that time the friends of the bridegroom will fast.... Some think this is the reason the fast should be held as soon as the forty days of the Pasch are over ... but to us the days of Pentecost and the coming of the Holy Spirit indicate immediately a time of festivity and joy.

[55]Text: PL 25.1528
[56]Cf. PL 26.378
[57]Text: PL 26.57

More clearly:

[58] *Would that we could fast at all times,* as we read in the *Acts of the Apostles* (Acts 13:3), Paul did, even on the days of Pentecost and Sundays, and his fellow believers likewise. Nor do I say this because I personally believe that the fast should be observed on the feast days, or because I want to suppress the *feriae* which make up the fifty days, but let each province abound in its own good sense.

> Thus, for Jerome, Pentecost was a season in change from the unity of the original fifty days to a variety of individual days within the season. Something of this division can be seen in the *Conferences* of John Cassian (d. 435). In one of these conferences Cassian has the monk Germanus ask Theonas: Why, then, do we relax the rigor of the fast by taking our meal in the middle of the day during the whole fifty days of Pentecost, seeing that the Lord only remained with His disciples for forty days after the Resurrection? Theonas replies:

[59]Your question is not without point and deserves to elicit a full response giving the truth in its entirety. After the Ascension of our Lord which took place on the fortieth day after the resurrection the apostles returned from Mount Olivet where He had granted them the sight of His return to the Father, as the reading in the Acts of the Apostles testifies. They entered Jerusalem and awaited the coming of the Holy Spirit for ten days. At the end of this period, that is, on the fiftieth day they received the Spirit with joy. Thus the number fifty consecrated to the present feast is obviously fulfilled.

We also read this number figuratively preshadowed in the Old Testament. There the priests were ordered to offer to the Lord the bread of first fruits at the end of seven weeks (cf. Deut. 16:9). But the true bread of first fruits was really offered to God on that day by the preaching of the apostles to the

[58]Text: CSEL 55
[59]Text: SC 64.94

crowd (cf. Acts 2). This bread was produced by the institution of the new doctrine on which the five thousand were generously nourished and satisfied and the new people of the Christians was offered to God as the first fruits of the Jews.

That is why these ten days should be celebrated with equal solemnity and joy as the previous forty. The tradition of this feast has been handed down to us by Christians of the apostolic age and should be observed in the same spirit. And so we should not genuflect in prayer during these days because kneeling is a sign of penitence and grief. And so we should preserve the same solemnity in all details on these (fifty) days as we do on Sundays on which our elders have handed down that we should not keep the fast or kneel out of reverence for the Lord's resurrection.

> Augustine is clear and specific: "We celebrate Pentecost, that is the fiftieth day from the Passion and resurrection of the Lord, the day on which He sent to us the Holy Spirit, the Paraclete, whom He had promised."[60] Elsewhere he says: "that which you now see on the altar of God, you also saw last night";[61] from this it is clear that Pentecost in Hippo had a vigil Mass and another Mass on the day itself, and the *descent of the Holy Spirit* was the text of Scripture read and the homily preached. Indeed, this same emphasis on the day of Pentecost can be seen also in the *Catechetical Instructions* of Augustine:

[62]Then, *having strenghtened His disciples and having sojourned with them for forty days, He ascended into heaven in their sight* (Acts 1:3); and when fifty days from His resurrection had been accomplished, He sent to them the Holy Spirit (cf. Acts 2:1), for so He had promised, that through *the love poured forth in their hearts* (Rom. 5:5) by Him, they might be able to fulfill the law not only without its being a burden but even with delight. Now this Law was given to the

---

[60]Cf. CSEL 25.770
[61]Cf. PL 38.1246
[62]Text: PL 40.340 = ACW 2.72

Jews in ten commandments, which they call the Decalogue. And these again reduced to two, namely, that we should love God with our whole heart, and with our whole soul, and with our whole mind; and that we should love our neighbor as ourselves. For that on these two commandments depend the whole Law and the prophets the Lord Himself has both said in the Gospel and made manifest by His own example. For in the case of the people of Israel likewise, from the day on which they first celebrated the Passover in a figure by killing and eating a sheep, with the blood of which their doorposts were marked to preserve them unharmed—from that day, I say, the fiftieth day was completed when they received the Law written by the finger of God, by which name we have already said that the Holy Spirit is typified; as after the Passion and Resurrection of our Lord, *who is the true Passover* (1 Cor. 5:7), on the fiftieth day the Holy Spirit Himself was sent to the disciples, no longer, however, typifying the hardness of their hearts by tables of stone; but when they were gathered together in one place in Jerusalem itself, *suddenly there came a sound from heaven as of a rushing mighty wind, and there appeared to them parted tongues as it were of fire, and they began with tongues* (Act 2:2), so that all who had come to them recognized each his own tongue; then preaching Christ with all confidence, they wrought many signs in His name, so that, as Peter was passing by, his shadow touched a certain dead man, and he rose again.

In this context Pasch and Pentecost were weeks apart: consequently the celebration of Christ and the Spirit became separate but equal solemnities with different rituals evoking different memories. In the one case the lamb of Exodus was joined with the *Unleavened Bread* of Spring, and in the other case the Law of the Covenant was seen as the *First Fruits* of Summer; the former ritualized the Christ of God and the latter the Spirit of God—two human expressions of the one divine mystery:

⁶³That will be the seventh day, just as if the first day in the whole era were the time from Adam to Noah; the second, from Noah to Abraham; the third, from Abraham to David, as the Gospel of Matthew divides it; the fourth, from David to the transmigration into Babylon; the fifth, from the transmigration to the coming of our Lord Jesus Christ. The sixth day, therefore, begins with the coming of the Lord, and we are living in that sixth day. Hence, just as in Genesis . . . man was fashioned in the image of God on the sixth day, so in our time, as if on the sixth day of the entire year, we are born again in baptism so that we may receive the image of our Creator. But, when that sixth day will have passed, rest will come after the judgment, and the holy and just ones of God will celebrate their Sabbath. After the seventh day, however, when the glory of the harvest, the brightness and the merit of the saints have appeared on the threshing floor, then we shall go to that life and rest of which the Scripture says: *Eye has not seen nor ear heard, nor has it entered into the heart of man, what things God has prepared for those who love him* (1 Cor. 2:9). Then we return, as if to the beginning, for just as when seven days have passed, the eighth becomes the first of a new week, so after the seven periods of this transitory world have been spent and completed, we shall return to that immortal blessedness from which man fell. Hence, octaves complete the sacraments of the newly baptized. Hence, too, the number seven multiplied by seven gives forty-nine and with one added it returns to the beginning and becomes fifty, the number of days which we celebrate in symbolic fashion up to the feast of Pentecost. The same number is reached in a different way according to that division whereby the tenfold reward is added to the number forty. Both methods of calculation lead to the same number, fifty.

In the time of Augustine Pentecost was a feast of equal rank with the Pasch, having its own vigil and octave and considered as suitable as the Pasch for baptism; yet the

---

⁶³Text: PL 38.1197 = FOTC 38.370

separation of the two solemnities created certain theological problems which Augustine discussed:

[64]Attend to this, my brethren: someone may ask me: 'Why did the Lord give the Holy Spirit twice?' Many men have said many things and , as men, they have asked questions. Within the bounds of faith they have had their discussions, one saying one thing, another stating something else, but both keeping within the rule of truth. If I should say that I know why the Lord gave the Holy Spirit twice, I would be lying to you. I do not know why He did this. He who says that He knows what he does not know is rash; he who denies that he knows what he knows is ungrateful. Therefore, I confess to you that I am still seeking the reason why the Lord gave the Holy Spirit twice; I desire to arrive at a more definite conclusion. May the Lord help me because of the instancy of your prayers and, because He deigns to grant favors, may He not be silent in your regard. Hence, I do not know the answer. Nevertheless, although I do not yet know what to think and although I do not yet hold any definite view as to your question, still I hold it as certain that He did give the Holy Spirit twice. Therefore I shall not be silent as to why I hold to this. If my view is correct, may the Lord confirm it; if there is another theory which seems closer to the truth, may the Lord grant me that knowledge.

Hence, I think (but this is merely my own view) that the Holy Spirit was given twice for the purpose of commending to us the two precepts of charity. For, though there are two precepts, there is only one love. . . . One love and two precepts; one Spirit and two bestowals of the Spirit.

Nevertheless the basic unity of the Pasch remained operative in the consciousness of Augustine in spite of the ritual separation that was taking place in the liturgical season:

[64]Text: *ibid.* 1222 = FOTC 38.416

[65]*Blessed*, therefore, *are they that suffer persecution for justice's sake, for theirs is the kingdom of heaven* (Mt. 5:10). This eighth maxim, which harks back to the first, and announces the perfected man, is perhaps expressed in the type in the Old Testament by circumcision on the eighth day and by the resurrection of the Lord after the Sabbath which is at once the eighth day of the week and the first; also by the celebration of the octave which we keep on occasion of the rebirth of the renewed man; and by the very name Pentecost. For to the number seven multiplied seven times—making forty-nine—an eighth is added, as it were, so that we have fifty and in a way a return to the beginning. It was on this day that the Holy Spirit was sent by whom we are brought into the kingdom of heaven.

> Pope Leo (c. 450) is, as has been already seen, the theologian of the solemnities that came out of the historical focus of the fourth century. Time—the day and the week, the season and the year—was for Leo a sacramental representation of biblical history, and every hour of time was a temporal facet of the eternal mystery. Pentecost was no mere memory; it was an event—the annual renewal in the hearts of the faithful of the apostolic experience in Jerusalem:

[66]The hearts of all Catholics, dearly beloved, realize that today's solemnity deserves to be honored among the most important feasts. One cannot exaggerate the esteem in which this day should be held, which the Holy Spirit has consecrated by the incomparable miracle of the gift of Himself. This day is the tenth from the day when the Lord ascended higher than the heavens ... and the fiftieth from the day of His resurrection, when indeed it began. In itself it contains great revelations of divine realities, of mysteries, both old and new ... for grace was hidden in the Law, and the Law is fulfilled through grace. In times past the Hebrew nation ... was delivered by the sacrifice of a lamb; on the fiftieth day afterwards the Law was

[65]Text: CCL 35.12 = ACW 5.21
[66]Text: SC 74. 144-145

given on Mount Sinai: similarly, Christ, the true Lamb of God, was first slain; then on the fiftieth day after the resurrection the Holy Spirit came down on the apostles. In this way all can see that the beginnings of the Old Testament were a type of the beginnings of the Gospel ... for indeed the second Covenant was made by the same spirit that had begun the first. Hence the testimony: *while the days of Pentecost were fulfilled ... they were all filled with the Holy Spirit* (Acts 2:1-4).

> This excerpt is from the first of three sermons on Pentecost by Leo which survive. According to the third of these, John's Gospel was read in Rome at this time: the Lord said to his disciples, as has been proclaimed in the Gospel reading, *if you truly loved me you would rejoice* (Jn. 14:28).[67] The theology of the Holy Spirit, developed by Basil and the Cappadocians, and the theology of the Trinity, enunciated by Athanasius in the East and Augustine in the West, enabled Leo to preach on Pentecost in a new language:

[68]Today's festival, dearly-beloved, which is celebrated throughout the whole world, has been hallowed by that advent of the Holy Spirit, which on the fiftieth day after the Lord's resurrection, descended on the apostles and the multitude of believers; the Lord Jesus had promised that He should come to fill with greater largess the hearts of those dedicated to Him, increasing and not just beginning.

The magnificence of the Holy Spirit is never separate from the omnipotence of the Father and the Son and whatever the divine order accomplishes proceeds from the providence of the whole Trinity. Therefore, what the Father enlightens the Son enlightens and the Holy Spirit enlightens: and while there is one Person of the Sent, another of the Sender, and another of the Promiser, both the Unity and the Trinity are at the same time ' revealed to us, so that the essence which possesses equality and does not admit of singularity is understood to

[67]Cf. *ibid.* 159
[68]Text: *ibid.* 157

belong to the same substance but not the same Person....

When, therefore, we fix our minds on confessing the Father and the Son and the Holy Spirit, let us keep far from our thoughts the forms of things visible, and the limitation of things born in time and space. Let that which is extended in space, that which is enclosed by limit, and whatever is not always everywhere and entire be banished from the heart. The conception of the Triune Godhead must put aside the idea of interval or of grade, and if a man has attained any worthy thought of God, let him not dare to withhold it from any Person therein, as if to ascribe with more honor to the Father that which he does not ascribe to the Son and the Spirit. It is not true godliness to put the Father before the Only-begotten: insult to the Son is insult to the Father: what is detracted from the one is detracted from both....

What the Father has the Son also has, and what the Father and the Son have, the Holy Spirit also has, because the whole Trinity together is One God. But this faith is not the discovery of earthly wisdom nor the conviction of man's opinion: the Only-begotten Son has taught it Himself.

> In the Rome of Leo, tradition and innovation in liturgical practice met without success, and the fast of the ancient week was maintained during the octave of the new feast:

[69]Therefore, after the days of holy rejoicing, which we have devoted to the celebration of the Lord rising from the dead and then ascending into heaven, and after receiving the gift of the Holy Spirit, a fast is ordained as a wholesome and needful practice, so that, if perchance through neglect or disorder even amid the joys of the festival any undue license has broken out, it may be corrected by the remedy of strict abstinence, which must be the more scrupulously carried out in order that what was on this day divinely bestowed on the Church may abide in us. For, being made the temple of the Holy Spirit, and watered with a greater supply than ever of the Divine Stream, we ought

---

[69]Text: SC 200.28

not to be conquered by any lust nor held in bondage by any vice....

Therefore, on Wednesday and Friday let us fast, and on Saturday let us keep vigil in the presence of the most blessed apostle, Peter, by whose prayers we surely trust to be set free from spiritual foes and bodily enemies; through our Lord Jesus Christ, who with the Father and the Holy Spirit, lives and reigns for ever and ever. Amen.

> In conclusion Leo wrote two letters, one to all the bishops of Campania, Samnium and Picenum, and another to the bishops of Sicily, rebuking them for baptizing outside the recognized times of Pasch and Pentecost. His understanding of Pentecost as a Paschal season is clear:

[70]The solemn season of Pentecost, hallowed by the coming of the Holy Spirit, is also a time for baptism, being, as it were, the sequel and completion of the Paschal feast. And while other festivals are held on other days of the week, this festival (of Pentecost) always occurs on a Sunday, which is marked by the Lord's resurrection: inviting those, who have been cut off from the Easter feast by disabling sickness, or length of journey, or difficulties of sailing, to gain the gift of the Holy Spirit. For the Only-begotten of God Himself wished no difference to be felt between Himself and the Holy Spirit in the Faith of believers and in the efficacy of His works....

When He, the Spirit of Truth, is come, He shall guide you into all the Truth (Jn. 16:13).

Thus, since Christ is the truth, and the Holy Spirit the Spirit of Truth, and the name of 'Comforter' appropriate to both, the two festivals are not dissimilar, where the sacrament is the same.

> The same devotion to Pasch and Pentecost, as two solemnities of the one season, can be seen in the sermons of Leo's contemporary, Maximus of Turin:

[70]Text: PL 54.699

[71]Brethren, I believe that you know the reason why this Pentecost day should be celebrated with no less joy than we devoted to the Pasch and why we should have recourse to the observance of this solemnity with the same devotion with which we discharged the responsibilities of that other festival. We did then as we do now; we fasted on the vigil, we celebrated and spent the whole night in prayer. And so a similar joy should follow a similar observance. . . .

> Again:

[72]During these days of Pentecost we do not fast because the Lord is with us; sons of the bridegroom, we cannot fast . . . rather, we are refreshed during Pentecost because He remains with us.

> In Caesarius of Arles (d. 542) the solemnity is permanent and complete, and Pentecost with its own vigil, fast and octave, and its own proper readings and prayers, is a feast as prominent as the Pasch.

[73]Today, dearest brethren, everything that has been read to us comes together along with the solemn feast. The psalm says: *Give me back the joy of your salvation, and with a perfect spirit sustain me.* (Ps. 51:14). Moreover, the Gospel says: *The Spirit of truth comes* (Jn. 16:13), while a passage in the Acts of the Apostles tells us: *All were filled with the Holy Spirit* (Acts 2:4). Now everything has been fulfilled and made perfect. The psalm asked the coming of the Holy Spirit, the Gospel promised that He would come, and the passage in the Acts related that He had already come. Therefore in the texts nothing is lacking to the order of the divine happenings, because there is a plea in the prophet, a promise in the Gospel, and fulfillment in the Acts. Concerning the same Holy Spirit, the blessed Apostle Paul also gives witness when he says: *To*

[71]Text: CCL 23.160
[72]Text: *ibid.* 178
[73]Text: CCL 104.841 = FOTC 66.98

one is given wisdom in discourse, to another the power to express knowledge, another receives faith through the same Spirit. But it is one and the same Spirit, who produces all these gifts, distributing them to each as He wills (1 Cor. 12:8). However, after the effort of the vigils, it is not necessary for you to be wearied still more by a longer sermon: whoever desires to hear a fuller sermon on the divinity of the Holy Spirit may come to church early tomorrow.

3. Advent and Quartertense

Among the most ancient institutions of the Roman liturgy were the four seasons of fast, the *quattuor tempora*, called quartertense in English, or Ember days from the German *Quatember*. They were a weeklong "Station," or observance, of fast, prayer and vigil that did for Summer, Autumn and Winter, in June, September and December, what Lent did for Spring. Opinion differs about their origin, which may go back to the harvest feasts of wheat, wine and oil of the ancient Romans. In fact the earliest reference to these fasts in Christian literature does not associate them with the four great feasts of Christian time: Philastrius, bishop of Brescia (d. 390), author of *Book on Various Heresies*, is our witness for both the feasts and the fasts and their divergence:

Feasts:

[74]Four greater feast days have been established for our salvation annually: first in order is the Nativity, secondly, the day of Christ's Epiphany, that is to say, twelve days later. Next, the day on which He suffered, the Pasch, and finally, the day on which He ascended into heaven around Pentecost, which is, of course, the consummation of His victory. Anyone who does not know and omits one of these days can also be doubtful about the other days, not having the fullness of truth, because,

[74]Text: CCL 9.304, Cabié, 188-189

in accordance with the four seasons of each year Christ our Lord has been for us the source of different joys, namely, first, the Nativity, second, the Epiphany, third, the day on which He suffered, rose, and appeared, and fourth, the day of His Ascension into heaven.

Fasts:

[75]In the course of the year four fasts are celebrated in the Church: the first at Christmas, the second at Easter, the third at Ascension, and the fourth at Pentecost. In fact we should fast at the birth of our Lord and Saviour, then likewise at Easter during Lent. It is the same at the Ascension into heaven, forty days after Easter, and the ten days which follow, up to Pentecost, or later; that is what the blessed apostles did after the Ascension, *persevering in fasting and in prayer* (Acts 1:14), as the Scripture says. They deserved at Pentecost to receive the fullness of the Spirit and the perfection of His power to such an extent that, when the Divine Spirit was poured upon them, armed with heavenly weapons, they laid aside all doubts which they held previously, they set forth. Thereupon they set forth to become invincible teachers and glorious martyrs of the Lord Himself.

> The December week of fast, or the *Fast of the Tenth Month* as it was then called, cannot be identified with the one day fast, mentioned by Augustine, of preparation for the feast of the Nativity. Many sermons of Pope Leo survive on those seasonal fasts, and those on the *Fast of the Tenth Month* make no reference to the feast of the Nativity that is nearing: indeed, this fast has its own meaning:

[76]And while all seasons are opportune for this duty, beloved, yet this present season is specially suitable and appropriate, at which our holy Fathers, being divinely inspired, sanctioned the fast of the tenth month, that when all the ingathering of the

[75]Text: *ibid.* 312, Cabié 248
[76]Text: PL 54.177

crops was complete, we might dedicate to God our reasonable service of abstinence, and each might remember so to use His abundance as to be more abstinent in himself and more open-handed towards the poor. For forgiveness of sins is most efficaciously prayed for with almsgiving and fasting, and supplications that are winged by such aids mount swiftly to God's ears: since as it is written, *the merciful man doeth good to his own soul* (Prov. 11:17), and nothing is so much a man's own as that which he spends on his neighbor. For that part of his material possessions with which he ministers to the needy, is transformed into eternal riches, and such wealth is begotten of this bountifulness as can never be diminished or in any way destroyed, for *blessed are the merciful, for God shall have mercy on them* (Mt. 5:7), and He Himself shall be their chief Reward, who is the model of His own command

Furthermore he explains:

[77]The transcendent power of God's grace, dearly beloved, is indeed daily effecting in Christian hearts the transference of our every desire from earthly to heavenly things. But this present life also is passed through the Creator's aid and sustained by His providence, because He who promises things eternal is also the giver of things temporal. Therefore, we ought to give God thanks for the hope of future happiness towards which we run by faith, because He raises us up to a perception of the happiness in store for us; so, for those things which we receive in the course of every year, God should be honored and praised, who from the beginning gave fertility to the earth and laid down laws of bearing fruit for every germ and seed, will never forsake His own decrees but will as Creator ever continue His kind administration of the things that He has made. Whatever therefore the cornfields, the vineyards and the olive groves have borne for man's purposes, all this God in His bounteous goodness has produced: for under the varying condition of the elements He has mercifully aided the uncertain toils of the husbandmen so that wind, and

[77]Text: *ibid.* 176

rain, cold and heat, day and night might serve our needs. For men's methods would not have sufficed to give effect to their works, had not God given the increases to their wonted plantings and waterings. And hence it is but godly and just that we, too, should help others with that which the Heavenly Father had mercifully bestowed on us. For there are full many, who have no fields, no vineyards, no olive groves, whose wants we must provide out of the store which God had given, that they too with us may bless God for the richness of the earth and rejoice at its possessors having received things which they have shared also with the poor and the stranger.

The meaning of the December fast is clearly expressed in the following sermon on the Fast of the tenth month:

[78]But there are three things which most belong to religious actions, namely prayer, fasting, and almsgiving, in the exercising of which while every time is accepted, yet that ought to be more zealously, which we have received as hallowed by tradition from the apostles: even as this tenth month brings round again to us the opportunity when according to the ancient practice we may give more diligent heed to those three things of which I have spoken. For by prayer we seek to propitiate God, by fasting we extinguish the lusts of the flesh, by alms we redeem our sins: and at the same time God's image is throughout renewed in us, if we are always ready to praise him, unfailingly intent on our purification and unceasingly active in cherishing our neighbor. This threefold round of duty, dearly beloved, brings all other virtues into action: it attains to God's image and likeness and unites us inseparably with the Holy Spirit. Because in prayer faith remains steadfast; in fasting life remains innocent; in almsgiving the mind remains kind. On Wednesday and Friday, therefore, let us fast: and on Saturday let us keep vigil with the most blessed Apostle Peter, who will deign to aid our supplications and fast and alms with his own prayers through our Lord Jesus Christ, who

[78]Text: *ibid.* 171

with the Father and the Holy Spirit lives and reigns for ever
and ever. Amen.

> One sermon on this fast mentions the Advent of God's
> kingdom, but not the Advent of the Nativity feast:

[79]Whenever the Savior would instruct His disciples about
the Advent of God's kingdom and the end of the world's times,
He said, *Take heed lest haply your hearts be overcharged with
surfeiting and drunkenness, and care of this life* (Lk. 21:34).
And assuredly, dearly beloved, we acknowledge that this
precept applies more especially to us, to whom undoubtedly
the day denounced is near, even though hidden. For the advent
of which it behooves every man to prepare himself, lest it find
him given over to gluttony, or entangled in cares of this life.

> As a season of fast in preparation for a feast, Advent first
> appeared in the early part of the sixth century in Gaul. St.
> Martin's Lent, as it was called, was a period of eight weeks,
> but only forty fast days, from the feast of St. Martin
> (November 11) to the feast of the Epiphany. This fast of
> forty days was in Gaul, like Lent elsewhere, a time of
> preparation for baptism at Epiphany. The importance of
> Christmas in the West, and the prohibition of baptism at
> Epiphany, made the forty days' fast of Gaul and Spain a
> season of preparation for the feast of the Nativity. This can
> be seen in the homilies of Caesarius of Arles (d. 542), *On the
> Coming of Christ*:

[80]Through the divine mercy, beloved brethren, the day on
which we long to celebrate with joy the birthday of our Lord
and Savior is almost at hand. Therefore I pray and advise that
with God's help we labor as much as we can, so that on that
day we may be able to approach the altar of the Lord with a
pure and upright conscience, a clean heart, and a chaste body.
Then we may merit to receive His Body and Blood, not to our

[79]Text: *ibid.* 185
[80]Text: CCL 104.763 = FOTC 66.7

judgment, but as a remedy for our souls. Truly our life depends upon the Body of Christ, as the Lord Himself said: *If you do not eat the flesh of the Son of Man and drink His blood, you have no life in you* (Jn. 6:53). Therefore, a man should change his life, if he wants to receive life, for if he does not change his life, he will receive it to his own judgment. Then he is corrupted by it more than he is healed; he is killed rather than given life. For thus the Apostle spoke: *He who eats and drinks without recognizing the body and blood of the Lord, eats and drinks a judgment on himself* (1 Cor. 11:29).

Although it is fitting for us to be adorned and distinguished by good works at all times, still on the day of the Lord's birth in particular, our good deeds, as He Himself said in the Gospel, ought to shine before men (cf. Mt. 5:16)

Again:

[81]Beloved brethren, as we are about to begin with sincerest devotion a holy and desirable, glorious and excellent feast, that is, the Nativity of our Lord and Savior, with His help we ought to prepare ourselves with all our strength. Let us carefully examine all the recesses of our soul, lest perchance there be some hidden sin within us to confound and gnaw at our conscience and to offend the eyes of the divine majesty. Although Christ our Lord arose from the dead after His Passion and ascended into heaven, nevertheless, as we believe, He considers and carefully notices how each one of His servants strives to prepare and dispose himself to celebrate His birthday without avarice, anger, pride, or dissipation. In proportion to the way He sees each one adorned with good works, in that measure He will dispense to him the grace of His mercy. If He sees a man clothed with the light of charity, adorned with the pearls of justice or mercy, chaste, humble, merciful, kind and prudent, through the ministry of His priests He will dispense His Body and Blood to such a man, not to His judgment, but as a remedy. But if He sees anyone adulterous, drunk, avaricious and proud, I am afraid that He may say to

---

[81]Text: *ibid.* 767 = FOTC 66.11

him what He Himself said in the Gospel: *My friend, how is it you came in here not having a wedding garment* (Mt. 22:12)?

Finally:

[82]Since the Lord's birthday is approaching, let us with Christ's help prepare ourselves for the nuptials and heavenly banquet by being clear of all dissipation and adorned with good works. Let us give alms to the poor, attend vigils more promptly, pray or chant the psalms standing in church; observe peace with all men, and recall to harmony those whom you know are at variance. If with the help of Christ you are willing to fulfill these things faithfully, you will be able to approach the Lord's altar in this life with an easy conscience and in the future life will happily arrive at eternal bliss.

> Outside of Rome, custom prevailed and the fast of preparation for Christmas was computed differently and varied accordingly. In Rome baptism at Epiphany was not the practice: consequently, the Fast before Christmas remained the Fast of the Tenth Month, preached by Pope Leo, and became only in the time Gregory the Great (d. 604), the four weeks' fast of Advent in preparation for the feast of the Nativity. This development of Advent, like that of Lent, overshadowed the fasts of the other Ember weeks which were the original Quartertense of Leo: "In the Spring we fast for forty days before Easter; in Summer we fast at Pentecost; in the Autumn during September, and in Winter during December."[83] But time does not stand still and the mystery of Christ leads us beyond the seasons of Winter, Spring, Summer and Autumn into the seasons of Christmas, Easter, Ascension and Pentecost—the *kairos* of redemption. Thus are the words of the prophet Zechariah fulfilled in time and made new in Christ: *The fast of the fourth month, the fast of the fifth, the fast of the seventh and the fast of the tenth are to become gladness and happiness and days of joyful feasting for the House of Judah. But love the truth and peace* (Zech. 8:19)!

[82]Text: *ibid.* 769 = 66.14

[83]Cf. PL 54.186

EPILOGUE

Isidore of Seville, *On Ecclesiastical Duties* (PL 83. 760-769)

Concerning Sunday

c. 24. These apostles sanctioned religious observance for Sunday, because on that day our Redeemer rose from the dead. And so this day is called the Lord's Day because on it, abstaining from mundane tasks and worldly attractions, we only give attention to divine worship, giving thereby to this day, honor and reverence because of the hope of our resurrection which we have on it.

For just as our Lord and Savior Jesus Christ rose from the dead on the third day, so also we hope to do at the end of time. Whence also, standing on the Lord's Day we pray, which is a sign of future resurrection. This the universal Church does, which has been established in the pilgrim state of mortality, awaiting the end of the world what has been shown beforehand in the body of Jesus Christ, Who is the firstborn from the dead.

Concerning the Sabbath

c. 25. The Sabbath was given to the first people to be celebrated in bodily leisure, so that it might be a figure for rest, whence also the etymology of the word 'Sabbath' is rest. The Lord's Day, however, was announced, not to the Jews but to the Christians, through the Lord's resurrection, and from that it began to be held as a festivity. For this is the first day which after seven is found to be the eighth. Whence also, in Ecclesiastes, to signify the two Testaments, it is said: these are seven, and those eight (cf. Eccles. 11:2).

For at first it was handed down that only the Sabbath should be celebrated because it was before the rest of the dead. For there was no resurrection of anyone who once raised from the dead will never die again; death has no more power over him (cf. Rom. 6:9). But after such a resurrection took place in the Lord's body, so that it would precede in the head of the Church what the body of the Church hoped for as its end, the Lord's Day, that is the eighth day which also is the first, succeeded as a feast.

It is apparent, however, that this day is a solemn one in the sacred Scriptures; for this is the first day of the age in which the angels were created, and this is also the day on which Christ rose from the dead. On that day also the Holy Spirit descended on the apostles from the heavens, and on this same day the manna was first given from the heavens in the desert. For so said the Lord: For six days you will collect manna; on the seventh, however, you will collect double (cf. Exod. 16, 5). On the sixth day is the day of preparation which is placed prior to the Sabbath. The Sabbath, however, is the seventh day, which is succeeded by the Lord's Day, on which the manna first came from heaven.

Whence let the Jews understand that already then our Sunday was preferred to the Jewish Sabbath; already then it was indicated that on their Sabbath no grace would descend on them from heaven, but on our Sunday instead, the day on which our Lord first rained manna.

Concerning the Lord's Nativity

c. 26. The day of our Lord's birth [Christmas] of votive solemnity was instituted for this reason that on it Christ wished to be born corporeally for the redemption of the world, coming forth from the virgin's womb, which was under the Father's order. This was why He assumed flesh. After our first parent had fallen through the envy of the devil, seduced by vain hope, he was immediately exiled and lost. He transmitted to all his descendants the first root of evil and of sin. The whole race of mortals increased more steadily in evil, their crimes spread far and wide and, what was worse, we became a slave to the cults of every idol. God, then, wishing to end sin, by Word, by the Law and the prophets, by signs, by plagues, by prodigies consulted man's interests. But since the world even when thus admonished did not recognize its erring ways, God sent His own Son, so that He might put on flesh and manifest Himself to humanity, and heal sins. He came thus to humanity because through Himself He could not gain their recognition. He assumed human nature, but did not thereby lose His divinity. And so, at the same time God and man, equal in divine nature to the Father and in human nature made mortal in humanity for Him.

This, then, is the great solemnity of the Lord's nativity. This is the new and glorious festivity of this day, the coming of God to humankind. Therefore, this day, in that Christ was born on it, is called the Nativity. We are accustomed to observe it annually as in solemn festivity as each year rolls around so that it may be recalled to memory that Christ was born on that day.

Concerning the Epiphany

c. 27. The apostles marked off the day of Epiphany for a solemn festival because on that day the Savior was manifested by a star, when the Magi found Christ lying in a manger, and in adoration offered Him gifts appropriate to the Trinity: gold, frankincense, and myrrh, as to a King, to God, and to one destined to suffer. And so therefore they sanctified this day with an annual celebration that the world might recognize the Lord whom the heavenly elements shewed forth. Seeing, then, that on that day this same Jesus was washed in the baptism of the Jordan and, when the heavens opened, declared by the testimony of the Holy Spirit coming down on Him that He was the Son of God (cf. Mt. 3:17). This day is named in Greek, Epiphany and in Latin, it is called Apparition or Showing

Forth. For three reasons, then, this day took this name; either because on that occasion in His baptism Christ was manifested to His peoples, or because on that day with the appearance of the star He was revealed to the Magi, or because with His first miracle, turning water into wine, He was manifested to many.

Cassian reports, however, that among the Egyptians the Nativity and Epiphany are celebrated as a one day festival, and not as two, as is done in the Western provinces.

Concerning Palm Sunday

c. 28. Palm Sunday is celebrated as a feast because on that day our Lord and Savior, as the Prophet foretold, is said to have gone toward Jerusalem riding on a donkey. Then a multitude of people advancing with palm branches went to meet him, exclaiming: Hosanna, blessed is He who comes in the name of the Lord, King of Israel (Zach. 9, Mt. 21, Jn. 12).

Victory is signified by the palm branches, the victory in which the Lord was to overcome death by Himself dying and triumphing over the devil, the prince of death, with the trophy of the cross.

The ass on which He sat as He approached Jerusalem indicates the simple hearts of the Gentiles. With Him sitting and directing it leads to a vision of peace. On this day the Creed is handed over to the instructed candidates for baptism on account of the approaching solemnity of the Pasch. This is given so that they may recognize the faith which they confess in that they are hastening toward the reception of God's grace. And so, ordinary people call that day *Capitilavium* (Washing the Head) because it is customary on that day to wash the heads of infants who are to be anointed lest they approach the anointing with heads blackened by the ashes of Lent.

Concerning Holy Thursday

c. 29. The Lord's Supper, that is on the last Thursday of Lent, when our Lord and Savior, after completing the Pasch in prototype, passed over to the true Pasch. First, He gave to His apostles the mystery of His body and blood (cf. Mt. 26), when, after the heavenly sacraments, the deceitful disciple, the traitor Judas accepted a price from the Jews and sold Christ's blood (cf. Jn. 13). And so on that day the Savior, rising from supper, washed the feet of His disciples in order to commend a form of humility which He had come to teach and He Himself subsequently explained. And this was particularly appropriate that He should teach by demonstration what He forewarned the disciples to observe. That is why on this same day the altars, walls, and pavements of the temple consecrated to the Lord are washed, and the vessels consecrated to the Lord are purified. On this day too the sacred chrism is produced because, two days before the Pasch, Mary is said to have anointed the Lord's head and feet. Whence also the Lord said to His disciples: You know that after two days will be the Pasch, and the Son of Man will be handed over to be crucified (Mt. 26:2).

Concerning Good Friday

c. 30. The Parasceve (Preparation), that is the Friday of Holy Week is kept as a holy day because on that day Christ fulfilled the mystery of the cross, on account of which He had come into this world so that we might be healed by the mystery of the wood of the cross because we had been smitten in Adam by the wood of the tree of knowledge. Because of this triumph, human weakness offers an annual celebration to Christ throughout the world because of the fact that He thought fit to redeem humanity by the blood of His passion and, with the overthrow of death by the cross, to absolve the sin of the world.

That substance of the divinity did not endure the injury of the cross, but only the human nature which had been assumed. For the passion pertained to the body, but the divinity remained outside of injury's way. A three-fold reason for the Lord's passion is offered. The first reason is that Christ was offered a victim for the redemption of the world and that the ancient enemy is caught, as it were, by the hook of the cross so that he might disgorge those whom he had swallowed up, and lose the booty which he held, vanquished, not by power but by justice, not by domination but by reason.

The second reason is that schooling in life should be given to men who were going to follow. For Christ ascended the cross to give us an example of suffering and resurrection: of suffering, to strengthen our patience; of resurrection, to arouse our hope, so that He might show us two lives in the flesh: one, laborious; the other, blessed. The troublesome one which we must endure, and the happy one which we must hope for.

The third reason for assuming the cross is that He by the foolish, as it was regarded, preaching of the cross, might crush the haughty and inflated worldly wisdom so that man might think that God's folly is wiser than men, and His weakness more powerful than men (cf. 1 Cor. 1:25).

The apostle Paul teaches that we ought to have the eyes of the heart illuminated to see how great is the breadth, and length, and heighth and depth of the cross (cf. Eph. 3:18). Its breadth is the transverse beam on which the arms are extended; its length is from the transverse down to the earth; its depth is what is hidden, fixed in the earth, by which sign of the cross the whole life of the saints is described.

For man is told, *Take up your cross and follow me.* Then indeed the flesh is crucified when our members are mortified on earth—fornication, uncleanness, luxury et cetera. Whenever the exterior man is corrected so that the interior man may daily be renewed there is a passion of the cross. And these deeds, although they are good, are nevertheless laborious, but their reward is rest. And so it is said, rejoicing in hope, so that, thinking of future rest we may work with joy even in our labors.

The breadth of the cross in its transverse beam, where the hands are nailed, signifies this joy. By the hands the work is signified, by the breadth, the joy of the work, because sadness leads to troubles. Furthermore, through the breadth of the cross to which the head is affixed, the expectation of eternal retribution from the sublime justice of God is signified. And so that these very good works are believed, must be done, not on account of God's earthly and temporal benefits, but rather because of that which faith hopes for above, which is achieved through charity.

And finally through the length of the cross, on which the whole body is extended, that tolerance is signified, so that we may remain magnanimous, whence also those who endure are called magnanimous. By the cross's depth, however, that is the part of the cross which is fixed hidden in the earth, but from which everything that can be seen rises, are indicated the inscrutable judgments of God. Concerning these, man is called by a hidden will to the participation of so much grace, one in one way, another in another.

Concerning Holy Saturday

c. 31. The feast of Easter Saturday is celebrated for the reason that on that day the Lord reposed in the tomb. Whence also in the Hebrew language the word Sabbath means rest, either because God rested on that day when the world had been created, or because on that day our Lord and redeemer rested in the tomb. This day comes between the death and resurrection of Christ, signifying a certain rest of souls from all toil and labor, and from all trouble after death, by which a transition is made through the resurrection of the flesh to that life which our Lord, Jesus Christ deigned to show us in advance by His own resurrection.

Concerning the Holy Day of the Pasch

c. 32. Now indeed the Paschal mystery, which at present most clearly is celebrated in the mystery of our Savior, at first was held in a figurative way in the Old Testament. There the people of God celebrated the Pasch in Egypt by killing the lamb (cf. Exod. 12). This figure was brought to full realization by Christ who was led like a lamb to the slaughter. When we anoint our doorposts with His blood, that is, when we sign our brows with the sign of the cross, we are liberated from the destruction of this life, as from the Egyptian captivity. We celebrate the mystical day of this resurrection not only to celebrate His resurrection which occurred on this day, but also for the other sacraments which are signified through it.

Because, as the apostle says, He died on account of our sins and He rose for our justification, the passover from death to life was made sacred in that passion and resurrection of the Lord. For the very word, 'Pasch' is not Greek, but Hebrew, and is derived, not from 'passion' (the Greek verb *pathein* means 'to suffer'), but from the Hebrew word which means passover. And this is very well expressed by the evangelist when the Pasch was celebrated by the Lord with His disciples: Jesus, when His hour was come that He was to pass over from this world to His Father (cf. Jn. 13:1).

. It is, then, a passing over from this mortal life to an immortal one, from death to life, that is indicated in the Lord's passion and resurrection. This passing over is now done by us through faith, which is given to us in the remission of sins, when we are buried with Christ in baptism, as it were, passing from the dead, from worse to better things, from bodily to spiritual, from the way of the present life to the hope of future resurrection and glory.

On account, therefore, of this beginning of a new life, to which we pass over, and on account of the new man which we are ordered to put on, and to put off the old, purging out the old yeast so that we may be a new sowing, since Christ our Pasch has been immolated; because of this newness of life, therefore, the first month of the months of the year is assigned to this celebration, for this is called the month of the new. And so, since in the whole span of time the third phase has now appeared, so the resurrection is for three days.

The first phase of time was what preceded the law, the second was under the law, and the third is what is under grace, when already the mystery is shown forth which was hidden in the enigma of the prophets. This also is signified in the lunar number. Because the number seven is wont to appear as a mystical number as a sign of a certain perfection, the Pasch is celebrated in the third week of the moon, that is, a day which shall occur between the fourteenth and the twenty-first.

But it is not only on account of the third period of time, because from there begins the third week, but also on account of the very conversion of the moon. Because the moon is converted from the lower to the higher parts, and we assume the same likeness from the moon, to pass over from visible to invisible things, from bodily to spiritual mysteries, so that more and more we die to this world, and our life is hidden with Christ, and we convert the whole light of our study, which verges on lower things to higher things, to that eternal contemplation of the immutable truth.

And so the Pasch is observed unto the twenty-first, because of the number seven, which is often a figure to signify the universe, which is also assigned to the Church itself, on account of its universal appearance; and so, in the Apocalypse, John the apostle wrote to the seven Churches. The Church, still constituted in this mortal flesh because of this mortality, is often called in scriptures by the name of the moon. That the annual celebration of the day of the Pasch does not occur on the same day each year as happens in the case of the day on which the Lord is believed to have been born so happens on account of the Lord's Day and the moon.

It is obvious, then, on what day Christ was crucified, and was buried, and rose again. The observance of these days was added by the Fathers of the Council of Nicaea and the whole of the Christian world was persuaded that the Pasch should be celebrated in this way so that we might await not only the Paschal moon but also the Lord's Day, on which He rose from the dead. Whence it is that the Pasch does not occur on the same day each year. For the Jews only observe the new month and the moon. But our Fathers thought that Sunday should be added, so that our feast should be different from that of the Jews.

Concerning the Ascension

c. 33. The solemnity of our Lord's ascension is celebrated because on that day, after the world's victory, after hell's retreat, Christ is said to have ascended into heaven, as the scripture says: He ascended into heaven, He captured His captive, He gave gifts to men (Ps. 68:19). This festivity is celebrated in the turn of the year's revolution to recall to memory that the humanity of the Lord's assumed flesh was placed at the right hand of the Father. We believe His body to be in heaven as it was when it ascended, which the voice of the angel proclaimed, saying: He will return, just as you saw Him go up into the heavens (Acts 1:11), that is, in the same kind and substance of body, the arrival of which gave bodily immortality, but did not take away its nature.

The right hand of the Father at which the same Son is believed to sit, is not a bodily one, for it is not lawful to talk of God in these terms. But the right hand of the Father is perpetual beatitude which is promised to the saints in the resurrection, that is to the universal Church, which is the body of Christ. Likewise His left hand is rightly understood as wretchedness and perpetual punishment which will be given to the impious.

Concerning Pentecost

c. 34. The beginning and origin of the feast of Pentecost must be sought a little further back. For the day of Pentecost received its origin when the voice of God was heard above on Mount Sinai and the law was given to Moses (cf. Exod. 20). In the New Testament Pentecost began with the arrival of the Holy Spirit which Christ promised, whom He said would not come unless He had ascended into heaven.

Then, when Christ entered the gate of heaven, after an interval of ten days, suddenly the place shook as the apostles were praying, and when the Holy Spirit descended on them they were so inflamed that they spoke the wonderful things of God in all the languages of all nations (cf. Acts 2). Therefore the arrival of the Holy Spirit from heaven on the apostles in a variety of tongues transmitted a solemnity to posterity, and for this reason Pentecost is celebrated and the day itself is held sacred.

This Gospel festival is in harmony with the feast of the Law;

for then, after the lamb was immolated and a period of fifteen days had elapsed, the law was given to Moses, written with the finger of God; now after Christ was immolated, who like a sheep was led to the slaughter, the true Pasch is celebrated, and after an interval of fifty days the Holy Spirit was given which is the finger of God over one hundred and twenty disciples, constituted from a number in the Mosaic law, seeing that this feast occupies another mystery.

Suggested Further Reading

General

N.M. Denis-Boulet, *The Christian Calendar,* tr. P. Hepburne-Scott, Hawthorne Books, New York, 1960

Odo Casel, *The Mystery of Christian Worship,* Newman Press, Md., 1959

Jean Daniélou, *The Bible and the Liturgy,* University of Notre Dame Press, 1956

Geoffrey Dix, *The Shape of the Liturgy,* Dacre Press, London, 1945

G. Martimort, *The Church at Prayer,* vols 1- IV, New York, 1968

A. Nocent, *The Liturgical Year,* vols. 1-4, tr. M.J. O'Connell, Collegeville, Minnesota, 1977

J. Quasten, *Patrology,* vols. I-IV, Westminster, Md., 1951-1986

M.F. Toal, *Sunday Sermons of the Great Fathers,* 3vols., Longman, London, 1957

Individual Chapters

Chapter 1. The Lord's Day and Week

D.A. Carson, *From Sabbath to Lord's Day,* Grand Rapids, Michigan, 1982

F.A. Regan, *Dies Dominica and Dies Solis, The Beginning of the Lord's Day in Christian Antiquity,* Catholic University of America Press, Washington, D.C., 1961

Chapter 2. The Lord's Night and Season

R. Cantalamessa, *La Pasqua della Nostra Salvezza,* Torino, 1971

A. Hamman, *The Paschal Mystery,* tr. T. Halton, Alba House, New York, 1969

Chapter 3. New Days of the Lord

A. Adam, *The Liturgical Year, its history and its meaning after the reform of the Liturgy,* tr. M.J. O'Connell, Pueblo, New York, 1981

T.J. Talley, *The Origin of the Liturgical Year,* Pueblo, New York, 1986

Chapter 4. New Weeks of the Lord

J.G. Davies, *Holy Week,* Lutterworth Press, London, 1961

P.T. Weller, *Selected Easter Sermons of St. Augustine,* Herder, St. Louis, 1959

Chapter 5. New Seasons of the Lord

J. Jungmann, *Public Worship,* Challoner, London, 1957

J. Jungmann, *The Early Liturgy to the Time of Gregory the Great,* University of Notre Dame Press, Indiana, 1959

Index

340